BY MATTHEW DESMOND

On the Fireline

Race in America (with Mustafa Emirbayer)

The Racial Order (with Mustafa Emirbayer)

Evicted

Poverty, by America

POVERTY, BY AMERICA

POVERTY,
BY AMERICA

———

MATTHEW
DESMOND

CROWN
NEW YORK

Published in the United States by Crown,
an imprint of Random House, a division of
Penguin Random House LLC, New York.

CROWN and the Crown colophon are registered
trademarks of Penguin Random House LLC.

Portions of this work are excerpted from *The New York Times Magazine*
(Matthew Desmond, "House Rules," May 9, 2017; Matthew Desmond,
"Dollars on the Margins," February 23, 2019; Matthew Desmond,
"Why Work Doesn't Work Anymore," September 11, 2018; Matthew Desmond,
"The Tenants Who Evicted Their Landlord," October 13, 2020), *The New York
Times* (Matthew Desmond, "'The Moratorium Saved Us. It Really Did,'"
September 30, 2021), and *American Journal of Sociology* (Matthew Desmond
and Nathan Wilmers, "Do the Poor Pay More for Housing?
Exploitation, Profit, and Risk in Rental Markets," 124 [2019]: 1090–124).

Grateful acknowledgment is made to the Russell Sage Foundation for
permission to reprint portions of "Severe Deprivation in America:
An Introduction," *RSF: The Russell Sage Foundation Journal of the Social Sciences*
Volume 1, Issue 1. Matthew Desmond, ed. © Russell Sage Foundation,
112 East 64th Street, New York, NY 10065,
https://www.rsfjournal.org/content/1/1/1.

Library of Congress Cataloging-in-Publication Data
Names: Desmond, Matthew, author.
Title: Poverty, by America / Matthew Desmond.
Description: First edition. | New York: Crown, 2023 | Includes index.
Identifiers: LCCN 2022052347 (print) | LCCN 2022052348 (ebook) |
ISBN 9780593239919 (hardcover) | ISBN 9780593239926 (ebook)
Subjects: LCSH: Poverty—United States. | Poverty—Prevention. |
Poor—United States.
Classification: LCC HC110.P6 D46 2023 (print) | LCC HC110.P6 (ebook) |
DDC 362.50973—dc23/eng/20230118
LC record available at https://lccn.loc.gov/2022052347

Printed in the United States of America on acid-free paper

crownpublishing.com

6 8 9 7 5

Book design by Barbara M. Bachman

For Devah

We imagine that their sufferings are one thing
and our life another.

—LEO TOLSTOY

CONTENTS

POVERTY, BY AMERICA

PROLOGUE

WHY IS THERE SO MUCH POVERTY IN AMERICA? I WROTE this book because I needed an answer to that question. For most of my adult life, I have researched and reported on poverty. I have lived in very poor neighborhoods, spent time with people living in poverty around the country, pored over statistical studies and government reports, listened to and learned from community organizers and union reps, drafted public policy, read up on the history of the welfare state and city planning and American racism, and taught courses on inequality at two universities. But even after all that, I still felt that I lacked a fundamental theory of the problem, a clear and convincing case as to why there is so much hardship in this land of abundance.

I began paying attention to poverty when I was a child. The home in which I grew up cost $60,000. It sat a couple of miles outside Winslow, Arizona, a small Route 66 town east of Flagstaff. It was small and wood paneled, surrounded by hard-packed dirt sprouting with thorny weeds. I loved it: the woodburning stove, the Russian olive trees. We had moved in after my father accepted a position as pastor of the First Christian Church. Scraping a salary from the offering plate never amounted to much, and Dad always griped that the railroad men in town got paid more than he did. He could read ancient Greek, but they had a union.

We learned to fix things ourselves or do without. When I put a hole through a window with my Red Ryder BB gun, it stayed broken. But a family friend and I once replaced the engine in my first truck, having found the right parts at a junkyard. After my father lost his job, the bank took our home, before it was all the rage, and we learned to do without that, too. Mostly I blamed Dad. But a part of me also wondered why this was our country's answer when a family fell on hard times.

I went to college, enrolling at Arizona State University (ASU) by applying for every scholarship and loan I could. And I worked: as a morning-shift barista at Starbucks, a telemarketer, you name it. In the summers, I decamped to a forest near my hometown and served as a wildland firefighter. When classes were in session, I began hanging out with homeless people around my campus—not serving them at soup kitchens or delivering socks, but just sitting with them, talking. I think it helped me process, in my own adolescent way, what I was seeing all around me, which was money. So much money. Back in Winslow, some families were better off than others, but not like this. My classmates were driving BMWs and convertible Mustangs. For most of college, I didn't have a car, and when I did, it was a 1978 Ford F-150 with that junkyard engine and decent-sized holes in the floorboard, allowing me to see the road rip past as I drove. My classmates were going out for sushi. I stocked canned sardines and saltine crackers in my dorm room. The town of Tempe, the Phoenix suburb where ASU's main campus sits, had spent hundreds of millions of dollars to construct a two-mile-long artificial lake in the middle of the desert, a giant puddle that loses two-thirds of its water to evaporation each year. A few blocks away, people were begging on the street. How could there be, I wondered, such bald scarcity amid such waste and opulence?

I began stalking this question in the classroom, enrolling in courses that I hoped would help me make sense of my country and its confounding, unblushing inequality. I kept it up in graduate school at the University of Wisconsin—the only program that accepted my application—where I focused on the housing crisis. To get as close as I could to that problem, I moved to Milwaukee, living in a mobile home park and then a rooming house. I befriended families who had been evicted, and I followed them for months and then years, sleeping on their floors, watching their children grow up, laughing and arguing with them, and, later, attending some of their funerals.

In Milwaukee, I met grandmothers living in trailers without heat. They spent the winter under blankets, praying that the space heaters didn't give out. I once saw an apartment full of kids, just kids, evicted on a rainy spring day. Their mother had died, and the children had chosen to go on living in the house until the sheriff came. In the years since, I have met poor Americans around the country striving for dignity and justice—or just plain survival, which can be hard enough: home health aides in New Jersey who belonged to the full-time working homeless, fast food workers in California fighting for a living wage, and undocumented immigrants in

Minneapolis organizing for affordable housing, communicating with their neighbors through the Google Translate app.

This is who we are: the richest country on earth, with more poverty than any other advanced democracy. If America's poor founded a country, that country would have a bigger population than Australia or Venezuela. Almost one in nine Americans—including one in eight children—live in poverty. There are more than 38 million people living in the United States who cannot afford basic necessities, and more than 108 million getting by on $55,000 a year or less, many stuck in that space between poverty and security.[1]

More than a million of our public schoolchildren are homeless, living in motels, cars, shelters, and abandoned buildings. After arriving in prison, many incarcerated Americans suddenly find that their health improves because the conditions they faced as free (but impoverished) citizens were worse. More than 2 million Americans don't have running water or a flushing toilet at home. West Virginians drink from polluted streams, while families on the Navajo Nation drive hours to fill water barrels. Tropical diseases long considered eradicated, like hookworm, have reemerged in rural America's poorest communities, often the result of broken sanitation systems that expose children to raw sewage.[2]

The United States annually produces $5.3 trillion more in goods and services than China. Our gross domestic product is larger than the combined economies of Japan, Germany, the United Kingdom, India, France, and Italy, which are the third, fourth, fifth, sixth, seventh, and eighth richest countries in the world. California alone has a bigger economy than Canada does; New York State's economy surpasses South Korea's.[3]

America's poverty is not for lack of resources. We lack something else.

Books about poverty tend to be books about the poor. It's been this way for more than a hundred years. In 1890, Jacob Riis wrote about "how the other half lives," documenting the horrid conditions of New York tenements and photographing filthy children asleep in alleyways. A decade later, Jane Addams wrote about the sorry state of Chicago's immigrant workforce: a thirteen-year-old girl from Russia who committed suicide because she couldn't repay a $3 loan; a new mother forced to work so many hours that her breast milk soaked through her shirt. The Depression-era reportage of James Agee and Walker Evans, and the photojournalism of Dorothea Lange, seared images of dusty, kicked-down sharecroppers into our collective memory. In 1962, Michael Harrington published *The Other America,* a book intended to make visible "tens of millions of human beings" who had "dropped out of sight and out of mind." Two years later, Lyndon and Lady Bird Johnson paid a visit to Appalachia and sat on the rough-hewn porch of a jobless sawmill worker surrounded by children with small clothes and big teeth.[4]

Bearing witness, these kinds of books help us understand the nature of poverty. They are vital. But they do not—and in fact cannot—answer the most fundamental question, which is: *Why?* Why all this American poverty? I've learned that this question requires a different approach. To understand the causes of poverty, we must look beyond the poor. Those of us living lives of privilege and plenty must examine ourselves. Are we—we the secure, the insured, the housed, the college educated, the protected, the lucky—connected to all this needless suffering? This book is my attempt to answer that question, addressed to that "we." Which makes this a book about poverty that is not just about the poor. Instead, it's a book about how the *other* other half lives, about how some lives are made small so that others may grow.

Drawing on years of my own research and reporting, as well as studies from across the social sciences, I lay out why there is so much poverty in America and make a case for how to eliminate it. Ending poverty will require new policies and renewed political movements, to be sure. But it will also require that each of us, in our own way, become *poverty abolitionists,* unwinding ourselves from our neighbors' deprivation and refusing to live as unwitting enemies of the poor.

CHAPTER I

THE KIND OF PROBLEM
POVERTY IS

I RECENTLY SPENT A DAY ON THE TENTH FLOOR OF NEWARK'S courthouse, the floor where the state decides child welfare cases. There I met a fifty-five-year-old father who had stayed up all night working at his warehouse job by the port. He told me his body felt heavy. Sometimes when pulling a double shift, he would snort a speedball—cocaine mixed with benzodiazepine and morphine, sometimes heroin—to stay awake or dull his pain. Its ugly recipe was laid bare in the authorities' toxicology reports, making him look like a career junkie and not what he was: an exhausted member of America's working poor. The authorities didn't think the father could care for his three children alone, and their mother, who had a serious mental illness and was using PCP, wasn't an option either. So the father gambled, surrendering his two older children to his stepmother and hoping the authorities would allow him to raise the youngest. They did. Outside the courtroom, he hugged his public defender, who considered what had happened a real victory. This is what winning looks like on the tenth floor of Newark's courthouse: giving up two of your children so you have a chance to raise the third alone and in poverty.

Technically, a person is considered "poor" when they can't afford life's necessities, like food and housing. The architect of the Official Poverty Measure—the poverty line—was a bureaucrat working at the Social Security Administration named Mollie Orshansky. Orshansky figured that if poverty was fundamentally about a lack of income that could cover the basics, and if nothing was more basic than food, then you could calculate poverty with two pieces of information: the cost of food in a given year and the share of a family's budget dedicated to it. Orshansky determined that bare-bones food expenditures accounted for roughly a third of an American family's budget. If a family of four needed, say, $1,000 a year in 1965 to feed themselves, then any family making less than $3,000 a year (or around $27,000 at the beginning of 2022) would be considered poor because they would be devoting more than a third of their income to food, forgoing other necessities. Orshansky published her findings in January of that year, writing, "There is thus a total of 50 million persons—of whom 22 million are young children—who live within the bleak circle of poverty or at least hover around its edge." It was a number that shocked affluent Americans.[1]

Today's Official Poverty Measure is still based on Orshansky's calculation, annually updated for inflation. In 2022, the poverty line was drawn at $13,590 a year for a single person and $27,750 a year for a family of four.

As I've said, we can't hope to understand why there is so much poverty in America solely by considering the lives of the poor. But we need to start there, to better understand the kind of problem poverty is—and grasp the stakes—because poverty is not simply a matter of small incomes. In the words of the poet Layli Long Soldier, that's just "the oil at the surface."[2]

I MET CRYSTAL MAYBERRY when I was living in Milwaukee and researching my last book, on eviction and the American housing crisis. Crystal was born prematurely on a spring day in 1990, shortly after her pregnant mother was stabbed eleven times in the back while being robbed. The attack induced labor. Both mother and daughter survived. It was not the first time Crystal's mother had been stabbed. For as far back as Crystal can remember, her father beat her mother. He smoked crack cocaine, and so did her mother; so did her mother's mother.[3]

Crystal's mother found a way to leave her father, and soon after, he began a lengthy prison stint. Crystal and her mother moved in with another man and his parents. That man's father began molesting Crystal. She told her mother, and her mother called her a liar. Not long after Crystal began kindergarten, Child Protective Services, the branch of government tasked with safeguarding children from maltreatment, stepped in. At five, Crystal was placed in foster care.

Crystal bounced around between dozens of group homes and sets of foster parents. She lived with her aunt for five years. Then her aunt returned her. After that, the longest Crystal lived anywhere was eight months. When she reached adolescence, Crystal fought with the other girls in the group homes. She picked up assault charges and a scar across her right cheekbone. People and their houses, pets, furniture, dishes—these came and went. Food was more stable, and Crystal began taking refuge in it. She put on weight. Because of her weight, she developed sleep apnea.

When Crystal was sixteen, she stopped going to high school. At seventeen, she was examined by a clinical psychologist, who diagnosed her with, among other things, bipolar disorder, post-traumatic stress disorder, reactive attachment disorder, and borderline intellectual functioning. When she turned eighteen, she aged out of foster care. By that time Crystal had passed through more than twenty-five foster placements. Because of her mental illness, she had been approved for Supplemental Security Income (SSI), a government income subsidy for low-income people who are old, blind, or who have a disability. She would receive $754 a month, or a little over $9,000 a year.

Crystal was barred from low-income housing for two years because of an assault charge she received for fighting in the group home. Even if she had not been barred, she would still have found herself at the bottom of a waiting list that was six years long. Crystal secured her first apartment in the private market: a run-down two-bedroom unit. The apartment was located in a majority-Black neighborhood that ranked among the city's poorest, but Crystal herself was Black and had been turned down for apartments in the Hispanic and white areas of town. Crystal's rent took 73 percent of her income, and it wasn't long before she fell behind. A few months after moving in, she experienced her first official eviction, which went on her record, making it likely that her application for housing assistance would be denied. After her eviction, Crystal met a woman at a homeless shelter and secured another apartment with her new friend. Then Crystal put that new friend's friend through a window, and the landlord told Crystal to leave.

Crystal spent nights in shelters, with friends, and with members of her church. She learned how to live on the streets, walking them at night and sleeping on the bus or in hospital waiting rooms during the day. She learned to survive by relying on strangers. She met a woman at a bus stop and ended up living with her for a month. People were attracted to Crystal. She was gregarious and funny, with an endearing habit of slapping her hands together and laughing at herself. She sang in public, gospel mostly.

Crystal had always believed that her SSI was secure. You couldn't get fired from SSI, and your hours couldn't get cut. "SSI always come," she said. Until one day it didn't. Crystal had been approved for SSI as a minor, but her adult reevaluation found her ineligible. Now her only source of income was food stamps. She tried donating plasma, but her veins were too small. She burned through the remaining ties she had from church and her foster families. When her SSI was not reinstated after several months, she descended into street homelessness and prostitution. Crystal had never been an early riser, but she learned that mornings were the best time to turn tricks, catching men on their way to work.

FOR CRYSTAL AND PEOPLE in similar situations, poverty is about money, of course, but it is also a relentless piling on of problems.

Poverty is pain, physical pain. It is in the backaches of home health aides and certified nursing assistants, who bend their bodies to hoist the old and sick out of beds and off toilets; it is in the feet and knees of cashiers made to stand while taking our orders and ringing up our items; it is in the skin rashes and migraines of maids who clean our office buildings, homes, and hotel rooms with products containing ammonia and triclosan.

In America's meatpacking plants, two amputations occur each week: A band saw lops off someone's finger or hand. Pickers in Amazon warehouses have access to vending machines dispensing free Advil and Tylenol. Slum housing spreads asthma, its mold and cockroach allergens seeping into young lungs and airways, and it poisons children with lead, causing irreversible damage to their tiny central nervous systems and brains. Poverty is the cancer that forms in the cells of those who live near petrochemical plants and waste incinerators. Roughly one in four children living in poverty have untreated cavities, which can morph into tooth decay, causing sharp pain and spreading infection to their faces and even brains. With public insurance reimbursing only a fraction of dental care costs, many families simply cannot afford regular trips to the dentist. Thirty million Americans remain completely uninsured a decade after the passage of the Affordable Care Act.[4]

Poverty is the colostomy bag and wheelchair, the night terrors and bullets that maimed but didn't finish their cunning work. In Chicago, gun violence killed 722 people in 2020 and injured another 3,339. By some estimates, eight in ten gunshot victims nationwide survive the attack, often forced to live out their days in pain. The lives of the poor are often marked by violence, including violence experienced as children. Among a sample of men and women released from prison in Massachusetts, over 40 percent had witnessed a murder as children. Among a sample of parents who had been investigated by Child Protective Services in New Jersey, over 34 percent grew up with violence in their homes, and 17 percent were victims of sexual abuse.[5]

Poverty is traumatic, and since society isn't investing in its treatment, poor people often have their own ways of coping with their pain. My friend Scott was sexually abused as a child. As an adult, he found pills, then fentanyl. He bought peace for $20 at a time. In his forties, he got sober and stayed that way for several years before relapsing and dying alone in a hotel room. My former roommate Kimball, or Woo, as everyone knew him, never did drugs and drank only on rare occasions. But he stepped on a nail one day in a run-down duplex apartment we used to share in Milwaukee, ignored the injury because he couldn't afford to pay it any mind, and lost his lower leg when the infection, accelerated by his diabetes, threatened to take all of him.[6]

On top of the pain, poverty is instability. Over the past twenty years, rents have soared while incomes have fallen for renters; yet the federal government provides housing assistance to only one in four of the families who qualify for it. Most renting families below the poverty line now spend at least half of their income on housing, with one in four spending more than 70 percent on rent and utility costs alone. These combined factors have transformed the United States into a nation where eviction is commonplace among low-income renters. Churn has become the status quo. More than 3.6 million eviction filings are taped to doors or handed to occupants in an average year in America, which is roughly equivalent to

the number of foreclosures initiated at the height of the financial crisis in 2010. Eviction movers, flanked by armed marshals
and watched by the family, do a quick business. They take
everything—the shower curtain, the mattresses on the floor,
the meat cuts in the freezer and bread in the cupboard—and
either lock it away in storage (usually to be hauled to the dump
after missed payments) or pile it high on the curb. People start
over as best they can.[7]

The job market asks us to start over more and more these
days, as well. Half of all new positions are eliminated within
the first year. Jobs that used to come with some guarantees,
even union membership, have been transformed into gigs.
Temp workers are not just found driving Ubers; they are in
hospitals and universities and insurance companies. The manufacturing sector—still widely mistaken as the fount of good,
sturdy, hard-hat jobs—now employs more than a million temp
workers. Long-term employment has declined steadily in the
private sector, particularly for men, and temp jobs are expected to grow faster than all others over the next several
years. Income volatility, the extent to which paychecks grow
or shrink over short periods of time, has doubled since 1970.
For scores of American workers, wages are now wobbly, fluctuating wildly not only year to year but month to month, even
week to week. America has welcomed the rise of bad jobs at
the bottom of the market—jobs offering low pay, no benefits,
and few guarantees. Some industries such as retail, leisure and
hospitality, and construction see more than half of their workforce turn over each year. Workers quickly learn they are ex-
pendable, easily replaced, while young people are graduating
into an economy characterized by deep uncertainty.[8]

Poverty is the constant fear that it will get even worse. A third of Americans live without much economic security, working as bus drivers, farmers, teachers, cashiers, cooks, nurses, security guards, social workers. Many are not officially counted among the "poor," but what then is the term for trying to raise two kids on $50,000 a year in Miami or Portland? What do you call it when you don't qualify for a housing voucher but can't get a mortgage either? When the rent takes half your paycheck, and your student loan debt takes another quarter? When you dip below the poverty line one month then rise a bit above it the next without ever feeling a sense of stability? As a lived reality, there is plenty of poverty above the poverty line.[9]

And plenty far, far below it. In the land of the free, you can drop all the way down, joining the ranks of the *lumpenproletariat* (literally the "ragged proletariat").[10] According to the latest national data, one in eighteen people in the United States lives in "deep poverty," a subterranean level of scarcity. Take the poverty line and cut it in half: Anything below that is considered deep poverty. The deep poverty line in 2020 was $6,380 annually for a single person and $13,100 for a family of four. That year, almost 18 million people in America survived under these conditions. The United States allows a much higher proportion of its children—over 5 million of them—to endure deep poverty than any of its peer nations.[11]

Economists have estimated that a person needs roughly $4 a day to afford the bare minimum of basic necessities in the United States, a figure meant to correspond to the $1.90-a-day poverty line the World Bank uses to identify the poorest people in countries like India or Bangladesh, which have lower

costs of living. Using this threshold, the Nobel laureate Angus
Deaton reported in 2018 that 5.3 million Americans were "ab-
solutely poor by global standards," getting by on $4 a day or
less. "There are millions of Americans," Deaton wrote,
"whose suffering, through material poverty and poor health,
is as bad or worse than that of the people in Africa or in Asia."[12]
In the years following the end of guaranteed cash welfare, the
United States has witnessed a shocking rise in extreme poverty, one that tracks with other grim indicators. Between 1995
and 2018, the number of households receiving Supplemental
Nutrition Assistance Program benefits (food stamps) but reporting no cash income increased from roughly 289,000 to
1.2 million, amounting to roughly one in fifty Americans. The
number of homeless children, as reported by the nation's public schools, rose from 794,617 in 2007 to 1.3 million in 2018.[13]
There is growing evidence that America harbors a hard bottom layer of deprivation, a kind of extreme poverty once
thought to exist only in faraway places of bare feet and swol-
len bellies.

Poverty is the loss of liberty. The American prison system
has no equal in any other country or any other epoch. Almost
2 million people sit in our prisons and jails each day. Another
3.7 million are on probation or parole. Hidden behind the system's vague abstractions—justice, law and order—is the fact
that the overwhelming majority of America's current and former prisoners are very poor. By the time they reach their mid-
thirties, almost seven in ten Black men who didn't finish high
school will have spent a portion of their life in a cage. Prison
robs people of the prime of their life, taking not only the
sleepy, slow years at the end but also the pulsing, hot years in

the middle. In prisons, of course, they will remain poor, earning in their prison jobs between 14 cents and $1.41 an hour on average, depending on the state. The United States doesn't just tuck its poor under overpasses and into mobile home parks far removed from central business districts. It disappears them into jails and prisons, effectively erasing them: The incarcerated are simply not counted in most national surveys, resulting in a falsely rosy statistical picture of American progress. Poverty measures exclude everyone in prison and jail—not to mention those housed in psych wards, halfway houses, and homeless shelters—which means there are millions more poor Americans than official statistics let on.[14]

Poverty is the feeling that your government is against you, not for you; that your country was designed to serve other people and that you are fated to be managed and processed, roughed up and handcuffed. In the late nineteenth and early twentieth centuries, cities passed "ugly laws" banning "unsightly beggars" from public places. In the first half of the twentieth century, vagrancy and loitering ordinances were used to expel the poor from park benches and street corners. Today, municipal regulations still allow the police to arrest the homeless for being seen in public, criminalizing abject poverty. In recent years, up to one in twelve people killed by a gun in the United States have been killed by a police officer. Three in four Black mothers worry that their children will be brutalized by the people charged with guaranteeing their safety. We remember some of those children's names—Tamir, George, Eric—and have forgotten, or were never told, others.[15]

The poor are subjected to takings by the state in the form of misdemeanor charges and citations: the price paid for missing a child support payment, jumping a subway turnstile, getting caught with a joint. One minor infraction can lead to another, then another—you might forget a court date or fail to make a payment and get slapped with another sanction, penalties on top of penalties—until you are embroiled in judgment and debt. Criminal justice agencies levy steep fines and fees on the poor, often making them pay for their own prosecution and incarceration. When payments are missed, courts issue warrants, mobilize private bill collectors, and even incarcerate as retribution. Today, scores languish in jail, not because they've been convicted of a crime, but because they missed a payment or can't make bail. Even light brushes with law enforcement can leave people feeling reduced in stature. The political scientist Vesla Weaver has shown that those stopped (but not arrested) by the police are less likely to vote. The criminal-legal system, Weaver has written, "trains people for a distinctive and lesser kind of citizenship."[16]

Poverty is embarrassing, shame inducing. Misery (*misère*), the French sociologist Eugène Buret once remarked, "is poverty felt morally." You feel it in the degradation rituals of the welfare office, where you are made to wait half a day for a ten-minute appointment with a caseworker who seems annoyed you showed up. You feel it when you go home to an apartment with cracked windows and cupboards full of cockroaches, an infestation the landlord blames on you. You feel it in how effortlessly poor people are omitted from movies and television shows and popular music and children's books, erasures reminding you of your own irrelevance to wider society. You may begin to believe, in the quieter moments, the lies told about you. You avoid public places—parks, beaches, shopping districts, sporting arenas—knowing they weren't built for you. Poverty might consume your life, but it's rarely embraced as an identity. It's more socially acceptable today to disclose a mental illness than to tell someone you're broke. When politicians propose antipoverty legislation, they say it will help "the middle class." When social movement organizers mobilize for higher wages or housing justice, they announce that they are fighting on behalf of "working people" or "families" or "tenants" or "the many." When the poor take to the streets, it's usually not under the banner of poverty. There is no flag for poor rights, after all.[17]

Poverty is diminished life and personhood. It changes how you think and prevents you from realizing your full potential. It shrinks the mental energy you can dedicate to decisions, forcing you to focus on the latest stressor—an overdue gas bill, a lost job—at the expense of everything else. When someone is shot dead, the children who live on that block perform much worse on cognitive tests in the days following the murder. The violence captures their minds. Time passes, and the effect fades until someone else is dropped.[18] Poverty can cause anyone to make decisions that look ill-advised and even downright stupid to those of us unbothered by scarcity. Have you ever sat in a hospital waiting room, watching the clock and praying for good news? You are there, locked on the present emergency, next to which all other concerns and responsibilities feel (and are) trivial. That experience is something like living in poverty. Behavioral scientists Sendhil Mullainathan and Eldar Shafir call this "the bandwidth tax." "Being poor," they write, "reduces a person's cognitive capacity more than going a full night without sleep." When we are preoccupied by poverty, "we have less mind to give to the rest of life." Poverty does not just deprive people of security and comfort; it siphons off their brainpower, too.[19]

Still, poverty is no equalizer. It can be intensified by racial disadvantages or eased by racial privileges. (And which is more primary, race or class? Which is the root of social inequity and which the branches? Which organ is more important to you, your heart or your brain?) Black poverty, Hispanic poverty, Native American poverty, Asian American poverty, and white poverty are all different. Black and Hispanic Americans are twice as likely to be poor, compared to white Americans, owing not only to the country's racial legacies but also to present-day discrimination. The Black unemployment rate remains nearly double the white unemployment rate, and studies have shown that Black jobseekers are just as likely to face discrimination in the labor market today as they were thirty years ago. There has been no progress in a generation.[20]

Poor white families tend to live in communities with lower poverty levels than poor Black and Hispanic families. There is no metropolitan area in the United States where whites experience extreme concentrations of disadvantage, living in neighborhoods with poverty rates in excess of 40 percent. But across the nation, many poor Black and Hispanic families live under these conditions. That means most poor white children attend better-resourced schools, live in safer communities, experience lower rates of police violence, and sleep in more dignified homes than their poor Black and Hispanic peers. Poverty not only resides in people; it lives in neighborhoods, too, with poor Black and Hispanic families being much more likely to experience the kind of hardship that results when personal poverty collides with community-level poverty. This is a big reason why the life expectancy of poor Black men in America is similar to that of men in Pakistan and Mongolia.[21]

Today, the wealth gap between Black and white families is as large as it was in the 1960s. Our legacy of systematically denying Black people access to the nation's land and riches has been passed from generation to generation. Most first-time home buyers get down-payment help from their parents. Many of those parents pitch in by refinancing their own homes, as their parents did for them after the government subsidized homeownership in white communities in the wake of World War II.[22] In 2019, the median white household had a net worth of $188,200, compared with $24,100 for the median Black household. The average white household headed by someone with a high school diploma has more wealth than the average Black household headed by someone with a college degree.[23]

Poverty is often material scarcity piled on chronic pain piled on incarceration piled on depression piled on addiction—on and on it goes. Poverty isn't a line. It's a tight knot of social maladies. It is connected to every social problem we care about—crime, health, education, housing—and its persistence in American life means that millions of families are denied safety and security and dignity in one of the richest nations in the history of the world.[24]

CHAPTER 2

WHY HAVEN'T WE MADE
MORE PROGRESS?

THE PAST FIFTY YEARS SAW SCIENTISTS MAP THE ENTIRE human genome and eradicate smallpox, a disease that had stalked the earth for millennia. During that time, infant mortality rates and deaths from heart disease in the United States fell by roughly 70 percent. The average American gained almost a decade of life. Climate change was recognized as an existential threat. The Internet was invented; smartphones, too.[1] And our progress on poverty? As estimated by the federal government's poverty line, 12.6 percent of the U.S. population was poor in 1970; two decades later it was 13.5 percent; in 2010, it was 15.1 percent; and in 2019, it was 10.5 percent. To graph the share of Americans living in poverty over the past half century amounts to drawing a line that resembles gently rolling hills. The line curves slightly up, then slightly down, then back up again over the years, staying steady through Democratic and Republican administrations, rising in recessions and falling in boom years. There is no real improvement here, just a long stasis.

What accounts for our lack of progress on poverty? It cannot be chalked up to how the poor are counted: Different measures spit out the same embarrassing result.[2] Maybe, then, it can be explained by how poverty is experienced—or, more precisely, how that experience has changed over time. Any fair assessment of poverty through the years must confront the breathtaking march of material progress. At least since the early twentieth century, commentators have observed that Karl Marx's "law of increasing misery"—the idea that workers' suffering would steadily rise as capitalism expanded and exploitation intensified—was forestalled in the West thanks to technological advances that transformed yesterday's luxuries into today's necessities. George Orwell once ventured that what kept young men going into the coal mines during the interwar years, instead of forming barricades and demanding a better life, was the spread of cheap sweets and electricity, which brought movies and radio to the masses.[3]

But the fact that standards of living have risen across the board doesn't mean that poverty itself has fallen. Forty years ago, only the rich could afford cell phones. But cell phones have become more affordable over the past few decades, and now most Americans have one, including many poor people, as cell phones have become increasingly necessary to finding jobs, housing, and lovers. This has led some observers to assert that "access to certain consumer goods (TV sets, microwave ovens, cell phones) show[s] that the poor are not quite so poor after all."[4]

No, it doesn't. You can't eat a cell phone. You can't trade one in for a living wage. A cell phone doesn't grant you stable housing, affordable medical and dental care, or adequate childcare. In fact, as the cost of items like cell phones and washing machines has fallen, the cost of the most necessary of life's necessities, such as healthcare and rent, has increased. Between 2000 and 2022, in the average American city the cost of fuel and utilities increased by 115 percent.[5] The American poor, living as they do in the epicenter of global capitalism, have access to cheap, mass-produced goods like every American does. But what good is a toaster oven if you can't afford the electricity to power it or a kitchen in which to use it? As Michael Harrington put it sixty years ago: "It is much easier in the United States to be decently dressed than it is to be decently housed, fed, or doctored."[6]

As a country on the move, it may seem unimaginable that we have stood still for so long when it comes to making real progress on poverty. So much has changed since the moon landing, since the Beatles broke up, since Vietnam and Watergate. But when it comes to poverty reduction, we've had fifty years of nothing.

When I first started looking into this depressing state of affairs, I figured America's efforts to reduce poverty had stalled because we had stopped trying to solve the problem. I bought into the idea, popular among progressives, that the election of President Ronald Reagan (as well as Prime Minister Margaret Thatcher in the United Kingdom) marked the ascendancy of market fundamentalism, or "neoliberalism," a time when governments cut aid to the poor, lowered taxes, and slashed regulations. If American poverty persisted, I thought, it was because we had reduced our spending on the poor.

But I came to realize that the reality was far messier. President Reagan expanded corporate power, massively cut taxes on the rich, and rolled back spending on some antipoverty initiatives, especially in housing. But he was unable to make large-scale, long-term cuts to many of the programs that make up the American welfare state. When the president proposed reducing Social Security benefits in 1981, Congress rebuffed him.[7] Throughout Reagan's eight years in office, antipoverty spending did not shrink. It grew and continued to grow after he left office. In fact, it grew significantly. Spending on the nation's thirteen largest means-tested programs—aid reserved for Americans who fall below a certain income level—went from $1,015 a person the year Ronald Reagan was elected president to $3,419 a person one year into Donald Trump's administration.[8] That's a 237 percent increase.

Admittedly, the lion's share of this increase was due to healthcare spending. Somehow, the United States has the unique distinction of lacking universal healthcare while still having the most expensive healthcare system in the world. Every year, we spend vastly more on healthcare for low-income Americans than we do on archetypical antipoverty programs, such as cash welfare and public housing. In 2021, for example, the federal government spent $521 billion on Medicaid, which provides health coverage to low-income Americans, compared to $61 billion on the Earned Income Tax Credit directed at the nation's poorest workers (and particularly those with children).[9]

Even so, welfare spending on programs not directly related to healthcare has also increased substantially in the past four decades. If we exclude Medicaid from the calculation, we find that federal investments in means-tested programs increased by 130 percent between 1980 and 2018, from $630 to $1,448 per person.[10] "Neoliberalism" is now part of the left's lexicon, but

I looked in vain to find it in the plain print of federal budgets, at least as far as aid to the poor was concerned. There is no evidence that the United States has become stingier over time. The opposite is true.[11]

This makes the country's stalled progress on poverty even more baffling. Decade after decade, the poverty rate has remained flat even as federal relief has surged. How could this be?

PART OF THE ANSWER, I learned, lies in the fact that a fair amount of government aid earmarked for the poor never reaches them. To understand why, consider welfare. When welfare was administered through the Aid to Families with Dependent Children program, almost all of its funds were used to provide single-parent families with cash assistance.[12] But when President Bill Clinton reformed welfare in 1996, replacing the old model with Temporary Assistance for Needy Families (TANF), he transformed the program into a block grant that gives states considerable leeway in deciding how to distribute the money. As a result, states have come up with rather creative ways to spend TANF dollars.

Nationwide, for every dollar budgeted for TANF in 2020, poor families directly received just 22 cents. Only Kentucky and the District of Columbia spent over half of their TANF funds on basic cash assistance. Of the $31.6 billion in welfare funding, just $7.1 billion was realized as dollars-in-hand relief to the poor.[13] Where did the rest of the money go? Some of it went to helping families in other ways, such as supporting job training and offsetting childcare costs. Other TANF dollars were dedicated to funding juvenile justice administration, promoting financial literacy, and a wide assortment of other activities that had little or nothing to do with reducing poverty. Between 1999 and 2016, Oklahoma spent more than $70 million in TANF funds on the Oklahoma Marriage Initiative, providing counseling services and organizing workshops open to everyone in the state, poor or not. Arizona used welfare dollars to pay for abstinence-only sex education. Pennsylvania diverted TANF funds to anti-abortion crisis pregnancy centers. Maine used the money to support a Christian summer camp.[14]

And then there's Mississippi. A 389-page audit released in 2020 found that money overseen by the Mississippi Department of Human Services (DHS) and intended for the state's poorest families was used to hire an evangelical worship singer who performed at rallies and church concerts; to purchase a Nissan Armada, Chevrolet Silverado, and Ford F-250 for the head of a local nonprofit and two of her family members; and even to pay the former NFL quarterback Brett Favre $1.1 million for speeches he never gave. (Favre later returned the money.) There's more. DHS contractors squandered TANF dollars on college football tickets, a private school, a twelve-week fitness camp that state legislators could attend free of charge ($1.3 million), and a donation to the University of Southern Mississippi for a wellness center ($5 million). Welfare funds also went to a ministry run by former professional wrestler Ted DiBiase—the Million Dollar Man and the author of the memoir *Every Man Has His Price*—for speeches and wrestling events. DiBiase's price was $2.1 million. Brett DiBiase, the Million Dollar Man's son, was serving as deputy administrator for Mississippi's Department of Human Services at the time.

He and five others have been indicted on fraud and embezzle-ment charges.[15]

States aren't required to spend all of their TANF dollars each year, and many don't, carrying over the unused money into the next year. In 2020, states had in their possession al-most $6 billion in unspent welfare funds. Nebraska was sitting on $91 million. Hawaii had $380 million, enough to provide every poor child in the state with $10,000. Tennessee topped the list with $790 million. That year only nine states in the Union had a higher child poverty rate than Tennessee. No state had a child poverty rate higher than Mississippi's, at roughly 28 percent, which is also the child poverty rate of Costa Rica.[16]

Or take Social Security Disability Insurance (SSDI), which provides a stipend to people with disabilities who contributed to Social Security during their working years. In 1996, roughly 1.28 million Americans applied for disability. By 2010, nearly 3 million people did. Demographic changes—especially popu-lation growth and aging baby boomers—seem to be behind this trend. Yet the number of new disability awards approved by the Social Security Administration did not keep pace with the steep rise in applications. Between 1996 and 2010, applica-tions rose by 130 percent, but new awards increased by just 68 percent. Many Americans were turning to disability for help, but the government was making it harder to get. In the mid-1990s, roughly half of new disability applications were ap-proved; today, roughly a third are.[17]

I remember watching my friend Woo go through the pro-cess of trying to secure disability after his leg was amputated. A backslapper with an irreverent laugh, Woo loved people. It's what made him a good security guard—that and the fact that he cleared six feet and wore XXL shirts. When we lived together in a rooming house on the North Side of Milwaukee, he called me Andy and told me to call him Red, like the friends (one white, as I am; the other Black, as Woo is) in the movie *The Shawshank Redemption,* which Woo always called *The Shawdank Reduction.*

In the hospital, I found Woo in a wheelchair, his half-leg wrapped in a temporary cast and propped up by a support. He looked small, and we cried together as he placed both hands next to his stump as if to say: *See?* "I been done so wrong, Matt," he kept saying.

Once released, Woo began learning to walk with a prosthesis, and he applied for disability. He was forty-one. At that age, you need twenty Social Security credits to qualify, which equates to five years in the formal workforce. Woo had worked more than full-time for well over five years—regularly pulling double shifts working security—but not at the kind of places that took down your Social Security number. So Woo applied for the nation's alternative disability program, Supplemental Security Income (SSI). Like SSDI, most SSI applications are rejected.[18] I helped Woo fill out the paperwork, but his first try was batted down. Woo wasn't surprised. "That's how it always be," he told me. Then he phoned a disability lawyer.

In poor communities, it is common knowledge that you must apply multiple times for disability, as if being denied over and over is part of the standard application process, and you'll need to hire an attorney. Working on contingency, lawyers can receive up to a quarter of the back pay their clients receive for the months they waited. As the odds of being approved for

disability have narrowed over the years, applicants have increasingly turned to attorneys to argue their claims. In 2001,
179,171 payments totaling $425 million were issued to "claimant
representatives," attorneys mostly, who represented people
applying for disability and other benefits. By 2019, 390,809
payments—totaling $1.2 billion—were issued.[19]

The second time Woo applied, he did it in person, at the
courthouse, with a lawyer by his side. "The lawyer used the
big words, but the wheelchair won the case," Woo remembered. His time in front of a judge lasted all of five minutes.
Woo received $3,600 in back pay, which he spent on a used
wheelchair-accessible van that ran for three years before catching on fire. His lawyer took home $400 for his efforts. Today,
Woo makes do on $800 a month in SSI payments, far less than
he made working. He isn't bothered that his lawyer got paid.
"He's the reason I'm on disability," Woo told me. But I can't
get over the fact that each year, over a billion dollars of Social
Security funds are spent not on getting people disability but
on getting people lawyers so that they can get disability.[20]

If we have more than doubled government spending on
poverty and achieved so little, one reason is because the American welfare state is a leaky bucket.[21] A dollar allocated to an
antipoverty program does not mean a dollar will ultimately
reach a needy family. But this does not completely solve the
puzzle of why poverty has been so stubbornly persistent. After
all, many of the country's largest social welfare programs distribute funds directly to people. Roughly 85 percent of the
Supplemental Nutrition Assistance Program budget is dedicated to funding food stamps themselves, and almost 93 percent of Medicaid and even Supplemental Security Income

dollars flow directly to beneficiaries.[22] There are, it would seem, other forces at play.

OVER THE COURSE OF American history, immigrants have served as a scapegoat for our economic anxieties. "The Chinese as a class are a detriment and a curse to our country," reads a newspaper column from 1877. "They have supplanted white labor and taken the bread out of the mouths of the white men and their families." In the early 1900s, native-born white Americans lashed out at Italian immigrants for landing jobs and working hard in them, even resorting to mob violence and lynching to drive them out of town. Conservatives today who cast blame on immigrants for dragging down wages and displacing native workers are carrying forward an old American tradition.[23]

Theoretically, immigrants could drive up a country's poverty rate in at least three ways: They could arrive poor and stay that way, forming a new underclass; they could make the native-born population poorer by depressing wages; or they could overburden the safety net, diluting antipoverty investments. Our foreign-born population has soared over the past half century. In 1960, one in twenty people in America was born in another country. Today, one in eight is. The United States now has more immigrants than any other nation on earth. Could this be why the poverty rate hasn't budged even as antipoverty aid has increased?[24]

Like European immigrants who crossed the Atlantic generations ago, many present-day immigrants arrive poor. If those newcomers and their children remained poor, increased immigration could push up the poverty rate. If this were happening, states that experienced the largest influx of immigrants should have seen their poverty rates climb. Almost half of America's foreign-born population now lives in just three states: California, Texas, and Florida. As those states took in more and more immigrants, did they become worse off? No, they did not. Between 1970 and 2019, the share of the immigrant population increased by nearly 18 percent in California, 14 percent in Texas, and 13 percent in Florida. But over that same period, California's poverty rate increased only marginally (by 0.7 percent), while poverty fell in both Texas and Florida: by 5 and almost 4 percent, respectively. The states that have taken in the most immigrants over the past half century have not grown poorer. In the case of Texas and Florida, they have grown more prosperous.[25]

If poor immigrants have settled in large numbers in California and Florida and Texas without making those states poorer over time, it's because immigrants have some of the highest rates of economic mobility in the country. This is especially true for the children of immigrants. How many of us have met software engineers and doctors and lawyers who are the children of migrant farmers and dishwashers and laundresses? Their collective success is a big reason why heightened immigration has not resulted in more poverty.[26]

But has their success come at the expense of other workers? Do immigrants compete with native-born Americans, driving down wages and pulling more people into poverty? The best research we have on this question finds that the long-term impact of immigration on wages is quite small, and its impact on employment is even smaller. If immigrants competed with native-born workers for jobs, this finding would be head-scratching, even dubious, but immigrants mainly compete with other immigrants for jobs, which means the workers most threatened by new arrivals are older arrivals.[27] For many Americans, wages have stagnated, but immigrants are not to blame.

Undocumented immigration has slowed in recent years. The push factors have waned, thanks to an aging population and stabilizing economy in Mexico, and the push *back* factors have grown stronger with increasingly militant border enforcement. The politicians who wring their hands about "the border crisis" know full well that the undocumented population peaked over fifteen years ago, in 2007. Yet employers have not responded to a shrinking undocumented workforce by hiring native-born workers at competitive wages. Instead, they have responded by automating their jobs (using machines instead), hiring other immigrants, like those on H-2A visas (Americans don't exactly queue up for immigrant jobs), or simply closing up shop.[28]

Regardless of their impact on the labor market, immigrants could make a country poorer by relying heavily on welfare benefits. But the poorest immigrants are undocumented, which makes them ineligible for many federal programs, including food stamps, non-emergency Medicaid, and Social Security. Over a typical lifetime, an immigrant will give more to the U.S. government in taxes than he or she will receive in federal welfare benefits.[29] Even if the opposite were true, the impact immigrants would have on overall government spending would be utterly, even comically, trivial compared to the stress the American upper class places on the welfare state. But I'm getting ahead of myself. For now, it's enough to concede that America's dismal track record on poverty reduction cannot be blamed on its immigrant workforce.

CAN WE PIN IT on the family? There was a time in America when most poor children grew up in a home with both of their biological parents. In 1959, about 70 percent of poor families were composed of a married couple. Today, the preachers of down-at-the-heels churches do far more funerals than weddings, as most poor children are born to single mothers. Roughly one in three families headed by a single mother is poor, compared to just one in seventeen married families.[30] This disparity has led some to conclude that single parenthood is a major cause of poverty in America.

But then, why isn't it a major cause in Ireland or Italy or Sweden? A study of eighteen rich democracies found that single mothers outside the United States were not poorer than the general population. Countries that make the deepest investments in their people, particularly through universal programs that benefit all citizens, have the lowest rates of poverty, including among households headed by single mothers. We could follow suit by investing in programs to help single parents balance work and family life, programs such as paid family leave, affordable childcare, and universal pre-K. Instead, we've increasingly privatized daycare and summer programming, effectively reserving these modern-day necessities for the affluent. In doing so, we've made it impossible for many single parents to go back to school or work full-time. Choosing to have a child outside of marriage may be an individual choice, but condemning many of those parents and their children to a life of poverty is a societal one.[31]

In America, marriage has become something of a luxury good. It comes after a couple believes they have achieved a level of financial stability. When couples don't reach that "marriage bar," they tend not to tie the knot. So pointing to lower rates of marriage among the poor as the main reason for their poverty is akin to pointing to higher rates of homeownership among the affluent as the primary reason for their prosperity, confusing effect for cause. Homeownership doesn't lead to financial stability; it leads to *more* financial stability. You can usually buy a home only after you've done well for yourself (or your parents have). Marriage works the same way.[32] It tends to lock in the security of the already secure. The bourgeois model of the two-parent family is made possible by the same stuff that made the bourgeoisie: money.[33]

When we extend real economic opportunities to poor Americans, marriage typically follows. Take the New Hope program, implemented in the mid-1990s in Milwaukee. This initiative gave residents from poor neighborhoods access to affordable health insurance and childcare, while also providing wage supplements to boost their incomes. Five years after New Hope launched, participants randomly selected into the program had significantly higher incomes and better jobs than those who weren't. They were also nearly twice as likely to be married. New Hope is one of several programs that have boosted marriage rates, not by offering relationship counseling or organizing workshops—initiatives that almost never work—but by providing couples with enough economic stability to try for a life together.[34]

But these programs are fleeting and experimental, while much of American social policy remains downright hostile to the family. The most antifamily social policies have been those fueling mass incarceration. Most people in prison are parents. Men have been taken from their families by the tens and hundreds of thousands, then by the millions. Poor Black and Hispanic families have paid the highest price.[35] Other countries, like Germany, permit their incarcerated citizens to visit family members outside detention centers, but the American prison system seems designed to break up all sorts of relationships. By one estimate, the number of marriages in the United States would increase by as much as 30 percent if we didn't imprison a single person.[36] America's obsession with incarceration has removed scores of poor people from their families, strictly controlling when they can call their children, spouses, and loved ones, and then releasing them back into society with a criminal record that impedes their already dim job and housing prospects. In the history of the nation, there has only been one other state-sponsored initiative more antifamily than mass incarceration, and that was slavery.

Many of our welfare policies, too, have an antifamily design. Supplemental Security Income checks are docked if recipients live with relatives. A mother can lose her rental assistance or public housing unit if she allows the father of her children to live with her in violation of her lease. Households receive a higher total allotment of food stamps if romantic partners apply separately for the benefit rather than as a married couple.[37] Then there is the Earned Income Tax Credit (EITC). Say there is a family of four, where Mom makes $30,000 a year and Dad makes $15,000. If Dad claimed the EITC benefit himself, he would receive the maximum amount ($5,920 in 2020). But if the couple married, the family would receive only around $2,000. So which decision is more "pro-family": choosing not to marry and bringing in considerably more money or choosing to get hitched and bringing in less?[38]

I don't mean to leave the wrong impression. There is not much evidence that the design of welfare programs plays a decisive role in discouraging marriage. Bad jobs, unobtainable college degrees, mass incarceration, and unaffordable child-care are far more consequential.[39] But I do wonder why the federal government fashions its welfare policies this way, even as many of its elected officials present marriage as the solution to the nation's deep and persistent poverty.

Instead of recognizing the effect of broader economic and social policies on the decision to marry, some commentators see marriage as a check-off item in an instructional manual for the Good Life. For example, young people are commonly told that they can avoid poverty in America by following three sim-ple steps: graduate from high school, obtain a full-time job, and wait until they get married to have children. A report pub-lished by the American Enterprise Institute, a conservative think tank, labeled the three steps "the success sequence." One study found that only 2 percent of people who completed the sequence were poor in 2007, compared to 76 percent of people who violated all three rules.[40]

I wish it were that simple. But when you dig into the data, you discover that there were more poor people who had fol-lowed all three rules than who had broken all of them and that Black Americans who had stuck to the success sequence were less likely to escape poverty than white Americans who did the same. You also learn that the step in the sequence responsible for nearly all the "success" is not marriage but securing a full-time job. The problem is that many single parents simply can't afford to work more because of childcare costs.[41] We do not devalue the importance of education or work or marriage by recognizing that when we ask a poor person—someone like Crystal, say—to just finish high school and land a good job and get married, we might as well be asking that person to just get a different life.

The real question about single-parent families isn't why so many poor parents are single but why we allow so many of them to remain poor. Wouldn't we prefer a country where all family types were protected from want, where single parenthood didn't so often come with a poverty sentence?[42]

Trees ramify a welter of gnarled, twisting roots, and there is something to be said for tracing each one that stretches and curls through the earth. It's a useful exercise, evaluating the merits of different explanations for poverty, like those having to do with immigration or the family. But I've found that doing so always leads me back to the taproot, the central feature from which all other rootlets spring, which in our case is the simple truth that poverty is an injury, a taking. Tens of millions of Americans do not end up poor by a mistake of history or personal conduct. Poverty persists because some wish and will it to.

CHAPTER 3

HOW WE UNDERCUT
WORKERS

W E TYPICALLY DON'T TALK ABOUT POVERTY AS A CON-
dition that benefits some of us. It seems we prefer more absolving theories of the problem. There is, of course, the old
habit of blaming the poor for their own miseries, as if Americans were made of lesser stuff than people in countries with
far less poverty. But structural explanations are more in fashion these days, explanations that trace widespread poverty
back to broken institutions or seismic economic transformations.

One popular theory for American poverty is deindustrialization, which caused the shuttering of factories and the hol-
lowing out of communities that had sprung up around them.
Such a passive word, "deindustrialization." It leaves the impression that it just happened somehow, as if the country got
deindustrialization the way a forest gets infested by bark bee-
tles. In this telling, poverty is "a by-product of social causes,"
as the sociologist Erik Olin Wright once put it. "No one intended this calamity, and no one really benefits from it."[1]

But if arrangements that harm the poor have endured over

the decades, doesn't that suggest that they were designed to do so? At the end of the day, aren't "systemic" problems—systemic racism, poverty, misogyny—made up of untold numbers of individual decisions motivated by real or imagined self-interest? "The system" doesn't force us to stiff the waiter or vote against affordable housing in our neighborhood, does it?

People benefit from poverty in all kinds of ways. It's the plainest social fact there is, and yet when you put it like this, the air becomes charged. You feel rude bringing it up. People shift in their chairs, and some respond by trying to quiet you the way mothers try to shush small children in public when they point out something that everyone sees but pretends not to—a man with one eye, a dog urinating on a car—or the way serious grown-ups shush young people when they offer blanket critiques of capitalism that, with the brutal clarity of a brick through glass, express a deep moral truth. People accuse you of inciting class warfare when you're merely pointing out the obvious.

As a theory of poverty, exploitation elicits a muddled response, causing us to think *of course* and *but, no* in the same instant. On the one hand, as the late composer Stephen Sondheim once wrote, "The history of the world, my sweet—is who gets eaten and who gets to eat." Clans, families, tribes, and nation-states collide, and one side is annihilated or enslaved or colonized or dispossessed to enrich the other. One side ascends to a higher place on the backs of the vanquished. Why should we think of poverty today as the result of anything different?[2] On the other hand, that was then. Notice how our voices, which can so effortlessly discuss exploitation that happened in the past, become garbled and halting when the conversation moves to how we get over on each other today. Perhaps because exploitation appears to us only in its most galling, extreme forms: enslaved Black field hands, young boys sent into the coal pits and young girls into the cotton mills. Perhaps we are captivated by a heroic narrative of progress, particularly racial progress, as if history, to quote the psychologist Jennifer Richeson, was "a ratchet that turns in one direction only."[3]

Or perhaps we connect the concept of exploitation with socialism and don't want to be associated with its tenets (or at least not its aesthetics). Years ago, I presented a paper titled "Exploiting the Inner City" at Harvard's Kennedy School of Government, a paper that documented the business strategies of landlords in poor neighborhoods. The paper was straightforward. It showed how some landlords make a living (and sometimes a killing) by renting shabby housing to very poor families. After my talk, a senior scholar looked rather alarmed. "You're going down a Marxist path," she said. "You know that, right?"

I didn't see it that way and still don't.[4] Our vulnerability to exploitation grows as our liberty shrinks. Inmates in states such as Arizona, Connecticut, and Kentucky can call their loved ones only on the prison phone, and they are charged $3 for a fifteen-minute in-state call. Those of us who are not incarcerated would never accept such terms; we have better alternatives. Because labor laws often fail to protect undocumented workers in practice, more than a third are paid below minimum wage, and nearly 85 percent are not paid overtime. Many of us who are U.S. citizens, or who crossed borders through official checkpoints, would not work for these wages. We don't have to. (Did the undocumented workers choose the terms of their arrangement? If they migrated as adults, yes, they did. But just because desperate people accept and even seek out exploitative conditions doesn't make those conditions any less exploitative.)[5]

More shifting in chairs. *It's more complicated than that,* some will say. Most social problems are complicated, of course, but a retreat into complexity is more often a reflection of our social standing than evidence of critical intelligence. Hungry people want bread. The rich convene a panel of experts. Complexity is the refuge of the powerful. I'm reminded of the tractor driver in *The Grapes of Wrath* who was ordered to plow a line straight through a tenant farmer's home. "You even come too close, and I'll pot you like a rabbit," the farmer threatened. "It's not me. There's nothing I can do," the tractor driver replied, explaining that there were dozens of men ready to replace him—and besides, he had orders from his boss, who had orders from the bank, which "gets orders from the East," and on it went. The matter was complicated. "But where does it stop? Who can we shoot?" the farmer asked, registering what the tractor driver refused to: that his family was not, as we like to say, "a victim of the times" or "unfortunate" or "disadvantaged" but under siege. He saw clearly that one man's poverty was another man's profit, nothing complicated about it.[6]

SEVERAL YEARS AGO, I met Julio Payes, a permanent resident from Guatemala who came to the United States on a work visa. He lived in Emeryville, California, a city of roughly twelve thousand residents, sandwiched between Oakland and Berkeley. In 2014, Julio was working eighty hours a week at two full-time jobs. He began his day with the graveyard shift at a twenty-four-hour McDonald's, where he served burgers and fries from 10 P.M. to 6 A.M. After his shift ended, he had two hours to rest and shower. Then he'd clock in at Aerotek, going anywhere the temp service sent him between 8 A.M. and 4 P.M. When that shift ended, he slept as much as he could. Then it was back to McDonald's. To stay awake, Julio loaded up on coffee and soda. Each job paid minimum wage.[7]

"I felt like a zombie," Julio told me. "No energy. Always sad." Yet to afford the single unfurnished room he shared with his mother and two siblings, he had to work up to sixteen hours a day, seven days a week. It seemed Julio was either working or sleeping, with no life in between. Once, his younger brother, Alexander, who was eight at the time, told him he was saving money. "I want to buy one hour of your time," Alexander told his older brother. "How much for one hour to play with me?" Julio looked at his brother and wept. Not long after that, he fainted from exhaustion in the aisle of a grocery store. He was twenty-four.

Julio ended up on a stretcher because his employers paid him so little. Did they have to? This is the more direct way of asking a question usually presented in the sterile terms of academic economics: If we increased the wages of the poorest workers, would that increase unemployment?

"In all probability, yes," was the answer economists gave to this question for years. In 1946, the *American Economic Review* published a paper entitled "The Economics of Minimum Wage Legislation" by George Stigler, a thirty-five-year-old

economist at the University of Minnesota. Inflation had diluted the 40-cent minimum wage, and people were calling for
an increase to 60 or even 75 cents an hour, which translates to
$9.51 and $11.88 in June 2022 dollars. "Economists have not
been very outspoken on this type of legislation," Stigler wrote.
"It is my fundamental thesis that they can and should be outspoken, and singularly agreed" that raising the minimum
wage was a bad idea. Stigler believed that if employers had to
pay workers more, they'd hire fewer of them, spurring unemployment among people who otherwise would have had bad
jobs, but jobs nonetheless.[8]

The young economist arrived at this conclusion not by relying on facts but by drawing on "hypothetical data," a nu-
merical story he invented to illustrate his theory. Other
economists were persuaded by Stigler's simple, elegant rea-
soning, and canonized it in the pages of their textbooks. The
prediction that raising the minimum wage would lead to
higher unemployment rates became economic orthodoxy.[9]

And yet it remained untested for nearly fifty years. Then, in
1992, ten years after Stigler was awarded the Nobel Prize, New
Jersey raised its minimum wage while neighboring Pennsylvania did not. This created a natural experiment that could be
leveraged to evaluate the effect of the wage increase on jobs.
To do so, David Card and Alan Krueger, both economists at
Princeton, surveyed 410 fast food restaurants in each state before and after the wage hike. They found that fast food jobs in
New Jersey did not decline after the state raised its minimum
wage. At least in this case, Stigler was wrong.[10] In the years
since, economists have churned out hundreds of similar studies, the bulk of them supporting the main finding of Card and

Krueger's bombshell paper by showing that increasing the minimum wage has negligible effects on employment.[11]

Democrats push the idea that raising the minimum wage will create jobs by increasing spending, as workers will have more money in their pockets. Republicans fret that raising the minimum wage will cost jobs, echoing Stigler. You can find studies that support both positions, but the bulk of the evidence suggests that the employment effect of raising the minimum wage is inconsequential.[12] Julio didn't have to be paid poverty wages for his job to exist. If he manned the grill at a McDonald's in Denmark, his paycheck would have been double what it was in Emeryville.[13]

IT WASN'T ALWAYS THIS BAD. Between the late 1940s and the late 1970s, the American economy expanded and shared its bounty. Honest work delivered a solid paycheck, and a big reason why had to do with union power. Throughout the 1950s and 1960s, nearly a third of all U.S. workers carried union cards. These were the days of the United Automobile Workers, led by Walter Reuther, once savagely beaten by Ford's brass knuckle boys, and of the mighty American Federation of Labor and Congress of Industrial Organizations that together represented around 15 million workers, more than the population of California at the time. These workers raised hell. The United Farm Workers' 1965 Delano grape strike and boycott lasted five years and captivated the American public. In 1970 alone, 2.4 million union members participated in work stoppages, wildcat strikes, and tense standoffs with company heads. Their efforts paid off. Worker pay climbed, CEO compensation was reined in, and the country experienced the most economically equitable period in modern history.[14]

But unions were often a white man's refuge. During the postwar years, most white women did not work outside the home, while many Black women couldn't afford not to. They tended to labor in caretaking roles—as cooks and nurses and housekeepers—without anything resembling union representation. As for Black men, organized labor remained hostile to them. In the 1930s, many unions outwardly discriminated against Black workers or segregated them into Jim Crow local chapters. In the 1960s, unions like the Brotherhood of Railway and Steamship Clerks and the United Brotherhood of Carpenters and Joiners of America enforced segregation within their ranks. By excluding Black workers, unions prevented the American labor movement from ever realizing its full potential.[15]

Things got worse during the painful stagflation crisis of the 1970s, when economic growth slowed but inflation did not. Unions harmed themselves through self-defeating racism and were further weakened by a changing economy. As the manufacturing sector continued to shrink, they lost their traditional power base. But organized labor was also attacked by political adversaries. As unions flagged, business interests sensed an opportunity. Corporate lobbyists made deep inroads in both parties, launching a public relations campaign that blamed labor for the slump and pressured policymakers to roll back worker protections.[16]

A national litmus test arrived in 1981, when thirteen thousand unionized air traffic controllers left their posts after contract negotiations with the Federal Aviation Administration broke down. When workers refused to return to work, President Reagan fired all of them. The public's response was muted, and corporate America learned that it could crush unions with minimal blowback. In 1985, Hormel Foods, of Spam and Dinty Moore beef stew fame, cut worker pay in its Austin, Minnesota, plant from $10.69 to $8.25 an hour and kneecapped the strike that followed by hiring replacements. "If the President of the United States can replace strikers, this must be socially acceptable," remarked one observer at the time.[17] And so it went, in one industry after another. As global trade expanded and plants shuttered, unions collapsed, and corporate interests made sure they remained weak.

Today, only around one in ten American workers belong to a union, and most of them are firefighters, nurses, cops, and other public sector workers. Almost all private sector employees (94 percent) are without a union, though roughly half of nonunion workers say they would organize if given the chance. They rarely are. Employers have at their disposal an arsenal of tactics designed to prevent collective bargaining, from hiring union-busting firms to telling employees that they could lose their jobs if they vote yes.[18] Those strategies are legal, but companies also make illegal moves to block unions, such as disciplining workers for trying to organize, or threatening to close. Between 2016 and 2017, the National Labor Relations Board charged 42 percent of employers with violating federal law during union campaigns. In nearly a third of cases, this involved illegally firing workers for organizing.

THEY TOLD US THAT organized labor was a drag on the economy, burdensome cargo preventing our ship from reaching flank speed. They said that once the companies had cleared out all these fusty, lumbering unions, the economy would rev up, boosting everyone's fortunes. But that didn't come to pass. The negative effects of unions have been wildly overstated, and there is now evidence that they play a role in boosting company productivity, for example by reducing turnover.[19] The American economy is less productive today than it was in the postwar period, when unions were at peak strength. The economies of other rich countries have slowed as well, including those with more highly unionized workforces, but it is clear that diluting labor power in America did not unleash economic growth or deliver prosperity to more people. "We were promised economic dynamism in exchange for inequality," write Eric Posner and Glen Weyl in their book, *Radical Markets*. "We got the inequality, but dynamism is actually declining."[20]

As workers lost power, their jobs got worse. Unions had kept caps on profits by raising workers' wages and compensation. But as labor power faded, those caps were lifted with predictable consequences. Since 1979, the bottom 90 percent of income earners—not the bottom 10, 20, or even 50 percent, but the bottom 90 *percent*—saw annual earnings gains of only 24 percent, while the wages of the top 1 percent of earners more than doubled. For several decades after World War II, ordinary workers' inflation-adjusted wages (known as "real wages") increased by 2 percent each year. But since 1979, real wages have grown by only 0.3 percent a year.[21] Astonishingly, the real wages for many Americans today are roughly what they were forty years ago. Ninety percent of Americans who entered college or the job market in the late 1960s would go on to earn more than their parents did, but this was the case for only 50 percent of Americans by the late 1990s. Upward mobility is no longer the overriding feature of the American experience. For far too many young people today, the future is fraught.[22]

The United States now offers some of the lowest wages in the industrialized world, a feature that has swelled the ranks of the working poor, most of whom are thirty-five or older. Workers with a high school diploma made 2.7 percent less in 2017 than they would have in 1979, adjusted for inflation. Workers without a diploma made nearly 10 percent less. These are not primarily teenagers bagging groceries or scooping ice cream. They are adults, and often parents, wiping down hotel showers and toilets, taking food orders and busing tables, minding children at twenty-four-hour daycare centers, picking berries, emptying trash cans, stacking grocery shelves at midnight, answering customer service calls, smoothing hot asphalt on freeways, and, yes, bagging groceries and scooping ice cream.[23]

Are poor-paying jobs simply the result of people not getting enough education? It's true that workers with college degrees fare much better in today's economy than those without. But the spread of bad jobs in America is not primarily the result of a so-called skills mismatch involving too many people lacking the right credentials or training for good jobs. We've expanded the Pell Grant program and other initiatives to bring more low-income students to college. In 1970, fewer than a third of young adults from families in the bottom 25 percent of the income distribution were enrolled in college; by 2020, roughly half were. Yet during this time, the share of decent-paying American jobs fell and the share of poverty jobs rose, especially for young people. In 2020, almost a third of full-time workers between the ages of twenty-five and sixty-four who had earned at least a bachelor's degree made less than the national median ($59,371). Roughly half of Americans between the ages of twenty-five and thirty-four have earned a bachelor's degree or more, which is also the case in the Netherlands, Switzerland, France, and several other rich democracies with far less poverty. In Germany, only 35 percent of people in that age range have graduated from college, yet the child poverty rate there is half what it is here.[24]

We can't reduce our country's economic problems to a matter of education, and we can't chalk up today's brutal job market to globalization and technological change, either. Economic forces framed as inexorable, like the acceleration of global trade, are often the result of policy decisions such as the 1994 North American Free Trade Agreement (NAFTA), which made it easier for companies to move their factories to Mexico and contributed to the loss of hundreds of thousands of American jobs. The world has changed, but it has changed for other countries as well. Yet Belgium, Canada, Italy, and many other countries haven't experienced the kind of wage stagnation and surge in income inequality that the United States has. Why? A big reason is that those countries managed to keep their unions.[25] Which means this is largely about power.

Lousy, underpaid work is not an indispensable, if regrettable, by-product of capitalism, as some pro-business defenders claim today. (This notion would have scandalized capitalism's earliest defenders. John Stuart Mill, arch advocate of free people and free markets, once said that if widespread scarcity was a hallmark of capitalism, he would become a communist.)[26] But capitalism is inherently about workers trying to get as much, and owners trying to give as little, as possible. With unions largely out of the picture, corporations have chipped away at the conventional mid-century work arrangement, which involved steady employment, opportunities for advancement and raises, and decent pay with some benefits. As the sociologist Gerald Davis has put it: Our grandparents had careers. Our parents had jobs. We complete tasks. That's been the story of the American working class and working poor, anyway.[27]

Unlike the companies that rose to prominence after World War II, where virtually all employees worked for the same owner or firm, today's businesses now farm out positions to independent contractors. Those who buff the floors at Microsoft or wash the sheets at the Sheraton or deliver packages for Amazon are typically not employed by Microsoft or Sheraton or Amazon. At Google, the software engineers work for Google, but the recruiters, product testers, and administrators work for contractors hired by the tech giant. Google relies more on temps and contract workers than on full-time employees. Of the roughly 750,000 workers around the globe who help make and sell Apple products, only around 63,000 work directly for Apple. Before the rise of this chopped-up or "fissured" workplace, large firms standardized wages and benefits for all their employees. This had an equalizing effect, raising the income of, say, a janitor at an automobile factory. Today, temp agencies compete over who can offer the cheapest labor. OnContracting, a staffing agency, estimates that U.S. tech companies like Google and Apple can save an average of

$100,000 each year per job by using their services. As corpora-
tions have increasingly come to rely on independent contractors, they have depressed wages and hindered workers' ability
to earn promotions. (Mobility rates from low-paying work
have fallen since the 1990s.) How can someone who works at
Microsoft climb the ladder at Microsoft when she isn't even
employed by the company?[28]

Many employers now discourage or outright prohibit
workers from discussing wages and salaries because they
know that this kind of transparency enables underpaid employees to discover they are underpaid. Companies also require new hires to sign noncompete clauses barring them
from working for a rival business for several months, or even
years, after leaving their job. For entry-level workers, noncompete clauses are not used to protect a company's intellectual
property but to intimidate poorly paid employees and dimin-
ish one of the few powers they have left: the power to quit. Or
let's say you're a technician at a Jiffy Lube station—and damn
good at your job: hardworking, friendly, fast. If the franchise
owner at another Jiffy Lube in the next town heard about you
and wanted to lure you to his shop by offering a promotion, he
couldn't. The no-poaching agreement he signed with the corporation prohibits it. Most major franchisors' contracts con-
tain such agreements.[29] The goal of such tactics is to restrict
competition as much as possible because competition breeds
choice, and choice makes exploitation difficult.

The rise of gig jobs is not a break from the norm as much
as an extension of it, a continuation of corporations finding
new ways to limit their obligations to workers. Platforms such
as Uber, DoorDash, and TaskRabbit force their employees

(sorry, their "independent contractors") to assume more responsibility on the job—they must supply their own car, buy their own gas, cover their own insurance—while simultaneously subjecting those workers to heightened supervision. Some countries, including the United Kingdom and the Netherlands, have classified Uber drivers as full-time employees, which entitles them to basic protections like minimum wage and holiday pay, while other countries, such as Hungary and Thailand, have banned Uber altogether. But in America, Uber drivers and other gig workers usually don't get sick days, overtime, vacation time, or worker compensation. They often aren't covered by minimum wage laws or the National Labor Relations Act, which regulates employment conditions, and are ineligible for unemployment insurance. These kinds of jobs, along with other alternative work arrangements like temp work, have surged in the United States since the turn of the century.[30]

Corporations have not only drastically reshaped the nature of work; they've also bent the rules that govern it, turning economic coin into political muscle. The most powerful lobbying force in the nation (as measured in sheer dollars spent) is the U.S. Chamber of Commerce, which has mobilized against proposals to raise the corporate tax rate and the minimum wage and has come out against legislation designed to make it easier for workers to organize. In 2022, the U.S. Chamber dedicated more than $35 million to influencing government policy, while unions spent a combined total of roughly $25 million. But keep in mind that the U.S. Chamber is just a single pro-business organization. All but five of the top one hundred organizations that spend the most on lobbying represent business interests. Just three corporations alone—Meta, Amazon, and Comcast—spent more in 2022 than all labor unions combined. That kind of money allows corporate lobbyists to be everywhere at once, stalking not only the halls of Congress but also state legislatures and city council offices, pushing hundreds of bills. In 2016, Uber had 370 lobbyists working in forty-four states. Against that, what chance did the taxi unions have?[31]

AS CORPORATIONS HAVE AMASSED more market power, they've made every effort to keep wages low and productivity high. Increasingly, workers are providing far more value to their companies than their pay reflects, and employers are constantly finding new avenues to squeeze their labor force. Algorithms have proven to be more exacting bosses than people. Those algorithms powering just-in-time scheduling have allowed bosses to fine-tune staffing levels to demand, leading to unpredictable hours that cause paychecks to grow and shrink from week to week. Companies have deployed programs that record workers' keystrokes and mouse clicks and capture screenshots at random intervals and have even made use of devices that sense heat and motion. Warehouse workers, cashiers, delivery drivers, fast food managers, copy editors, and millions of other kinds of workers—even therapists and hospice chaplains—are now monitored by software with names like Time Doctor and WorkSmart. Most large private firms track worker productivity, sometimes docking pay for "idle time," including when employees use the bathroom or consult with clients. Such technological advances have increased workers' efficiency and their precarity: You produce

more profit but enjoy less of it, which is the textbook defini-
tion of exploitation.[32]

Economists have developed a way to put a price tag on
how much this costs workers. In 2018, the median annual compensation was $30,500. In a paper published that year, research-
ers estimated that in a perfectly competitive market, it would
be closer to $41,000 and could be as high as $92,000. These are
numbers to pause over: incomes rising by at least a third, just
from making markets fair. But as big corporations have gotten
bigger, buying up competitors or putting them out of business, workers have fewer and fewer options. Many are vastly
underpaid and don't even realize it. Do you know who does?
The bosses and investors.[33]

Work is not what keeps scores of low-paid Americans from
plunging into deep poverty. The government is. It's the government that helps these families access healthcare (through
Medicaid), that helps them eat (food stamps), and that boosts
their incomes (the Earned Income Tax Credit). The Government Accountability Office recently analyzed data from
eleven states and found that roughly 12 million American
workers relied on Medicaid for their health insurance and
9 million lived in homes receiving food stamps. Most of the
workers enrolled in each program worked full-time for part of
the year; roughly half worked full-time year-round.[34] In 2020,
one in seventeen Food Lion workers in North Carolina drew
on food stamps; almost one in ten Stop & Shop employees in
Massachusetts was enrolled in Medicaid, as was nearly one in
seven Oklahomans who worked at Dollar General.[35]

Our biggest antipoverty program for the working poor is
the Earned Income Tax Credit. In 2021, 25 million workers and

families received this subsidy, the average payment being $2,411.[36] The EITC is one of the nation's most enduring anti-poverty programs, in large part because of its strong bipartisan backing. But perhaps the primary reason the EITC enjoys such widespread support is because it functions as a generous handout to corporations. Among the loudest champions of the EITC have been multinational businesses, whose low wages are effectively subsidized through the program. Walmart has established initiatives to help their employees claim the EITC and has supported legislation that requires large employers to notify their workers about the benefit. (It also has a SWAT team ready to deploy to any store via corporate jet to squash the slightest whiff of organizing.) The U.S. Chamber of Commerce along with the National Restaurant Association, the world's largest food service trade association, have pushed for EITC expansion. A report issued by the Institute for a Competitive Workforce, an affiliate of the U.S. Chamber, encourages employers to make sure their workers know about the EITC because "by introducing employees to these benefits, businesses help their employees—and help themselves."[37]

CORPORATE PROFITS RISE WHEN labor costs fall. This is why Wall Street is so quick to pummel companies when they bump up wages. When Walmart announced in 2015 that it planned to increase its starting wage to at least $9 an hour, largely in response to public pressure, investors dumped the stock. Shares fell by 10 percent, erasing $20 billion in market value. It was the company's biggest single-day loss on record. The same thing happened in 2021. After the retailer pledged to raise its average hourly wage to $15 to compete with Amazon and other companies that had responded to the Fight for $15 campaign, shareholders bailed, causing the stock to fall 6 percent on a Thursday morning. Investors were putting Walmart, and every other publicly traded company, on notice: If you raise wages, you'll pay for it.[38]

Who benefits from this? The shareholders, of course, but who are they? It's tempting to picture them as a group of men in pinstriped suits and power ties, gathered in some high-rise Manhattan boardroom. But over half of U.S. households are vested in the stock market (though it should be said that the richest 10 percent of families own over 80 percent of the total value of all stocks). *We* are the shareholders, we lucky 53 percent who have a pension, a 401(k), a 403(b), or any other kind of investment—or we who have parents using 529 plans to fund our education or are enrolled in universities whose endowments pay for residential dormitories and study abroad trips. Don't we benefit when we see our savings go up and up, even when those returns require a kind of human sacrifice?[39]

Consumers benefit from worker exploitation, too. We can now, with a few clicks, summon rides and groceries and Chinese takeout and a handyman, all at cut rates. We have become masters in this new servant economy, where an anonymized and underpaid workforce does the bidding of the affluent. "Uber" is now a verb. Americans rank Amazon as one of the most trusted institutions in the country, second only to the military. These companies have become ascendant because we love them. I still find myself, after all these years, mystified that I'm able to have just about anything I can think of arrive on my doorstep in twenty-four hours. This is the closest thing to magic that we have.[40]

Even as more and more of us are shopping according to our values, economic justice does not seem to be among our top priorities. We know if our vegetables are local and organic, but we don't ask what the farmworkers made picking them. When we purchase a plane ticket, we are shown the carbon emissions for the flight, but we aren't told if the flight attendants are unionized. We reward companies that run antiracist marketing campaigns without recognizing how these campaigns can distract from those companies' abysmal labor practices, as if shortchanging workers isn't often itself a kind of racism. (The economists Valerie Wilson and William Darity, Jr., have shown that the Black-white pay gap has increased since 2000, and today, the average Black worker makes roughly 74 cents for every dollar the average white worker does.) We recognize the kind of coffee we should drink or the kind of shoes we should wear to signal our political affiliations, but we are often unaware of what difference that makes for the workers themselves, if it makes a difference at all. My family stopped shopping at Home Depot after learning about the company's hefty donations to Republican lawmakers who refused to certify the results of the 2020 presidential election. We have yet to inquire about the pay and benefits offered at Ace Hardware.[41]

AROUND THE TIME JULIO collapsed in the grocery store, the Emeryville City Council started to consider raising the city's minimum wage. Oakland had just passed a ballot initiative to increase it from $9 to $12.25 an hour, and Emeryville set out to match it. Then the mayor, Ruth Atkin, began asking if her city could do more. What if they mandated a real living wage? When Julio caught wind of this possibility, he began to pray. He prayed during Sunday and Wednesday revival services, where he danced and shouted as the spirit moved him. He prayed in quiet moments at home. "God, he believes in justice," Julio told me. "I have faith. But I also have politics." Julio became active in the Fight for $15, participating in marches and other shows of collective strength. "The first time we did a strike, I felt very nervous," he told me. But when he showed up in his work uniform and saw thousands of other fast food workers in theirs, he found his voice. It felt like church.

On a Tuesday night in May 2015, the Emeryville City Council voted to raise the city's minimum wage to almost $16 an hour by 2019. In July 2022, the city's minimum wage was set at $17.68, among the highest in the nation.

When I spoke to Julio in the winter of 2019, he was making $15 an hour at Burger King and $15.69 at a large hotel, where he worked as a room attendant. He could now afford to work less, logging around forty-eight hours a week when things were slow and sixty hours when they weren't. He slept more, took walks in the park. "It's had a big impact on my life," he told me. "I feel better."

When poor workers receive a pay raise, their health improves dramatically. Studies have found that when minimum wages go up, rates of child neglect, underage alcohol consumption, and teen births go down.[42] Smoking, too, decreases. Big Tobacco has long targeted low-income communities, but there is strong evidence that minimum wage increases are associated with decreased rates of smoking among low-income workers. Higher wages ease the grind of poverty, freeing people up to quit.

The chronic stress that accompanies poverty can be detected at the cellular level. One study found that up to 5,500 premature deaths that occurred in New York City from 2008 to 2012 could have been prevented if the city's minimum wage had been $15 an hour during that time, instead of just over $7. A higher minimum wage is an antidepressant. It is a sleep aid. A stress reliever. Vocal segments of the American public, those with brain space to spare, seem to believe the poor should change their behavior to escape poverty. *Get a better job. Stop having children. Make smarter financial decisions.* In truth, it's the other way around: Economic security leads to better choices.[43]

After his wages were increased, Julio opened a modest savings account for emergencies and began spending more time with Alexander, often picking him up from school. "Before, I felt like a slave," Julio told me. "But now I feel, *¿Cómo se dice, más seguro?*" Safer, he said. "I feel safer."

What do we deny workers when we deny them living wages so that we may enjoy more wealth and cheap goods? Happiness, health—life itself. Is this the capitalism we want, the capitalism we deserve?

CHAPTER 4

HOW WE FORCE THE POOR
TO PAY MORE

THERE ARE MANY WAYS TO BE EXPLOITED. WHEN WE ARE underpaid relative to the value of what we produce, we experience labor exploitation. And when we are overcharged relative to the value of something we purchase, we experience consumer exploitation. Our economic freedom is limited when we don't have resources at our disposal. When we don't own property or can't access credit, we become dependent on people who do and can, which in turn invites exploitation because a bad deal for you is a good deal for me. When someone has us over a barrel, we are at their mercy.[1]

Perhaps nowhere is this more apparent than in the rental housing market.

As people flocked to cities throughout the late eighteenth and early nineteenth centuries, urban land values soared, and landlords began subdividing their properties to make room for more renters. The Panic of 1837, a financial crisis that led the country into a major depression, encouraged even more partitioning. Cellars, attics, and storage sheds were fashioned into single-room apartments, and renting to poor families proved to be a lucrative enterprise even through the catastrophic downturn. The poor in major cities across the West had high rents extracted from them. When tenements began appearing in New York City in the mid-1800s, their rent was as much as 30 percent higher than that of better apartments uptown. This was true even in the poorest slums.[2]

Racism and exploitation feed on each other, and Black families who moved north during the Great Migration, which stretched from 1915 to 1970, experienced this fact afresh when they arrived in cities like Cleveland and Philadelphia. There, they were hemmed into ghettos, forced to accept housing options no one else wanted. The districts where Black families could live were written into the law and enforced by the police. Ghetto landlords had a captive tenant base, and because they could charge more, they did. For much of the migration, Blacks often paid double what white tenants had previously been charged for the worst housing in the city. As late as 1960, median rent in Detroit was higher for Blacks than for whites. In *The Warmth of Other Suns*, Isabel Wilkerson sums up the pattern: "The least-paid people were forced to pay the highest rents for the most dilapidated housing owned by absentee landlords trying to wring the most money out of a place nobody cared about." As the Black population in northern cities grew, real estate developers saw an opportunity to make even more by buying up properties on the edges of the ghetto and slicing them into apartments, pulling as much as they could out of the old housing stock until it was finally condemned (or should have been).[3]

There exists a long history of slum exploitation in America. Money made slums because slums made money.[4] What about today? Poor Americans continue to be crippled by the high cost of housing. Rent has more than doubled over the past two decades, rising much faster than renters' incomes. Median rent rose from $483 in 2000 to $1,216 in 2021. All regions of the country have experienced a surge in housing costs. Since 2000, median rent has increased by 112 percent in the Midwest, 135 percent in the South, 189 percent in the Northeast, and 192 percent in the West.[5] Why have rents shot up so fast? Experts tend to offer the same rote answers to this question. *There's not enough housing supply,* they say, *and too much demand. Government regulation and zoning restrictions have made building more expensive, and these costs are passed on to renters. Landlords must charge more just to earn a decent rate of return.* Must they? How do we know? Were landholders of old driven by money and profit while their contemporaries are merely steered by invisible market forces and pinched by government bureaucracy?

We need more housing; no one can deny that. But rents have jumped even in cities with plenty of apartments to go around. At the end of 2021, almost 19 percent of rental units in Birmingham, Alabama, sat vacant, as did 12 percent of those in Syracuse, New York. Yet rent in those areas increased by roughly 14 and 8 percent, respectively, over the previous two years.[6] The data also show that rental revenues have far outpaced property owners' expenses in recent years, especially in multifamily properties located in poor neighborhoods. Rising rents are not simply a reflection of rising operating costs.[7] There's another dynamic at work, one that has to do with the fact that poor people—and particularly poor Black families— don't have much choice when it comes to where they can live. Because of that, landlords can overcharge them, and they do.

To see if hard data supported this idea, I worked with Nathan Wilmers, now a professor at MIT, to gain access to the restricted version of the Rental Housing Finance Survey, conducted by the U.S. Census Bureau. The survey includes a battery of questions about landlords' revenues and expenses, and captures the experiences of small-time operators who own a couple of rental units, major players managing multiple large complexes, and everyone in between. These data allowed us to estimate landlord profits by deducting their expenses from their revenue.[8] We found that landlords in poor neighborhoods earn roughly $300 a month per apartment unit after regular expenses are deducted from rent. Landlords in middle-class neighborhoods take home $225 a month per apartment unit, and landlords in rich neighborhoods take home $250 a month per unit after regular expenses.[9]

But perhaps down-market landlords incur large maintenance costs because their buildings are older, and perhaps they regularly lose money on account of missed payments and high vacancy rates. Those landlords might adjust to these realities by bumping up rents. We investigated this as well, accounting for all the money lost to roof patches, plumbing issues, busted furnaces, cracked windows, electrical systems, and dozens of other costly issues property owners face. We also adjusted for nonpayment of rent and vacancies. After deducting all expenses—both routine (water bill, taxes, insurance) and irregular (installation of a new toilet, three months of vacancy)—we still found that apartments in poor neighborhoods generated roughly $100 a month in profit, while those in rich neighborhoods generated only $50 a month. Across the United States, landlords in poor neighborhoods do not just come out ahead. After accounting for all their costs, they typically enjoy profits that are double those of landlords operating in affluent communities.[10]

In the hottest housing markets in the country, this pattern reverses itself. In New York City, it's better to be a landlord in SoHo than in the South Bronx. But New York City and other high-cost metropolitan areas are the outliers. In cities with more typical home values, like Orlando, Little Rock, or Tulsa, it *is* better to be a landlord in the South Bronx, so to speak—to rent out property in low-income neighborhoods. This is especially true in the cities with the lowest housing values in the nation.

Why do landlords in poor neighborhoods make more? Because their regular expenses (especially their mortgages and property tax bills) are considerably lower than those in more affluent neighborhoods, but their rents are only slightly lower. In many cities with average or below-average housing costs— think Buffalo, not Boston—rents in the poorest neighborhoods are not drastically lower than rents in the middle-class sections of town. Between 2015 and 2019, median monthly rent for a two-bedroom apartment in the Indianapolis metropolitan area was $991; it was $816 in neighborhoods with poverty rates above 40 percent, just around 17 percent less. Rents are lower in extremely poor neighborhoods, but not by as much as you'd think.[11]

A theory of the problem isn't a theory of the person. Some landlords to the poor will milk dilapidated housing for all it's worth and move on, gutting cities along the way. A small number of these predatory landlords are responsible for a disproportionate share of our housing woes. In cities like Tucson,

Arizona, and Fayetteville, North Carolina, for example, the top one hundred buildings where the most evictions occur account for 40 percent of all evictions in those cities.[12] I've met landlords who have more than earned the moniker "slumlord," but I've also met landlords trying their best to provide decent housing to low-income families. I've met small-time property owners who keep their rents low and larger operators striving for a zero-percent eviction rate by developing diversion programs.

Many property owners start investing in real estate because they don't have enough saved for retirement or have little interest in holding down a "normal" job that comes with a boss and regular hours. When people in these situations become landlords, they transform an investment traditionally intended as a side hustle, a source of "passive income," into their main hustle, "active income" that they believe should pay the bills and support them in their silver years. This overworks the asset and pressures landlords to make as much as they can, which would be far less problematic if the asset didn't happen to be someone's home and if raising the rent didn't result in tenants becoming poorer. This doesn't necessarily mean that your average landlord makes as much as, say, an accountant. But it does mean that those who try to make as much money landlording as they would make in a conventional job—or who try to reproduce the security that comes with saving for retirement for most of your adult life by investing in rental housing—can often only do so by squeezing their tenants. The landlords who are successful are not just the bad apples. Exploitation can be brought about by the prudence of landlords just as much as by their greed, especially if everyone is doing it, which is just another way of saying "if that's what the market will bear."

Why don't poor families move to better neighborhoods if rents there are not that much higher? This question assumes that poor families move like affluent families do: to secure better homes, neighborhoods, schools. But it's more often the case that poor families experience moves not as opportunities but emergencies, even traumas. They move under trying circumstances because they have to—their landlord evicted them, the city condemned their place, their block grew too dangerous—and scramble to stay out of the worst neighborhoods, often accepting the first place that approves their application.[13] When they do attempt to move out of neighborhoods of last resort, they encounter numerous obstacles that bar their entry into better ones. Poor renters often have eviction and conviction records, bad credit or no credit at all, and no access to cosigners who appear on paper as safer bets. Those who are not white, and those who have children, face discrimination by landlords as well. The U.S. Department of Housing and Urban Development has conducted a massive audit of housing discrimination every decade since the 1970s. These studies involve hundreds of matched pairs of actors, similar in every way except for race, applying for the same apartment in several major cities. A recent review of these studies and similar research concluded that, while levels of discrimination have fallen over time, Black renters continue to face routine discrimination when searching for apartments.[14]

Poor renters are also excluded from homeownership, not because they are too poor to make regular mortgage payments—if people can pay rent, they almost certainly can

afford a mortgage—but because several factors discourage
them from even trying. I met Lakia Higbee in the fall of 2021.
At that time, Lakia worked as a picker in an Amazon warehouse and lived with her two adult daughters, her sixteen-
year-old son, and her two granddaughters in a four-bedroom
home in Cleveland. The rent was $950 a month. Not bad, Lakia
thought, even if the windows were so thin and drafty that the
monthly heating bill could reach $500. But if Lakia had bought
that home under conventional terms, her monthly mortgage
payment would have been around $577, inclusive of property
taxes and insurance fees.[15] With an additional $373 in her pocket
each month, Lakia might have been able to save enough to
replace those windows.

Even if Lakia had had a decent credit score, and even if
she'd managed to save enough for a down payment, her
chances of securing a mortgage for an affordable home would
have remained slim because banks aren't interested in financing the kind of homes she could afford. With no access to such
mortgages, poor families must pay high rents on otherwise
affordable homes. In the not-so-distant past (from 1934 to
1968), banks didn't do business in poor and Black communities
because the federal government refused to insure mortgages
there. Today, banks don't do much business in these same
neighborhoods because they can make more money elsewhere. Redlining may no longer be official U.S. policy, but
poor and predominately Black neighborhoods, and even
whole towns, continue to function as "mortgage deserts." If
millions of poor renters accept exploitative housing conditions, it's not because they can't afford better alternatives; it's
because they often aren't offered any.[16]

———

YOU CAN READ INJUNCTIONS against usury in the Vedic texts of ancient India, in the sutra scriptures of Buddhism, and in the Torah. Aristotle and Aquinas both rebuked the practice. Dante sent moneylenders to the seventh circle of hell. None of these efforts did much to stem the practice, but they do reveal that the unprincipled act of trapping the poor in a cycle of debt has existed at least as long as the written word. It might be the oldest form of exploitation after slavery. Many writers have depicted America's poor as unseen, shadowed, and forgotten people: as "other" or "invisible." But markets have never failed to notice the poor, and this has been particularly true of the market for money itself.[17]

The deregulation of the banking system in the 1980s heightened competition between banks. Many responded by raising fees and requiring that customers carry minimum balances. In 1977, over a third of banks offered accounts with no service charge. By the early 1990s, only 5 percent did. Big banks grew bigger as community banks shuttered, and in 2019, the largest banks in America charged customers $11.68 billion in overdraft fees. Just 9 percent of account holders pay 84 percent of these types of fees. Who were the unlucky 9 percent? Customers who carried an average balance of less than $350. The poor were made to pay for their poverty.[18]

In 2021, the average fee for overdrawing your account was $33.58. Because banks often issue multiple charges a day, it's not uncommon to overdraw your account by $20 and end up paying $200 for it. Banks could (and do) deny accounts to people who have a history of overextending their money, but those customers also provide a steady revenue stream for some of the most powerful financial institutions in the world.[19]

For much of the nation's history, banks were for white people, and even today banking while Black can be a harrowing experience. Black customers have been profiled and accused of fraud by bank tellers. They are denied mortgages in greater numbers than any other racial or ethnic group, and they pay higher interest rates on the loans they do secure. A 2021 study found that middle-class Black homeowners (with incomes between $75,000 and $100,000) carried higher interest rates on their mortgages than white homeowners with incomes at or below $30,000.[20] According to the Federal Deposit Insurance Corporation (FDIC), one in nineteen U.S. households had no bank account in 2019, amounting to over 7 million families. Compared to white families, Black and Hispanic families were nearly five times more likely to lack a bank account.[21]

Where there is exclusion, there is exploitation. Unbanked Americans have created a market, and thousands of check cashing outlets now serve that market. Their formula is simple. The first step is to open stores in low-income and non-white neighborhoods. As banks have fled Black communities, and as Black customers have sworn off banks, fringe institutions have filled the gap. The humble and quietly proud community bank, reliable sponsor of Little League teams and Boy Scout troops, has been replaced by storefronts with bright yellow and red signs announcing CHECKS CASHED. Payday loan stores and check cashing outlets are more prevalent in low-poverty Black neighborhoods than in high-poverty white ones, but the reverse is true for traditional banks.[22]

The second part of the formula: Stay open longer than traditional banks, even 24/7, and keep weekend hours, because if a check comes on a Friday, many cannot afford to sit on their money until Monday. Third, cash almost everything—work checks, government checks, personal checks—without requiring a credit check or a bank account.

Last, charge for the service. Check cashing stores charge between 1 and 10 percent of the total, depending on the type of check. That means a worker paid $10 an hour who takes a $1,000 check to a check cashing outlet after clocking one hundred hours over two weeks will pay between $10 and $100 just to receive the money he has earned, effectively losing one to ten hours of work. (For many, this is preferable to the less predictable exploitation of traditional banks, with their automatic deductions. It's the devil you know.) Major corporations have gotten in on the action. Walmart will now cash checks up to $1,000. In 2020, Americans spent $1.6 billion just to cash checks. If the poor had a costless way to access their own money, over a billion dollars would have remained in their pockets during the pandemic-induced recession.[23]

New online financial services have found ways to profit off financial insecurity, too, targeting a younger, tech-savvy clientele. Apps like Dave and Earnin allow workers to access some of their wages before payday. These apps may help workers avoid expensive overdraft fees, but some users end up paying fees and tips that exceed 100 percent of the annual percentage rate (APR) of the loan. Borrowers used pay-advance products 56 million times in 2020, up from 18.6 million times in 2018. Buy-now-pay-later (BNPL) companies like Afterpay and Klarna allow consumers to pay for online items in interest-free, bimonthly installments, but missing a payment can bring late fees and impact your credit. Over 40 percent of people who use BNPL services have made at least one late payment.[24]

We live and die by credit. It's how we afford the big necessities, like homes and cars, and sometimes the smaller ones, too, like when we use our Visa to pay for medication or a winter jacket. My mother used to postdate checks, floating our family between paydays. The proliferation of credit cards has made it so you don't have to ask the shop owner's permission to do that.

Poverty can mean missed payments, which can ruin your credit. But just as troublesome as bad credit is having no credit score at all, which is the case for 26 million adults in the United States. Another 19 million possess a credit history too thin or outdated to be scored.[25] Having no credit (or bad credit) can prevent you from securing an apartment, purchasing insurance, and even landing a job, as employers are increasingly relying on credit checks during the hiring process. And when the inevitable happens—when you lose hours at work or when the car refuses to start—the payday loan industry steps in.[26]

For most of American history, regulators prohibited lending institutions from charging exorbitant interest on loans. Because of these limits, banks kept interest rates between 6 and 12 percent and didn't do much business with the poor, who in a pinch took their valuables to the pawnbroker or the loan shark. But the deregulation of the banking sector in the 1980s ushered the money changers back into the temple by removing strict usury limits. Interest rates soon reached 300 percent, then 500 percent, then 700. Suddenly, some were very interested in launching businesses that lent to the poor. In recent years, seventeen states have brought back strong usury limits, capping interest rates and effectively prohibiting payday lending. But the trade thrives in most places. The APR for a two-week $300 loan can reach 664 percent in Texas, 516 percent in Wisconsin, and 460 percent in California.[27]

To qualify for a payday loan, you need a pay stub and valid identification. You also need a bank account, which should clue us in to the fact that this industry serves low-income Americans but not the unbanked bottommost level of the market. (The average payday loan customer has an annual income of around $30,000.) You take out a small loan, usually for less than $500, and are typically charged a percentage or fee per $100 borrowed. A charge of $15 per $100 lent might sound reasonable, but it equates to an APR of 400 percent. The loan officer requires a way to claim payment when time is up—access to a bank account or a postdated check for the full amount of the loan plus fees. Most loans are for two to four weeks, until the next payday, hence their name.[28]

Except that when the loan comes due, you usually still happen to be broke. So you ask for an extension, which will cost you. If you took out a two-week $400 loan with a $60 fee ($15 per $100), the loan officer might allow an extension if you pay the $60 fee when the original loan comes due. Then he will issue another fee, say for an additional $60. Just like that, you are charged $120 for borrowing $400, and that's if you ask for only a single extension. Four in five payday loans are rolled over or renewed. Because payday loan services have access to your bank account, they can overdraw your account, piling bank fees on top of loan fees. Roughly a third of all payday loans are now issued online, and almost half of borrowers who have taken out online loans have had lenders overdraw their accounts. The average borrower stays indebted for five months, paying $520 in fees to borrow $375. Keeping people indebted is, of course, the ideal outcome for the payday lender. It's how they turn a $15 profit into a $150 one.[29]

The products of the fringe banking industry rely on the feverish present-mindedness of the vulnerable, and the industry's precognition that its customers will remain that way longer than they can bring themselves to admit. When you walk into a payday loan store, you are focused on the present. Your rent is overdue, and you're facing eviction. Your lights are about to be shut off. (That's why seven in ten people take out these loans, by the way: to pay for rent, utilities, or basic expenses.) But the payday loan company is focused on your future. It sees you rushing through its doors on the fourteenth day of your loan, unable to pay in full. It sees you signing the extension papers. It sees you signing them again next month. It knows you're not in for a penny. You're in for a pound.

Lenders compete over things like location, store hours, and how fast they can process applications—but not cost. They know their customers are too desperate to comparison shop. This means fees stay high and borrowers get a bad deal anywhere they go. Given this, conventional banks could undercut the industry, offering short-term loans with much lower fees. By one estimate, commercial banks could offer payday loans with fees up to eight times less than the standard market price and still turn a profit.[30] But so far, they've shown no interest in doing so. It's one thing to soak low-income customers with overdraft fees because those fees apply to everybody, even if they are borne primarily by the poorest customers. But getting into the payday loan business would

mean offering financial products designed specifically for a
down-market clientele, loans that would come with APRs between 40 and 80 percent and serious reputational baggage. So
far, the suits at JPMorgan Chase and Citigroup have decided
it's not worth it. If payday borrowers are price insensitive (as
most of us are when circling the drain) and if most commercial banks maintain their lack of interest in serving the poor,
then the market failures that benefit the payday lending industry will persist. Payday lenders do not charge high fees because
lending to the poor is risky—even after multiple extensions,
most borrowers pay up. Lenders extort because they can.[31]

Every year: over $11 billion in overdraft fees, $1.6 billion in
check cashing fees, and up to $9.8 billion in payday loan fees.
That's over $61 million in fees collected predominately from
low-income Americans *each day*—not even counting the annual revenue collected by pawnshops and title loan services
and rent-to-own schemes. When James Baldwin remarked in
1961 how "extremely expensive it is to be poor," he couldn't
have imagined these receipts.[32]

"Predatory inclusion" is what historian Keeanga-Yamahtta
Taylor calls it in her book *Race for Profit*, describing the long-
standing American tradition of incorporating marginalized
people into housing and financial schemes through bad deals
when they are denied good ones. The exclusion of poor people from traditional banking and credit systems has forced
them to find alternative ways to cash checks and secure loans,
which has led to a normalization of their exploitation. This is
all perfectly legal, after all, and subsidized by the nation's richest commercial banks. The fringe banking sector would not
exist without lines of credit extended by the conventional one.

Wells Fargo and JPMorgan Chase bankroll payday lenders like
Advance America and Cash America. It's expropriators all the
way down, *orders from the East* and all that. Everybody gets a
cut.[33]

THERE IS NOT ONE banking sector. There are two—one for
the poor and one for the rest of us—just as there are two housing markets and two labor markets. The duality of American
life can make it difficult for some of us who benefit from the
current arrangement to remember that the poor are exploited
laborers, exploited consumers, and exploited borrowers, precisely because we are not. Many features of our society are not
broken, just bifurcated. For some, a home creates wealth; for
others, a home drains it. For some, access to credit extends financial power; for others, it destroys it. It is quite understand-
able, then, that well-fed Americans can be perplexed by the
poor, even disappointed in them, believing that they accept
stupidly bad deals on impulse or because they don't know any
better. But what if those deals are the only ones on offer?
What good is financial literacy training for people forced to
choose the best bad option?[34]

Poverty isn't simply the condition of not having enough
money. It's the condition of not having enough choice and
being taken advantage of because of that. When we ignore
the role that exploitation plays in trapping people in poverty,
we end up designing policy that is weak at best and ineffective
at worst. When legislation lifts incomes at the bottom—say,
by expanding the Child Tax Credit or by raising the minimum
wage—without addressing the housing crisis, those gains are

often recouped by landlords, not wholly by the families the legislation was intended to help. A 2019 study conducted by the Federal Reserve Bank of Philadelphia found that when states raised minimum wages, families found it easier to pay rent. But landlords quickly responded to the wage bumps by increasing rents, which diluted the effect of the policy. (This happened after the COVID-19 rescue packages, too, but commentators preferred discussing the matter using the bloodless language of inflation.)[35]

In Tommy Orange's début novel, *There There,* a man trying to describe the problem of suicides on Native American reservations says, "Kids are jumping out the windows of burning buildings, falling to their deaths. And we think the problem is that they're jumping."[36] The poverty debate has suffered from a similar kind of myopia. For the past half century, we've approached the poverty question by attending to the poor themselves—posing questions about their work ethic, say, or their welfare benefits—when we should have been focusing on the fire. The question that should serve as a looping incantation, the one we should ask every time we drive past a tent encampment, those tarped American slums smelling of asphalt and bodies, every time we see someone asleep on the bus, slumped over in work clothes, is simply: *Who benefits?* Not *Why don't you find a better job?* or *Why don't you move?* or *Why don't you stop taking out such bad loans?* but *Who is feeding off this?*[37]

CHAPTER 5

HOW WE RELY ON WELFARE

WHEN THE COVID-19 PANDEMIC STRUCK THE UNITED States, the economy went into a tailspin. Social distancing protocols caused businesses to shutter, and millions of Americans lost their jobs. Between February and April 2020, the unemployment rate doubled, then doubled again, rivaling levels not seen since the bread lines and banker suicides of the 1930s. During the worst week of the Great Recession of the late aughts, 661,000 Americans filed for unemployment insurance. During the week of March 16, 2020, more than 3.3 million Americans did. The country was in freefall.[1]

The federal government responded with bold relief. It expanded the time laid-off workers could collect unemployment, and in a rare recognition of the inadequacy of the benefit, added supplementary payments. For four months at the beginning of the pandemic, unemployed Americans received $600 a week on top of their regular stipend, nearly tripling the average amount of the benefit. In August, the government reduced the bonuses to $300 a week. In the summer of 2021, the U.S. Chamber of Commerce estimated that one in four recipients of the expanded unemployment insurance were receiving more from being out of work than they would have if they had been working.[2]

Because of the generous unemployment benefits—alongside stimulus checks, rental assistance, expanded Child Tax Credit, and other forms of relief—poverty did not increase during the worst economic downturn in nearly a century. Instead, it fell, and by a tremendous amount. The U.S. economy lost millions of jobs during the COVID-19 pandemic, but there were roughly 16 million fewer Americans in poverty in 2021 than in 2018. Poverty fell for all racial and ethnic groups. It fell for people who lived in cities and those who lived in rural areas. It fell for the young and old. It fell the most for children.[3] Swift government action didn't just prevent economic disaster; it helped to cut child poverty by more than *half.*

I thought this would be major cause for celebration: After years of inaction, the United States had finally made a major dent in the poverty rate. But many people weren't celebrating. A vocal subset of Americans seemed troubled that the government was doing so much to help its people. In particular, they blamed the souped-up unemployment checks for the nation's sluggish economic recovery. David Rouzer, a Republican congressman from North Carolina, tweeted a picture of a closed Hardee's with the caption: "This is what happens when you extend unemployment benefits for too long and add a $1400 stimulus payment to it." Kevin McCarthy, the House minority leader, wrote that unemployment insurance "had demonized work so Americans would become dependent on big government." *The Wall Street Journal* ran an opinion essay with the headline "Covid Unemployment Relief Makes Help Impossible to Find." Reporters fanned out across the country and interviewed small business owners, who attributed their hiring headaches to the federal aid. "We had employees that still chose to take the unemployment and not stay on, which I thought was just unbelievable," said Colin Davis, the owner of Chico Hot Springs Resort in Montana. "I just—when did everyone get so lazy?"[4]

That was our leading theory of the case. It made sense. Frankly, it sounded obvious: America wasn't getting back to work because we were paying people to stay home. But it was wrong, and the fact that so many of us thought otherwise reveals how conditioned we are to assume the worst about one another when it comes to receiving help from the government.

During June and July 2021, twenty-five states stopped some or all of the emergency benefits rolled out during the pandemic, including expanded unemployment insurance. This created an opportunity to see whether those states enjoyed a significant jump in their employment rates. It's what you'd expect if the benefits were discouraging Americans from returning to work. But there was no jump. When the Labor Department released the August data, we learned that in the race among states for the best job numbers, it was basically a tie. The five states with the fastest job growth (Alaska, Hawaii, North Carolina, Rhode Island, and Vermont) had retained some or all of the benefits. States that had cut unemployment benefits did not experience significant job growth. What they did experience was a decline in consumer spending, since the cuts left their citizens with less money, which slowed local economies.[5]

Other studies found no evidence that unemployment benefits were causing workers to stay home, and at the time several European countries were also experiencing labor shortages even though they hadn't done much to expand unemployment benefits.[6] Why, I wonder, did we so readily embrace a narrative that blamed high unemployment on government aid when so many other explanations were available to us? Why didn't we figure people weren't returning to work because they didn't want to get sick and die? Or because their jobs were lousy to begin with? Or because they were tired of sexual harassment and mistreatment? Or because their children's schools had closed, and they lacked reliable childcare? When asked why many Americans weren't returning to work as fast as some people would have liked, why was our answer *Because they are getting $300 extra each week*?

PERHAPS IT'S BECAUSE WE'VE been trained since the earliest days of capitalism to see the poor as idle and unmotivated. The world's first capitalists faced a problem that titans of industry still face today: how to get the masses to file into their mills and slaughterhouses to work for as little pay as the law and market allow. Hunger was the capitalists' solution to the labor question. "The poor know little of the motives which stimulate the higher ranks to action—pride, honour, and ambition. In general it is only hunger which can spur and goad them on to labour." So wrote the English doctor and clergyman Joseph Townsend in his 1786 treatise, *A Dissertation on the Poor Laws, By a Well-Wisher of Mankind,* asserting a position that would become common sense, then common law, throughout the early modern period. The "unremitted pressure" of hunger, Townsend continued, offered "the most natural motive to industry."[7]

Once you got the poor into factories, you needed laws to protect your property and law men to arrest trespassers and court systems to prosecute them and prisons to hold them. If you were going to fashion an economic system that required the movement of labor, capital, and products around the globe, you needed a system of tariffs and policies to govern the flow of trade, not to mention a standing army to uphold national sovereignty. Big money required big government. But big government could also hand out bread. Realizing this, early capitalists decried the corrosive effects of government aid long before it was extended to the so-called able-bodied poor. In 1704, the English writer Daniel Defoe published a pamphlet arguing that the poor would not work for wages if they were given alms. This argument was repeated over and again by leading thinkers, including Thomas Malthus in his famous 1798 treatise, *An Essay on the Principle of Population*.[8] Early converts to capitalism saw poor aid not merely as a burden or as bad policy but as an existential threat, something that could sever the reliance of workers on owners.

Fast-forward to the modern era, and you still hear the same neurotic arguments. The idea is to protect one kind of dependency, that of the worker on the company, by debasing another, that of citizens on the state. (An irony of capitalism is that work, which early Americans rejected as a barrier to independence—"wage slavery," they called it—is now seen as our only means of acquiring it.) When President Franklin Roosevelt, originator of the American safety net, called welfare a drug and "subtle destroyer of the human spirit"; or when Arizona senator Barry Goldwater said in 1961 that he didn't like how his "taxes paid for children born out of wedlock" and complained about "professional chiselers walking up and down the streets who don't work and have no intention of working"; or when Ronald Reagan, campaigning for the presidential nomination in the late 1970s, kept telling audiences about a public housing complex in New York City where "you can get an apartment with eleven-foot ceilings, with a twenty-foot balcony, a swimming pool and gymnasium"; or when in 1980 the American Psychiatric Association made "dependent personality disorder" an official diagnostic category; or when conservative writer Charles Murray wrote in his influential 1984 book, *Losing Ground,* that "we tried to provide more for the poor and produced more poor instead"; or when President Bill Clinton in 1996 announced his plan to "end welfare as we know it" because the program created a "cycle of dependency that has existed for millions and millions of our fellow citizens, exiling them from the world of work"; or when President Donald Trump's Council of Economic Advisers issued a report endorsing work requirements for the nation's largest welfare programs and claiming that America's welfare policies have brought about a "decline in self-sufficiency"; or when Kansas senator Roger Marshall in June 2021 said that the "number one impediment" to his state's slack labor market was unemployment insurance that effectively meant "paying [people] more to stay home than to go to work," they were rehashing an old story—call it the propaganda of capitalism—a story that has been handed down from one generation to the next: that our medicine (aid to the poor) is poison. The message has been received. Half the country appears to believe that social benefits from the government make people lazy.[9]

Who we think benefits from that aid also deeply colors our views. Studies have consistently identified two long-standing beliefs harbored by the American public. First, Americans tend to believe (wrongly) that most welfare recipients are Black. This is true for both liberals and conservatives. Second, many Americans still believe Blacks have a low work ethic. In 1972, social scientists conducted a survey of adults called the General Social Survey. The survey is still going strong, allowing us to track trends over time. In 1990, the survey asked Americans to rate how lazy or hardworking they thought different groups were, based on a seven-point scale, with 7 representing the belief that almost everyone in the group is lazy. That year, 6 percent of Americans who cared to answer the question thought whites were generally lazy (giving them a score of 5, 6, or 7), but 44 percent reported feeling that way about Black Americans. The most recent iteration of the survey, conducted in 2021, found that more than one in seven Americans still saw Black Americans as lazy. Anti-Black racism hardens Americans' antagonism toward social benefits.[10]

Arguments about the debasing effects of government support for the poor have long relied on anecdote and appeals to common sense. A sober empiricist on other matters, Malthus didn't bother much with the facts when opining on the corrupting power of poor aid, admitting that "little more appears to [me] to be necessary than a plain statement." Similarly, when in 2021 a journalist asked Michael Strain, who holds a PhD in economics and directs Economic Policy Studies at the American Enterprise Institute, what evidence led him to assert that he was "not eager to pay taxes so that somebody can buy drugs or buy alcohol or go to Vegas," Strain responded, "This is kind of an evidence-free topic."[11]

It's not. The U.S. Bureau of Labor Statistics (BLS) has meticulously tracked the spending patterns of families receiving means-tested government assistance. Not surprisingly, those receiving assistance spend a larger share of their income on necessities (housing, food) and a smaller share on entertainment, alcohol, and tobacco than other American families. The BLS also found that families with incomes in the top 20 percent of the distribution dedicate twice as much of their budget to alcohol as families with incomes in the bottom 20 percent. It's been this way for generations. In 1899, the sociologist Thorstein Veblen wrote about rich people's taste for "intoxicating beverages and narcotics" and the poor's "enforced continence," on account of the cost of booze and other drugs.[12]

We can also examine how poor people respond when their benefits increase substantially. For example, researchers have recently evaluated the results of a universal basic income experiment in Stockton, California. A random sample of 125 residents of the city's low-income neighborhoods were selected to receive $500 a month, no strings attached. What did they do with the cash? Pretty boring stuff. They took it to the grocery store and to Costco or used it to pay utility bills and fix up their cars. Less than 1 percent of purchases were for tobacco or alcohol.[13]

When I lived in poor Milwaukee communities, one thing that struck me about the people I met—people often enduring grinding hardship, even homelessness—was how few of them took the edge off their pain with anything more than a cigarette. I did get to know people addicted to heroin, and there were plenty of liquor stores around, but most of my neighbors faced their poverty dead sober. Honestly, it was disappointing. *I* wanted to take the edge off, and when I did, with a beer or a glass of whiskey, my friends in Milwaukee did not approve. "I didn't know you *drank*," Crystal once scolded me after I stopped by a liquor store to pick up a six-pack. I looked at everyone else in the car: Crystal, along with her friend Vanetta, whom Crystal had met at the Salvation Army homeless shelter, and Vanetta's mother, who had raised her kids in Chicago public housing. We were planning on cooking a Sunday meal together.

"Um, can I get anyone anything?" I asked.

Everyone shook their heads no. None of them drank. They wouldn't have even known what to ask for. I bought my beer, feeling like I had scandalized our supper.[14]

WE ALSO HAVE SOLID data on welfare dependency. Researchers set out to study the issue in the 1980s and '90s, when it dominated public debate. They didn't find much evidence for it. Most young mothers on welfare stopped relying on it within two years of starting the program. Most of those mothers returned to welfare sometime down the road, leaning on it for limited periods of time when between jobs or after a divorce. Some stayed on the rolls for long stretches, but they were the exception to the norm. Even at its peak, welfare did not generally function as a dependency trap. A review of the research in *Science* concluded that "the welfare system does not foster reliance on welfare so much as it acts as insurance against tempo-rary misfortune."[15] Today as then, the able-bodied jobless adult on welfare remains a rare creature. According to one study, only three in one hundred poor people in America are working-age adults disconnected from the labor market for unknown reasons.[16]

If you dig into the data, you quickly realize that the prob-lem isn't welfare dependency but welfare avoidance. Simply put, many poor families don't take advantage of aid that's available to them. Only a quarter of families who qualify for Temporary Assistance for Needy Families apply for it. Less than half (48 percent) of elderly Americans who qualify for food stamps sign up to receive them. One in five parents eli-gible for government health insurance (in the form of Medic-aid and the Children's Health Insurance Program) do not enroll, just as one in five workers who qualify for the Earned Income Tax Credit do not claim it.[17] Welfare avoidance persists through bumper years and downturns. At the height of the Great Recession, one in ten Americans was out of work, but only one in three drew unemployment.[18]

There are no official estimates of the total amount of gov-ernment aid that goes unclaimed by low-income Americans, but the number is in the hundreds of billions of dollars a year. Consider the amount of money left on the table by low-income workers who don't apply for the Earned Income Tax Credit. Roughly 7 million people who could receive the credit don't claim it, collectively passing up $17.3 billion annually. Combine that with the amount of money unclaimed each year by people who deny themselves food stamps ($13.4 bil-lion), government health insurance ($62.2 billion), unemployment insurance when between jobs ($9.9 billion), and Supplemental Security Income ($38.9 billion), and you are already up to nearly $142 billion in unused aid.[19]

The problem is so persistent and perplexing that an entire subfield of behavioral science has emerged with the goal of boosting what policy wonks call "take-up rates" for social programs. Psychologists and economists have designed sophisticated experiments, organized conferences, supervised doctoral dissertations, published peer-reviewed studies, and written books all with the aim of encouraging more low-income Americans to reach out and claim money set aside for them.

This is decidedly not a picture of welfare dependency. If poor people in America really knew how to pull every nickel and dime they could from the system, why do they pass on billions of dollars in aid every year? When politicians and pundits fume about long-term welfare addiction among the poor, or the social safety net functioning like "a hammock that lulls able-bodied people into lives of dependency and complacency," to quote former Republican congressman Paul Ryan, they are either deeply misinformed, or they are lying.[20] The American poor are terrible at being welfare dependent. I wish they were better at it, just as I wish that we as a nation devoted the same amount of thoughtfulness, creativity, and tenacity to connecting poor families with programs that would alleviate their hunger and ease their hardships as multinational corporations devote to convincing us to buy their potato chips and car tires.

THE REST OF US, on the other hand—we members of the protected classes—have grown increasingly dependent on our welfare programs. In 2020 the federal government spent more than $193 billion on homeowner subsidies, a figure that far exceeded the amount spent on direct housing assistance for low-income families ($53 billion). Most families who enjoy those subsidies have six-figure incomes and are white. Poor families lucky enough to live in government-owned apartments often have to deal with mold and even lead paint, while rich families are claiming the mortgage interest deduction on first and second homes. The lifetime limit for cash welfare to poor parents is five years, but families claiming the mortgage interest deduction may do so for the length of the mortgage, typically thirty years. A fifteen-story public housing tower and a mortgaged suburban home are both government subsidized, but only one looks (and feels) that way.[21]

If you count all benefits, America's welfare state (as a share of its gross domestic product) is the second biggest in the world, after France's. But that's true only if you include things like government-subsidized retirement benefits provided by employers, student loans and 529 college savings plans, child tax credits, and homeowner subsidies: benefits disproportionately flowing to Americans well above the poverty line. If you put aside these tax breaks and judge the United States solely by the share of its GDP allocated to programs directed at low-income citizens, then our investment in poverty reduction is much smaller than that of other rich nations. The American welfare state is lopsided.[22]

Our country is not divided into "makers," who can support themselves through work, and "takers," content to eke out a small life on government handouts. Virtually all Americans

benefit from some form of public aid. Republicans and Democrats rely on government programs at equivalent rates, as do
white, Hispanic, and Black families.[23] We're all on the dole.

In her book *The Government-Citizen Disconnect,* the political
scientist Suzanne Mettler reports that 96 percent of American
adults have relied on a major government program at some
point in their lives. Rich, middle-class, and poor families depend on different kinds of programs, but the average rich and
middle-class family draws on the same number of government benefits as the average poor family. Student loans look
like they were issued from a bank, but the only reason banks
hand out money to eighteen-year-olds with no jobs, no credit,
and no collateral is because the federal government guarantees the loans and pays half their interest. Financial advisers at
Edward Jones or Prudential can help you sign up for 529 college savings plans, but those plans' generous tax benefits will
cost the federal government an estimated $28.5 billion between
2017 and 2026. For most Americans under the age of sixty-five,
health insurance appears to come from their jobs, but supporting this arrangement is one of the single largest tax breaks
issued by the federal government, one that exempts the cost
of employer-sponsored health insurance from taxable incomes. In 2022, this benefit is estimated to have cost the government $316 billion for those under sixty-five. By 2032, its
price tag is projected to exceed $600 billion. Almost half of all
Americans receive government-subsidized health benefits
through their employers, and over a third are enrolled in
government-subsidized retirement benefits. These participation rates, driven primarily by rich and middle-class Americans, far exceed those of even the largest programs directed at

low-income families, such as food stamps (14 percent of Americans) and the Earned Income Tax Credit (19 percent).[24]

Altogether, the United States spent $1.8 trillion on tax breaks in 2021. That amount exceeded total spending on law enforcement, education, housing, healthcare, diplomacy, and everything else that makes up our discretionary budget.[25] Roughly half the benefits of the thirteen largest individual tax breaks accrue to the richest families, those with incomes that put them in the top 20 percent. The top 1 percent of income earners take home more than all middle-class families and double that of families in the bottom 20 percent. I can't tell you how many times someone has informed me that we should reduce military spending and redirect the savings to the poor. When this suggestion is made in a public venue, it always garners applause. I've met far fewer people who have suggested we boost aid to the poor by reducing tax breaks that mostly benefit the upper class, even though we spend over twice as much on them as on the military and national defense.[26]

Today, the biggest beneficiaries of federal aid are affluent families. To benefit from employer-sponsored health insurance, you need a good job, usually one that requires a college degree. To benefit from the mortgage interest deduction, you need to be able to afford a home, and those who can afford the biggest mortgages reap the biggest deductions. To benefit from a 529 plan, you need to be able to squirrel away cash for your children's college costs, and the more you save, the bigger your tax break, which is why this subsidy is almost exclusively used by the well-off.[27] As far as I know, there are no PhD dissertations being drafted, no studies being conducted, no

grant applications being submitted to figure out how to increase take-up rates for the mortgage interest deduction, student loans, or employer-sponsored health insurance, because
the participation rates for these kinds of programs are quite
impressive already.

But the rich pay more taxes, one might say. Yes, they do—
because they have more money. But that's not the same thing
as paying a larger share of taxes. The federal income tax is
progressive, meaning that tax burdens grow as incomes increase—in 2020, it was 10 percent for the poorest individuals
(with incomes at or below $9,875), 24 percent for middle-
income individuals (with incomes between $85,526 and
$163,300), and 37 percent for the richest individuals (with in-
comes at or above $518,401)—but other taxes are regressive,
forcing the poor to hand over a larger share of their earnings.
Take sales taxes. These hit the poor hardest, for two reasons.
First, poor families can't afford to save, but rich families can
and do. Families that spend all of their money every year will
automatically dedicate a higher share of their income to sales
tax than families who spend only a portion of theirs. Second,
when rich families do spend money, they consume more services than poor families, who spend their money on goods
(gas, food), which are subject to more sales tax. The progressive design of the federal income tax is offset by the regressive
nature of other taxes, including the fact that wealth (in the
form of capital gains) is taxed at a lower rate than wages.
When all taxes are accounted for, we're all effectively taxed at
the same rate. On average, poor and middle-class Americans
dedicate approximately 25 percent of their income to taxes,

while rich families are taxed at an effective rate of 28 percent, just slightly higher. The four hundred richest Americans are taxed at 23 percent, the lowest rate of all.[28]

THE AMERICAN GOVERNMENT GIVES the most help to those who need it least. This is the true nature of our welfare state, and it has far-reaching implications, not only for our bank accounts and poverty levels, but also for our psychology and civic spirit.

Studies have found that Americans who claimed the Earned Income Tax Credit weren't more likely to see themselves as government beneficiaries than those with a similar background who didn't or couldn't claim the benefit. But people who received cash welfare did see themselves as beneficiaries of government aid. Similarly, those who relied on student loans or drew on 529 plans were not more likely to recognize the government's role in their lives than people from similar walks of life who didn't rely on these programs. But Americans who benefitted from the GI Bill had a clear sense that they had been granted new opportunities through state action. In fact, Americans who rely on the most *visible* social programs (like public housing or food stamps) are also the most likely to recognize that the government had been a force for good in their lives, but Americans who rely on the most *invisible* programs (namely tax breaks) are the least likely to believe that the government had given them a leg up.[29]

Those who benefit most from government largesse—generally white families with accountants—harbor the strongest antigovernment sentiments. And those people vote at higher rates than their fellow citizens who appreciate the role of government in their lives. They lend their support to politicians who promise to cut government spending, knowing full well that it won't be *their* benefits that get the ax. Overwhelmingly, voters who claim the mortgage interest deduction are the very ones who oppose deeper investments in affordable housing, just as those who received employer-sponsored health insurance were the ones pushing to repeal the Affordable Care Act. It's one of the more maddening paradoxes of political life.[30]

But every so often, policies that disproportionately benefit nonpoor Americans are placed on the chopping block. When that happens, the "invisible" welfare state suddenly flies into view. In 2015, President Obama proposed to do away with the tax benefits attached to 529 college savings plans, but Democrats from affluent parts of the country immediately mobilized against his plan, fearing potential blowback from their constituents. The administration quashed the proposal the day after announcing it.[31] What Democratic leadership understood was that if the federal government took away 529 benefits or reduced the mortgage interest deduction or began taxing employer-sponsored health insurance, middle- and upper-class families would be outraged, which of course means those benefits aren't so invisible after all.

How do we square this? How do we reconcile the fact that massive government tax benefits go unnoticed by middle- and upper-class families who claim them, which in turn spreads resentment among those families toward a government perceived to be giving handouts to poor families, which in turn leads well-off voters to mobilize against government spending on the poor while also protecting their own tax breaks that supposedly aren't even noticed in the first place?

As I see it, there are three possibilities. The first is that many of us understandably have a hard time viewing a tax break as something akin to a government check. We see taxation as a burden and tax breaks as the state allowing us to keep more of what is rightfully ours. Psychologists have shown that we tend to feel losses more acutely than gains. The pain of losing \$1,000 is stronger than the satisfaction of winning that amount.[32] It's no different with taxes. We're apt to think much more about the taxes we have to pay (the loss) than about the money delivered to us through tax breaks (the gain).

This is by design, the result of the United States intentionally making tax filing exasperating and time-consuming. In Japan, Great Britain, Estonia, the Netherlands, and several other countries, citizens don't file taxes; the government does it automatically. In those countries, taxpayers check the government's math, sign the form, and mail it back in. The process can be completed in a matter of minutes, and more important, it better ensures that citizens pay the taxes they owe and receive the benefits owed to them. If Japanese or Dutch taxpayers believe their government has overcharged them, they can appeal their bill, but most don't. There's no reason Americans' taxes couldn't be collected this way, except for the fact that corporate lobbyists and many Republican lawmakers want the process to be painful. "Taxes should hurt," President Reagan famously said. If they don't, we might come to see taxpaying as a normal and straightforward part of membership in society, instead of what happens that irksome time of year when the government takes our money.[33]

This is a case where the packaging is just as important as the gift, and I don't doubt that the way benefits are delivered and taxes are collected affects how we see them. Paying taxes does hurt, and perceiving a tax break as fundamentally different from government aid is easy to do. But it's a bit of magical thinking. Both welfare checks and tax breaks boost a household's income; both contribute to the deficit; and both are designed to incentivize behavior, like seeing a doctor (Medicaid) or saving for college (529 plans). We could flip the delivery system to achieve the same ends, extending welfare to the poor by cutting payroll taxes for low-income workers (as France has) while replacing the mortgage interest deduction with a check mailed out to homeowners each month. The federal budget is a giant circle of money, a whirl of funds flowing to the state from taxpayers and back to taxpayers from the state. You can benefit a family by lowering its tax burden or by increasing its benefits, same difference.[34]

With respect to the federal income tax, some believe that middle-class taxpayers are carrying the poor on their backs. But let's look at the data. In 2018, the average middle-class family had an income of $63,900, paid $9,900 in federal taxes after all deductions, and received $13,600 in social insurance benefits (like disability and unemployment) along with $3,400 from means-tested programs (like Medicaid and food stamps). In other words, the average middle-class family received $7,100 more in government aid than it paid in federal taxes, a serious return on investment. The claim that middle-class Americans are subsidizing the poor with their tax dollars and receiving nothing in return just isn't true.[35]

But more fundamentally, looking only at the federal income tax is like counting calories only by recording what you ate for breakfast. When commentators focus exclusively on this tax to claim that the poor make up a "non-taxpaying class" because their tax burdens approach zero after the standard deduction and tax credits are applied, they intentionally ignore all the other ways the poor pay taxes as well as all the ways the rich don't. Here's the bottom line: The most recent data compiling spending on social insurance, means-tested programs, tax benefits, and financial aid for higher education show that the average household in the bottom 20 percent of the income distribution receives roughly $25,733 in government benefits a year, while the average household in the top 20 percent receives about $35,363.[36] Every year, the richest American families receive almost 40 percent more in government subsidies than the poorest American families.

Given this, I suspect there might be something deeper at work, another reason for our unwillingness to acknowledge the invisible welfare state: that middle- and upper-class Americans believe they—but not the poor—are entitled to government help. This has been a long-standing explanation among liberal thinkers: that Americans' hardwired belief in meritocracy drives them to conflate material success with deservingness. I don't buy it. We are bombarded with too much clear evidence to the contrary. Do we really believe the top 1 percent are more deserving than the rest of the country? Are we really, in 2023, going to argue that white people have far more wealth than Black people because white people have worked harder for it—or that women are paid less because they deserve less? Do we have the audacity to point to housekeepers with skin peeling from chemicals or berry pickers who can no longer stand up straight or the millions of other poor working Americans and claim that they are stuck at the bottom because they are lazy? "I've worked hard to get where I am," you might say. Well, sure. But we know that untold numbers of poor people have worked hard to get where they are, too.[37]

Even in our personal lives, we see people getting ahead not because of their gumption and effort but because they are tall or attractive or know a guy or received a fat inheritance. A brilliant coworker is passed over for a promotion, while someone with dimmer lights is given the corner suite. A family falls on hard times after a gutting medical diagnosis or a car crash. Our lives are tangibly impacted in countless ways—not only by things beyond our control but also by the relentless irrationality of the world. Every day we confront the capriciousness of life, the unfair, stupid ways our future is determined by background or chance.

Most of us believe that working hard helps us get ahead—because of course it does—but most of us also recognize that advantages flow from being white or having highly educated parents or knowing the right people. We sense that our bootstraps can be pulled up only so far, that self-help platitudes about grit and self-control and putting in the hours is fine advice for our children, but it's no substitute for a theory of how the world works. For as long as there has been poverty alongside great wealth, the winners have cultivated rationalizations for that arrangement. *Those who remain poor haven't tried hard enough. Welfare creates long-term dependency. Expanding opportunity to the poor is an act of destruction, leading to socialism and tyranny.* Such propaganda was repeated not because these ideas persuaded us but because they organized us, allowing us to avoid a more painful truth, which is that our lives are interlaced with the lives of the poor.[38] But these old tropes and stereotypes are dying. We've seen through them. Most Democrats and most Republicans today believe that poverty is caused by unfair circumstances, not by a lack of work ethic.[39]

This brings us to the third possible explanation for why we accept the current state of affairs: We like it.

It's the rudest explanation, I know, which is probably why we cloak it behind all sorts of justifications and quick evasions. But as the civil rights activist Ella Baker once put it, "Those who are well-heeled don't want to get un-well-heeled," no matter how they came by their coin. Frankly, tax breaks are nice to have if you can get them. In 2020, the mortgage interest deduction allowed more than 13 million Americans to keep $24.7 billion. Homeowners with annual family incomes below $20,000 enjoyed $4 million in savings, and those with annual incomes above $200,000 enjoyed $15.5 billion. Also in 2020, more than 11 million taxpayers deducted interest on their student loans, saving low-income borrowers $12 million and those with incomes between $100,000 and $200,000 $432 million. In all, the top 20 percent of income earners receives six times what the bottom 20 percent receives in tax breaks. Money granted by bizarre government subsidies is still money, and once we have it, we prefer to keep it.[40]

Help from the government is a zero-sum affair. The biggest government subsidies are not directed at families trying to climb out of poverty but instead go to ensure that well-off families stay well-off. This leaves fewer resources for the poor. If this is our design, our social contract, then we should at least own up to it. We should at least stand up and profess, *Yes, this is the kind of nation we want.* What we cannot do is look the American poor in the face and say, *We'd love to help you, but we just can't afford to,* because that is a lie.

CHAPTER 6

HOW WE BUY OPPORTUNITY

IN THE EARLY AUGHTS, BEFORE THE FINANCIAL CRISIS, OUR newspapers announced that the country was entering a Second Gilded Age. In October 2007, *The New York Times Magazine* ran a cover featuring a gold-plated manhole cover, as if New Yorkers were shitting money. That narrative was incomplete, of course, but it contained a blunt truth that Americans today seem bent on avoiding: that many of us are rich.[1] Colossally rich. In 2020, Americans bought more than 310,000 new powerboats. We spent over $100 billion on our pets and over $550 billion on leisure travel—down from $723 billion the previous year, owing to COVID-19. Our cars are bigger than everyone else's in the world. Our homes are, too. You could fit three newly built English homes into the average new American home. More than one in eight American families own property besides their primary residence, including second homes and timeshares.[2]

We are much richer than citizens of other countries, including other wealthy ones, and we're much richer than our forebearers. And yet, the dominant mood among the American middle and upper classes is one of fret and worry. In past eras, the rich used to flaunt their wealth, including by showing their indifference to work. The American aristocracy of today seem to prefer complaining to one another and working non-stop. Has there ever been another time, in the full sweep of human history, when so many people had so much and yet felt so deprived and anxious?

Those feelings have proven incredibly effective at preventing us from seeing ourselves as authors of inequality. We like healthy returns. We like smart products. We like low prices and raise a fuss when they creep up. Fast and cheap—that's how we prefer to consume in America. But somebody has to pay for it, and that somebody is the rag-and-bone American worker. Poverty wages allow rock-bottom prices. Relentless supervision and control facilitate fast service. The working class and working poor—and, now, even the working homeless—bear the costs of our appetites and amusements.[3]

It's just as tempting to blame rising housing costs on anything other than the fact that more than a few of us have a god-awful amount of money and are driving prices higher and higher through bidding wars. For several years now, I have been traveling across the United States and speaking with community organizers and political leaders about the nation's housing crisis. Everywhere I go, when searching for a reason for skyrocketing costs, someone will bring up Russian oligarchs. I go to New York and hear about the oligarchs gobbling up the Upper West Side. Mayor Bill de Blasio even complained about them. I fly to Los Angeles, and someone will mention the oligarchs. They are haunting the housing markets of Seattle and Honolulu and Austin, Texas, too. *How many Russian oligarchs are there to go around?* I began to wonder. Truth is, no one knows much about the oligarchs. It's just easier to talk about them than to talk about us. I mean, we don't even call our homegrown oligarchs "oligarchs."[4]

There are countries far poorer than the United States and countries with far less poverty and far less wealth, too. Among advanced democracies, America stands out for its embrace of class extremities. Here, social mobility can cut both ways: The forces that launch us into the upper air can also drop us into a deep pit. What happens to a country when fortunes diverge so sharply, when millions of poor people live alongside millions of rich ones? In a country with such vast inequality, the poor increasingly come to depend on public services and the rich increasingly seek to divest from them. This leads to "private opulence and public squalor," a self-reinforcing dynamic that transforms our communities in ways that pull us further apart.

It's an old problem, one documented by the Roman historian Sallust in his first monograph, *Bellum Catilinae,* which recounts the political turmoil that roiled Rome in 63 B.C.E., during the time of Julius Caesar.[5] But the mid-century economist John Kenneth Galbraith popularized the predicament in his 1958 book, *The Affluent Society.* Galbraith did not spill much ink (or any ink, really) on the issue of exploitation. His great concern had to do with the fact that private fortunes were significantly outpacing investments in public services like schools, parks, and safety net programs. The process tends to begin gradually before accelerating under its own momentum. As people accumulate more money, they become less dependent on public goods and, in turn, less interested in supporting them. If they get their way, through tax breaks and other means, personal fortunes grow while public goods are allowed to deteriorate. As public housing, public education, and public transportation become poorer, they become increasingly, then almost exclusively, used only by the poor themselves.[6]

People then begin to denigrate the public sector altogether, as if it were rotten at the root and not something the rich had found it in their interest to destroy. The rich and the poor soon unite in their animosity toward public goods—the rich because they are made to pay for things they don't need and the poor because what they need has become shabby and broken. Things collectively shared, especially if they are shared across class and racial divides, come to be seen as lesser. In America, a clear marker of poverty is one's reliance on public services, and a clear marker of affluence is one's degree of distance from them. Enough money brings "financial independence," which tellingly does not signal independence from work but from the public sector. There was a time when Americans wished to be free of bosses. Now we wish to be free of bus drivers. We wish for the freedom to withdraw from the wider community and sequester ourselves in a more exclusive one, pulling further and further away from the poor until the world they inhabit becomes utterly unrecognizable to us.[7]

Extreme displays of private opulence and public squalor are seen throughout the sprawling, buzzing cities of the developing world. Think of those massive homes in Lagos wrapped in barbed wire and surrounded by men with machine guns, or those air-conditioned chauffeured cars cruising past throngs of begging children on their way to private hospitals in Delhi. But we have our fair share of displays in America, too, those violent juxtapositions of wealth and destitution. We drive our

Apple CarPlay–equipped SUVs past homeless encampments by the sides of highways. We spend an enormous amount of time stuck in traffic because we've neglected to invest in public transportation projects like high-speed trains. We step from our Manhattan condo, nod to the doorman, and walk streets piled with trash, perhaps hopping on a derelict subway car to meet friends for sushi. We avoid public parks, some of which we've allowed to become dangerous and unsettling, but have memberships to private clubs and golf courses. We finish our basements and remodel our kitchens, while public housing is allowed to fester and fall to pieces. When we find ourselves in legal entanglements, we hire a team of lawyers from white-shoe firms but defund legal services for the indigent. This somehow feels normal to us: that those most in need of aggressive, committed legal defense get assigned attorneys with massive caseloads who sometimes can't remember their names. When legislators in Michigan accommodated their affluent political base by refusing to raise taxes, the state balanced its books by canceling infrastructure upgrades and firing safety inspectors, factors that directly contributed to the Flint water crisis, which exposed upward of twelve thousand children—most of them poor and Black—to lead poisoning.[8]

Follow the money, all of it, and you can see how a trend toward private opulence and public squalor has come to define not simply a handful of communities, but the whole nation. Over the past fifty years, personal incomes in the United States have increased by 317 percent, and yet federal revenue has increased by only 252 percent. Personal fortunes have outpaced the public purse, slowly choking public investments. This trend has occurred in red and blue states alike. Between George

H. W. Bush's time in the Oval Office and Donald Trump's, incomes in Oregon grew by 112 percent, far outpacing increases
in education spending, which grew by only 54 percent. During
that time, incomes in Montana grew by 114 percent, but education spending in the state grew by only 37 percent.[9]

As our incomes have grown, we've chosen to spend more
on personal consumption and less on public works. Our vaca-
tions are more lavish, but schoolteachers must now buy their
own school supplies. We put more money into savings to fuel
intergenerational wealth creation but collectively spend less
on expanding opportunity to all children. In 1955, government
spending accounted for roughly 22 percent of the economy,
and it stayed that way for years. But during the last quarter of
the twentieth century, public investments began to decline. By
2021, government spending on all public goods—including national defense, transportation, health expenditures, and programs to ease the pain of poverty—made up just 17.6 percent
of GDP. Meanwhile, personal consumption grew from about
60 percent of GDP to 69 percent over that same period.[10] A
9 percentage point increase might not look like much, but in
2021 that amounted to more than $2 trillion.

What happened? A major driver of this trend was the biggest tax cut in U.S. history. The Economic Recovery Tax Act of
1981, proposed by Congressman Jack Kemp and signed into
law by President Reagan, reduced federal tax revenues by
more than 13 percent over four years. The act included across-
the-board cuts to income taxes, including a 20 percentage
point reduction in the top marginal tax rate, and slashed estate
taxes as well. Republican overexuberance rocked the economy. In the immediate aftermath of this legislation, the deficit

began to expand, interest rates climbed, and markets flagged. Reagan was forced to right the ship, somewhat, by raising taxes on businesses the following year. But it was the public sector that paid the biggest price for the president's budgetary reprioritization. Reagan reduced funding for the Department of Housing and Urban Development, not by 20 or 40 percent, but by almost 70 percent. The agency whose budget was once second only to the Department of Defense, the agency that had replaced slums with (once) safe and dependable housing, soon couldn't pay for its buildings' trash collection or elevator repair.[11]

Tax cuts are one of the main engines of private opulence and public squalor, and in recent decades we have grown used to the Republican Party delivering them. But this is a recent trend—President Kennedy cut taxes; Nixon and Ford raised them—and if the modern flight from public investments can be said to have started anywhere, it started in a state that had elected a Democratic governor and a Democratic legislature: California. That's where a full-blown tax revolt broke out in the 1970s, amid rising inflation and property taxes. Proposition 13, which capped property taxes at 1 percent of a property's assessed value and froze that value at the property's original purchase price, passed with 65 percent of the vote. Democrats and Republicans voted for it; rich and middle-class homeowners, too. The law boosted private fortunes and gutted public services. If property owners won, public school kids lost. California was forced to cancel summer school, which the state hadn't done since the Great Depression, and dropped from first in the nation in education funding to ninth from the bottom.[12]

The passage of Proposition 13 inspired a nationwide revolt that led to Reagan's 1981 cutting spree. It was a white-led revolt. (The only two groups who had opposed Proposition 13 were public sector employees and African Americans.) Massive tax cuts, which fundamentally reshaped the agendas of the nation's two major political parties and resulted in the rise of private fortunes alongside public poverty, were not simply a response to government overreach. They were a response to white people being ordered to share public goods with Black people.[13]

The major accomplishments of the civil rights movement outlawed racial segregation in the public sector: first in public schools, with the passage of *Brown v. Board of Education* (1954); then in public parks and buildings, as well as restaurants and theaters, with the signing of the Civil Rights Act of 1964; then in housing, through the Civil Rights Act of 1968, better known as the Fair Housing Act. These changes terrified many white families. En masse, whites responded to racial integration by withdrawing from public spaces, then from entire cities, taking their tax dollars with them. Many came to view taxes as something like compulsory donations to Black people. White families felt that they were not only being ordered to integrate; they were being made to pay for it, too. Chafing at this, white voters across the class spectrum came together in their opposition to taxes, breaking the working-class Democratic coalition that had united around the New Deal. White parents also had children in public schools, of course, but in the wake of the civil rights era, most whites began voting according to their perceived racial interests rather than their economic ones.[14]

"In the end," writes historian Kevin Kruse, "court-ordered

desegregation of public spaces brought about not actual racial integration, but instead a new division in which the public world was increasingly abandoned to Blacks and a new private one was created for whites." When public schools were ordered to integrate, white parents first protested, then either retreated into private schools or decamped to the suburbs. In major cities, public schools lost nearly all their white students. For example, by the early aughts most of Atlanta's public schools had less than three white students. In 2022, 16 percent of Atlanta's public school students were white, in a city with a 38 percent white population.[15]

The drive toward private opulence and public squalor harms the poor not only because it leads to widespread disinvestment in public goods but also because that disinvestment creates new private enterprises that eventually replace public institutions as the primary suppliers of opportunity. As more affluent citizens come to rely on those private enterprises, they withdraw their support from public institutions even more. In this way, disinvestment from public goods does not spur renewed attention or motivate reinvestment; it brings further disinvestment and, at the extreme, energizes calls to privatize even our most treasured public institutions such as the U.S. Postal Service and popular programs like Social Security.[16] Equal opportunity is possible only if everyone can access childcare centers, good schools, and safe neighborhoods—all of which serve as engines of social mobility. But private opulence and public squalor leads to "the commodification of opportunity," where those engines of social mobility now cost something. The best way to ensure that opportunity is unequal and unfair is to charge for it.[17]

Proposition 13 is still on the books in California. The nation has never recovered from Reagan's tax cuts, and many of us pine for more. President Trump called his signature policy achievement "the biggest tax cut in U.S. history." It wasn't, but it was plenty big and will reduce public investment by an estimated $1.9 trillion by 2027.[18] More for me. Less for we.

OF COURSE, PUBLIC SQUALOR is not found in equal measure across the United States. In many communities—most, in fact—the parks are well fertilized and manicured, the snow and trash are removed in a timely fashion, the schools have new textbooks in the fall and heat in the winter, and 911 calls summon ambulances. Things work, at least by American standards (which, you learn from riding the trains in Europe or connecting to the Internet in Seoul, are not the highest in the world). Opportunity can be hoarded, then, not only by abandoning public goods for private ones, but also by leveraging individual fortunes to acquire access to exclusive public goods, buying yourself into an upscale community. In many corners of America, a pricey mortgage doesn't just buy a home; it also buys a good education, a well-run soccer league, and public safety so thick and expected it appears natural, instead of the product of social design.[19]

For decades, social scientists and policymakers have tried to engineer ways to pluck low-income families out of high-crime and high-poverty blocks and relocate them to neighborhoods brimming with promise. We started with the kids, busing them across town to integrate public schools. Forced busing turned out to be one of the most loathed domestic policies of the second half of the twentieth century, particularly among the white working class, who were most affected by the change. When busing didn't work, we tried to devise ways for whole families to "move to opportunity" (as the effort was called) by doing things like passing out housing vouchers that could be used anywhere, including in upscale communities. This helped families keep a roof over their heads, but it did little to pull families out of poor neighborhoods. People used their vouchers to rent nicer apartments around the block. We then figured that if we couldn't move the poor to opportunity, maybe we could move opportunity to the poor. This line of thought gave rise to programs like "opportunity zones," which offer tax breaks to developers and people who invest in distressed neighborhoods (very broadly defined). Each of these social policies has accomplished important ends. But none of them did much to integrate neighborhoods or social networks along the lines of race or class.[20] Why? Because most of us who live in safe, prosperous communities don't want poor people for neighbors, particularly if we are white and they are Black.

You can learn a lot about a town from its walls. Our first walls were primitive things: sharpened tree trunks, mud and stone. We learned to dig trenches and build parapets. Someone in the American West invented barbed wire. Today, we fashion our walls out of something much more durable and dispiriting: money and laws. Zoning laws govern what kinds of properties can be built in a community, and because different kinds of properties generally house different kinds of people, those laws also govern who gets in and who does not. Like all walls, they determine so much; and like all walls, they are boring. There may be no phrase more soulless in the English language than "municipal zoning ordinance." Yet there is perhaps no better way to grasp the soul of a community than this.

American cities had zoning ordinances in the 1920s, but they tended to be the general kind that organized the urban landscape—build your factory here, the shops go there, the people live here—not the kind we have today, which ban certain kinds of residences from residential space. Exclusionary zoning ordinances of that sort began appearing in response to the Great Migration. As millions of Black families fled racial terrorism in the South, the cities to which they moved began erecting walls between Black and white neighborhoods via zoning ordinances. After the U.S. Supreme Court outlawed explicit racial segregation in zoning, Atlanta changed its two residential zones from "R-1 white district" and "R-2 colored district" to "R-1 dwelling house district" and "R-2 apartment house district." Exclusionary zoning laws metastasized across the nation after Congress passed federal legislation abolishing housing discrimination in 1968.[21] We went from banning certain kinds of people from our communities to banning the kinds of housing in which those people lived—namely, apartment buildings designed for multiple families—achieving the same ends.

Today, many American cities remain in large part "R-1 dwelling house districts." As *The New York Times* put it in 2019: "It is illegal on 75 percent of the residential land in many American cities to build anything other than a detached single-family home." A 2021 study of one hundred large cities found that the median central city permitted apartment dwellers to live on only 12 percent of its residential land. This is a distinctly American approach to city planning. Greece and Bulgaria don't distinguish between single-family and multifamily housing in their zoning laws, for example, while Germany has outwardly acknowledged the benefits of integrating different housing types in the same neighborhood.[22]

Progressive cities have built the highest walls, passing a tangle of exclusionary zoning policies. This isn't because liberals have a stronger taste for segregation but because these cities experienced the largest increases to their Black populations in the wake of the Great Migration. In the North, especially, cities became more liberal when they gained more Black voters, which is why the liberalization of cities and the segregation of cities went hand in hand. The fact that this pattern has been so sticky—that it characterizes not just American cities of yesteryear but those of today—raises questions about our commitment to fairness and equality.[23]

Most Americans want the country to build more public housing for low-income families, but they do not want that public housing (or any sort of multifamily housing) in their neighborhood. Democrats are more likely than Republicans to champion public housing in the abstract, but among homeowners, they are no more likely to welcome new housing developments in their own backyards. One study found that conservative renters were in fact more likely to support a proposal for a 120-unit apartment building in their community than liberal homeowners.[24] Perhaps we are not so polarized after all. Maybe above a certain income level, we are all segregationists.

The progressive policies that well-off white liberals have

tended to support have been those that pose no real threat to their affluence. During the civil rights era, white elites supported the desegregation of public parks and pools because they didn't use those spaces anyway. They had private clubs. This enraged working-class whites, who called it "integration for everyone but the rich." In the 1970s, wealthy white liberals resisted rezoning their communities to be more inclusive but supported forced busing because their suburban neighborhoods were not subjected to the policy. In the Boston metro area, they didn't bus white students from the leafy enclaves of Newton and Lexington but from the double- and triple-deckers of Dorchester and Southie.[25] This kind of circumscribed liberalism, which ends at your property line, not only denied low-income Americans access to some of the nation's best public schools and safest streets: It also meant that working-class white families were asked to bear the costs of integration in a way that white professionals never were. This bred among blue-collar whites a festering resentment toward elites and their institutions—the university and its science, professional journalism and its standards, government and its decorum—which gave rise to a new political alignment and a new politicized anger still very much with us today.

It is true, as Heather McGhee has argued in her book, *The Sum of Us,* that one group's gain need not always come at another group's expense and that adopting such a zero-sum mindset has time and again led poor whites to choose poverty and sickness over parity with Black Americans.[26] But it is also true that hoarding resources and passing laws that block the less fortunate from those resources is an incredibly effective way to grow wealthier while the undesirables languish outside the wall.

If you erect a community of expensive, beautiful homes and prop up the value of those homes by making it illegal to build more housing, which turns your home into a resource so scarce that potential buyers do things like write pleading letters or make cash offers above the asking price or bid sight unseen—behavior that has become commonplace in liberal cities like Austin, Seattle, and Cambridge—then you pretty much want to keep things as they are.[27] If you design a public school system such that it primarily serves students of professional parents, who have the time and know-how to invest in their children's schooling, and who can afford to pay for extra tutoring and college prep coaches and out-of-state field trips and therapy, you can create an enriching educational environment and pipeline to college. Economically integrating schools would challenge this design, this social status preservation machine, requiring rich students to share classrooms with poor students who might carry some of the traumas of poverty, speak English as a second language, and spend their summers watching a lot of television because going outside is dangerous. One study found that growing up in a severely disadvantaged neighborhood is equivalent to missing a year of school when it comes to verbal ability. Another found that achievement gaps between rich and poor children form and harden before kindergarten.[28]

It has become fashionable these days to pitch social change to the privileged classes by appealing to their material self-interest. *The right thing to do is also the best thing to do! Integrat-*

ing our schools is antiracist, and it improves the overall learning environment, preparing your children for a diverse workforce! Raising the minimum wage allows workers to buy enough food, and it's good for business, stabilizing the company's labor force and saving on turnover costs! When then-presidential-candidate Joe Biden told a room of wealthy donors that "nothing would fundamentally change" if he were to be elected, he was repeating a familiar liberal talking point: *If you join me in this effort to reduce the inequality you yourself benefit from, you won't have to give up a thing.* These "everybody wins" arguments ring false because they are. If ameliorating poverty and racial division would get rich kids into better colleges or bump up a company's stock price, wouldn't well-off Americans already be doing it?

It cannot both be true that excluding poor people from high-opportunity communities enriches the lives of the people inside the wall while degrading the lives of people outside of it *and* that tearing down the wall and welcoming the poor into those communities will come at no cost to the current residents. Affluence allowed those residents to climb over the wall, and the wall protected and grew their affluence. As the sociologist Tressie McMillan Cottom has put it: "The families that can hoard do, and the neighborhoods in which they live benefit."[29] Let's be honest. Sharing opportunities previously hoarded doesn't mean everyone wins. It means that those who have benefitted from the nation's excesses will have to take less so that others may share in the bounty.

CHAPTER 7

INVEST IN ENDING POVERTY

I N 1881, HAVING PUBLISHED *WAR AND PEACE* AND *ANNA Karenina,* Leo Tolstoy moved to Moscow from the Russian countryside. He was fifty-three and a man of means, able to employ a team of servants who ran his household. One of the first things Tolstoy noticed about Moscow was its poverty. "I knew country poverty," he wrote, "but town poverty was new and incomprehensible to me." He was shocked to walk the streets of the city and see such hunger and hopelessness commingling with such ostentation and frivolity. The problem haunted Tolstoy, and he went looking for an answer. He visited houses of prostitution, questioned a police officer who had arrested a beggar, and even adopted a young boy, who eventually ran away. The problem wasn't work, the great writer quickly learned. The poor seemed to never stop working. The problem, he ultimately decided, was himself and his fellow affluents, who lived idle lives. "I sit on a man's back, choking him and making him carry me, and yet assure myself and others that I am very sorry for him and wish to ease his lot by all possible means—except by getting off his back."[1]

True then and there, and true now and here. There is so much poverty in this land not in spite of our wealth but because of it. Which is to say, it's not about them. It's about *us*. "It is really so simple," Tolstoy wrote. "If I want to aid the poor, that is, to help the poor not to be poor, I ought not to make them poor."[2]

How do we, today, make the poor in America poor? In at least three ways. First, we exploit them. We constrain their choice and power in the labor market, the housing market, and the financial market, driving down wages while forcing the poor to overpay for housing and access to cash and credit. Those of us who are not poor benefit from these arrangements. Corporations benefit from worker exploitation, sure, but so do consumers who buy the cheap goods and services the working poor produce, and so do those of us directly or indirectly invested in the stock market. Landlords are not the only ones who benefit from housing exploitation; many homeowners do, too, their property values propped up by the collective effort to make housing scarce and expensive. The banking and payday lending industries profit from the financial exploitation of the poor, but so do those of us with free checking accounts at Bank of America or Wells Fargo, as those accounts are subsidized by billions of dollars in overdraft fees.[3] If we burn coal, we get electricity, but we get sulfur dioxide and nitrogen oxide and other airborne toxins, too. We can't have the electricity without producing the pollution. Opulence in America works the same way. Someone bears the cost.

Second, we prioritize the subsidization of affluence over the alleviation of poverty. The United States could effectively end poverty in America tomorrow without increasing the deficit if it cracked down on corporations and families who cheat on their taxes, reallocating the newfound revenue to those most in need of it.[4] Instead, we let the rich slide and give the most to those who have plenty already, creating a welfare state that heavily favors the upper class. And then our elected officials have the audacity—the shamelessness, really—to fabricate stories about poor people's dependency on government aid and shoot down proposals to reduce poverty because they would cost too much. Glancing at the price tag of some program that would cut child poverty in half or give all Americans access to a doctor, they suck their teeth and ask, "But how can we afford it?" *How can we afford it?* What a sinful question. What a selfish, dishonest question, one asked as if the answer wasn't staring us straight in the face. We could afford it if we allowed the IRS to do its job. We could afford it if the well-off among us took less from the government. We could afford it if we designed our welfare state to expand opportunity and not guard fortunes.

Third, we create prosperous and exclusive communities. And in doing so, we not only create neighborhoods with concentrated riches but also neighborhoods with concentrated despair—the externality of stockpiled opportunity. Wealth traps breed poverty traps.[5] The concentration of affluence breeds more affluence, and the concentration of poverty, more poverty. To be poor is miserable, but to be poor and surrounded by poverty on all sides is a much deeper cut.[6] Likewise, to be rich and surrounded by riches on all sides is a level of privilege of another order. We need not be debt collectors or private prison wardens to play a role in producing poverty in America. We need only to vote yes on policies that lead to private opulence and public squalor and, with that opulence, build a life behind a wall that we tend and maintain. We may plaster our wall with Gadsden flags or rainbow flags, ALL LIVES MATTER signs or BLACK LIVES MATTER signs. The wall remains the wall, indifferent to our decorations.[7]

We know there is far too much scarcity in this rich land. What good is all this money when so many of us take four buses to work and turn cars into homes and deal with tooth-aches by waiting for the rot to dull the nerves and drink water we know is poisoned? We should significantly deepen our col-lective investment in economic stability and basic dignity, pro-moting "a right to a decent existence—to some minimum standard of nutrition, healthcare, and other essentials of life," to quote the economist Arthur Okun. "Starvation and dignity do not mix well."[8]

THE LOW-HANGING FRUIT HERE is to make sure low-income Americans get connected to the aid for which they qualify. We used to believe that welfare avoidance came down to stigma, that people weren't signing up for food stamps or claiming the Earned Income Tax Credit because they found the experience too shaming. But research has started to chip away at this theory. It turns out that take-up rates of means-tested programs like food stamps are similar to those of some more universal (and less stigmatized) social insurance pro-grams, like unemployment. And when the government switched from issuing food stamps in the form of actual stamps that you would conspicuously hand to a grocery store

cashier to issuing them through discreet Electronic Benefits
Transfer (EBT) cards that looked like any other debit card,
there wasn't a conclusive uptick in applications. There appar-
ently weren't scores of poor Americans sitting at home thinking, "I would definitely use food stamps if no one in the
checkout line noticed." Speaking of food stamps, in Oregon
virtually everyone who is eligible for the program enrolls in
it. But cross the border into California and roughly a third of
residents who qualify for food stamps don't use them. Are
food stamps more stigmatized in California than in Oregon?
Of course not.[9]

If the answer isn't stigma, what is going on? The bulk of
the evidence indicates that low-income Americans are not taking full advantage of government programs for a much more
banal reason: We've made it hard and confusing. People often
don't know about aid designated for them or are burdened by
the application process. When it comes to increasing enrollment in social programs, the most successful behavioral adjustments have been those that simply raised awareness and
cut through red tape and hassle.[10]

A little can go a long way. One intervention tripled the rate
of elderly people enrolled in food stamps by providing information about the program and offering sign-up assistance. Elderly households received a letter informing them they could
apply for food stamps along with a number to call. Those who
dialed the number were connected to a benefits specialist who
helped callers fill out the application and collect the necessary
documentation. Again, this nothing-to-it intervention *tripled*
enrollment. Another initiative significantly increased the number of workers who claimed the Earned Income Tax Credit

just by sending out mailers, reducing the amount of text on the application, and using a more readable font. No kidding: Using Frutiger font—that sturdy, confident typeface adorning Swiss road signs and prescription labels—helped bring millions of more dollars to low-income working families.[11]

Private industry in the United States knows a thing or two about advertising services and building distribution channels that seamlessly connect customers with products. The federal government should take note. It should be just as easy for a new mother to apply for the Special Supplemental Nutrition Program for Women, Infants, and Children (WIC), which provides diapers and formula, or a laid-off father to apply for unemployment, as it is for me to have birdseed or mouthwash delivered to my home from an app on my phone.

BUT LET'S REACH FOR something more. How much would it cost to end poverty—not to reduce it by 10 percent or even cut it in half, but to abolish it entirely? In 2020, the gap separating everyone in America below the poverty line and the poverty line itself amounted to $177 billion. I arrived at this rough estimate by multiplying the number of families and individuals below the line with the average amount they would need to rise above it.[12] Now, this figure is on top of current welfare spending, and it doesn't account for either the administrative costs of delivering aid (which would raise the estimate) or gains made by addressing issues like labor and housing exploitation (which would lower it). Really nailing down the cost of ensuring that every American enjoys a decent level of economic security would take a lot more calculating. But $177 billion is a good place to start. It helps us begin to understand what we're talking about when we talk about ending poverty in America. And what we're talking about is a goal that is irresistibly attainable. One hundred and seventy-seven billion dollars is less than 1 percent of our GDP. Americans throw away more than that amount in food every year.[13]

What could $177 billion buy? Quite a lot. We could ensure that every person in America had a safer and more affordable place to live. Every single one of us. We could put a real dent in ending homelessness in America, and we could end hunger. We could provide every child with a fairer shot at security and success. We could make immense headway in driving down the many agonizing correlates of poverty, like violence, sickness, and despair. Crime rates would plummet. Eviction rates, too. Neighborhoods would stabilize and come alive. Schools could focus more on education instead of dedicating so many resources to triaging the deep needs of their students.

Where would the money come from? The best place to start, in my view, is with the cheaters. The IRS now estimates that the United States loses more than $1 trillion a year in unpaid taxes, most of it owing to tax avoidance by multinational corporations and wealthy families. Congress hasn't given the agency the resources it needs to hunt down tax criminals, leaving the IRS outgunned and outmatched.[14]

In recent decades, corporations have parked more and more of their profits in shell companies registered in countries with bottom-level tax rates. The trick is to pretend that a sizable part of your Silicon Valley– or Wall Street–based company is really located in places like Ireland and Bermuda. Facebook recently logged $15 billion in profit in Ireland, which amounted to $10 million per Irish employee, while Bristol Myers Squibb reported making $5 billion on the Emerald Isle, or roughly $7.5 million per employee. Clearly, companies are doing all they can to avoid paying what they owe. Wealthy families, too, have found new ways to weasel out of paying taxes. Studies have shown that most Americans pay 90 percent of the taxes they owe, but the ultra-rich pay only 75 percent. This is possible because affluents have increasingly come to rely on a burgeoning industry of tax professionals who have devised ingenious ways to get around investing in the common welfare.[15] When corporations hide profits in tax havens, and when rich families stash valuable assets in offshore accounts, they defraud the American public, forcing everyone else to pay for their greed. Congress should crack down on such corruption, writing the IRS a blank check to go after tax cheats, and it should pass legislation mandating that corporations pay a minimum tax on their profits—say, 25 percent—no matter what country they're registered in.

Income inequality has endowed rich families with more political power, which they have used to campaign for lower taxes, which in turn boosts their economic and political power even more, locking in an undemocratic and unjust cycle.[16] We need to interrupt that cycle, which is why I also support increasing the top marginal tax rate and the corporate tax rate. Since 1962, the effective tax rate for poor, working-class, and middle-class Americans has increased, while it has decreased for the top 10 percent of income earners, and particularly for the richest among us. This is absurd. We should bump up the top marginal tax rate—perhaps to 50 percent, as it was in 1986; or 70 percent, as it was in 1975—and expand our tax brackets so that an investment banker's income is taxed differently than a dentist's. Meanwhile, at 21 percent, the corporate tax rate in America is the lowest it's been in more than eighty years. We could fund a good deal of antipoverty initiatives by increasing it to 35 percent, as it was from 1993 through 2017, or to 46 percent, as it was from 1979 through 1986.[17]

Some claim that such proposals would hamstring the economy by disincentivizing innovation and entrepreneurship. But no serious social scientist believes that the economy slows down when we reasonably increase taxes on the rich or on multinational corporations. There were go-getters aplenty in past decades, when top tax rates were much higher, while in recent years productivity has declined right alongside taxes on wealthy individuals and companies. Commentators have taken to describing today's America as having entered "The Age of Decadence" or "A Dark Age of Invention and Innovation," a time of stagnation and slowdown. Since the rich haven't given the country all that economic dynamism they promised when we cut their taxes, they can at least put in more for public investments.[18]

Would those wealthy Americans respond by picking up the phone and dialing their lawyers and accountants? Sure. Would they adjust their investment strategies to minimize the damage? Of course. But—so what? I've never understood the fatalistic criticisms that swat away calls for tax fairness because implementing it would be a challenge.[19] I once got into a yelling match with an economist in a New York City restaurant over this point. My tablemates and I were discussing Elizabeth Warren's wealth tax proposal, and the economist, who had ventured over to say hello, said it would never work. The rich would find a way to squirm out of it. I told him he was being defeatist and boring. Things escalated from there. Chests may have been poked.[20]

It turns out that addressing the most urgent problems of our time is, well, hard. But what is maddening about this debate is not how difficult fair-tax implementation would be but how utterly easy it is to find enough money to defeat poverty by closing nonsensical tax loopholes. If you don't like the changes I suggested above, I can propose twenty smaller reforms, or fifty tinier ones, or a hundred even more innocuous nudges to get us there. We could raise $25 billion by winding down the mortgage interest deduction, which disproportionately benefits high-income families and does nothing to promote homeownership. We could find $64.7 billion by increasing the maximum taxable amount of earnings for Social Security so that high- and low-income workers are taxed at the same rate. We could scratch out another $37.3 billion if we treated capital gains and dividends for wealthy Americans the same way we treat income for tax purposes.[21]

Now I'm the one being boring. But this is the fine print of civilization, and slogging through it gives form to an otherwise amorphous debate, allowing us to notice just how misshapen the American safety net truly is. There are countless ways to deepen our investments in economic opportunity and security without increasing the deficit. We just have to stop spending so much on the rich. This, to me, is what it truly means to be fiscally responsible.

REFASHIONING THE AMERICAN WELFARE state to support an aggressive, uncompromising antipoverty agenda could take many forms. We could significantly expand the Child Tax Credit to poor, working-class, and middle-class families, a program that functions like guaranteed income to households with kids. We could finally confront the affordable housing crisis, which has devastated the poor and dashed the hopes of countless young people shut out of homeownership, by investing in new construction and public housing. We could make deeper investments in public education and childcare and transportation infrastructure.

Should we seek out more targeted programs or more universal ones? This is an old question in the policy debate. Targeted programs (like food stamps) are reserved for the poorest families. Because they direct themselves to marginalized people with specific needs (like hunger), they are cost-efficient and typically successful. But they are also divisive, as families just above an arbitrary income cutoff are denied help, causing a rift to form between officially poor families and a much larger group of Americans who live above the poverty line but without much economic security. We saw this happen during the rollout of the Affordable Care Act. Some working-class families had to pay upward of $1,000 a month for coverage, while poorer families qualified for free Medicaid. After seeing her healthcare costs jump, Gwen Hurd, a worker at an outlet mall, told a reporter in 2018: "It seems to me that people who earn nothing and contribute nothing get everything for free. And the people who work hard and struggle for every penny barely end up surviving."[22] Universal programs, like a universal basic income (UBI), get rid of this baggage. Designed to benefit a large number of people, sometimes irrespective of their standing, universal programs are less polarizing and so are considered more politically durable. ("Programs for the poor are poor programs," the old policy-school adage goes.) But universal programs are also much more expensive—some popular UBI proposals would cost north of $1 trillion a year— and their one-size-fits-all design can underserve the neediest families.[23]

Recently, community organizers and policy wonks have developed innovative ideas that move beyond the targeted-universal binary. One is what might be called *broader* or *bigger tent targeting*. These are simply targeted programs with a higher income threshold, allowing aid to flow not just to the poor, but also to the working and middle class. In providing benefits to working families with annual incomes up to $57,414 (as of 2022), the Earned Income Tax Credit is one such program. The credit reaches the poor, but it reaches families well above the poverty line, too. Broader targeting policies have proven to be quite popular over the past several decades, and they're difficult for Congress to cancel when political winds shift (as happened with cash welfare in the 1990s).[24]

Another approach is what legal scholar john a. powell calls "targeted universalism." This entails setting a goal, determining what it would take to meet that goal, and recognizing that different groups will require different kinds and levels of aid if the goal is to be realized. One size does not fit all. Let's say we want every American family to have access to the Internet. A targeted approach might provide vouchers for free Internet services to all families with incomes under $25,000, leaving everyone bringing in at least $25,001 out in the cold. A universal approach might provide all families with vouchers, supplying affluent families with something they don't need, while bankrolling Internet providers and underserving the poorest families who need more than a voucher to gain reliable access. What about families who live in very rural communities? Or those who struggle to pay the electric bill or who lack a computer? What about those in prison? A targeted universal approach, on the other hand, takes such things into account, acknowledging that for our goal to be met, different groups will need different interventions: some shallow and some deep, some generic and some tailor-made.[25]

For me, the fundamental lesson that emerges from this debate is that if we want to abolish poverty, we need to embrace policies that foster goodwill and be suspicious of those that kindle resentment. *Will the policy unite people struggling with economic insecurity, those below the poverty line and those above it? Will it drive down poverty and promote economic opportunity?* A policy that checks both of these boxes deserves serious consideration. In fact, a guiding set of principles for an antipoverty agenda might be the following: *Rebalance the safety net and insist on tax fairness* in order to *make significant investments* in eliminating poverty through policies supported by *broad coalitions.* We should go big: No more nudges, no more tinkering, no more underfunding an initiative and then asking why it didn't work. Ambitious interventions should be funded by progressive tax policies and a redesigned welfare state and delivered in ways that do not sow division among struggling families who should for all intents and purposes be political allies.

Are you calling for the redistribution of wealth?

"Redistribution." I hate the word. It distracts and triggers, causing us to instinctively fly to our respective political corners and regurgitate the same old talking points. *No one should be that rich! Ingenuity and hard work should be rewarded!* It's tiresome. Even worse, the notion of redistribution has the pernicious effect of framing social progress as a taking, as if the government were a greedy, many-tentacled monster seeking to reach deeper into your pocket. The truth is that the government is devoting a considerable amount of effort—far too much effort, if you ask me—to underwriting the portfolios and estates of the American aristocracy.

This country of ours should be in the business of helping its people create wealth, but it should not be in the business of heavily subsidizing it. Why are we so focused on increasing the wealth of the already wealthy when millions languish in poverty? PayPal founder Peter Thiel's Roth IRA is worth $5 billion. That money is completely tax free if the billionaire doesn't withdraw it before he is fifty-nine and a half. This is just an obscenely exaggerated example of the kind of problem we should seek to rectify, a problem having to do with what used to be called "socialism for the rich and free enterprise for the poor."[26]

I'm not calling for "redistribution." I'm calling for the rich to pay their taxes. I'm calling for a rebalancing of our social safety net. I'm calling for a return to a time when America made bigger investments in the general welfare. I'm calling for more poor aid and less rich aid.

POLITICS IN AMERICA IS a dismal, ugly business these days. During a time of intense polarization, disturbing threats to democratic institutions, and partisan gridlock in Washington, calling for transformative federal policies to abolish poverty might sound hopelessly naïve. Then again, Congress responded with bold, bipartisan relief during the pandemic, making more progress on poverty than we've seen in generations. After the Great Recession that began in 2008, families in the bottom half of the income distribution had to wait nearly ten years before their incomes returned to pre-recession levels. After the COVID-19-induced recession, they waited just a year and a half. Government aid played a major role in the recovery.[27]

It is worth recognizing how consequential the antipoverty policies passed during the pandemic truly were. Consider just one: Emergency Rental Assistance (ERA). When COVID-19 spread across the United States, it triggered a national eviction crisis, which eventually led to the passage of a federal eviction moratorium. But everyone knew the moratorium wouldn't last forever, which raised the question: When the bill eventually comes due, what will happen to all those families who have fallen months behind in rent? The National Low Income Housing Coalition, along with dozens of like-minded organizations across the country, demanded action, and the federal government responded with $46.5 billion in rental assistance. This amounted to a colossal investment in housing stability, one that exceeded the entire budget of the Department of Housing and Urban Development in 2020.[28] To make sure funds ended up in the right hands, distribution channels had to be created from scratch in every community in America. Some states (Texas, Virginia) established these channels quickly; others (Ohio, Georgia) did not. As a result, the initial rollout of the ERA program was disappointing. Journalists criticized the "slow-asmolasses distribution" and declared that "the rent help is too damn slow."[29]

But then, thanks to the hard work of community organizers, heroic government bureaucrats, and housing advocates around the country, the distribution channels opened, and funds started flowing, eventually reaching millions of renting families. As a result, eviction filings remained well below historical levels months after the eviction moratorium ended, even as rent and inflation rose. In December 2021, eviction filings were down 39 percent in Minneapolis, 53 percent in Albuquerque, and 64 percent in Austin. This was astonishing. The Emergency Rental Assistance program, in tandem with other pandemic aid like the expanded Child Tax Credit, had cut the eviction filing rate *in half* in city after city across the United States. Eviction rates were lower than they had ever been on record.[30]

It was a real win. I thought the bureaucrats who had overseen the Emergency Rental Assistance program deserved a parade. They had to settle for scattered applause. When the ERA program was sputtering in the unsteady early days, it seemed that everyone was writing and tweeting about it. Later, when the rollout was working, it was ignored. Because journalists and pundits and social influencers did not celebrate the program, ERA garnered few champions in Washington. Elected leaders learned that they could direct serious federal resources to fighting evictions, make a real dent in the problem, and reap little credit for it. So, the Emergency Rental Assistance program became a temporary program, and we returned to normal, to a society where seven eviction filings are issued every minute.[31] Imagine if we had met the results of the ERA program with loud cheers. Imagine if we had taken to social media and gushed over what a difference it had made. Imagine if newspapers had run headlines that read, "Biden Administration Passes Most Important Eviction Prevention Measure in American History." Imagine if we'd worked together to ensure that the low eviction regime established during the pandemic became the new normal. But we chose to shrug instead. Poor renters in the future will pay for this, as will the Democratic Party, incessantly blamed for having a "messaging problem" when perhaps the matter is that liberals have a despondency problem: fluent in the language of grievance and bumbling in the language of repair.

Meaningful, tangible change had arrived, and we couldn't see it. When we refuse to recognize what works, we risk swallowing the lie that nothing does. We risk imagining the future only as more of the same. We risk giving in to despair, perhaps the most exculpating of all emotions, and submitting to cynicism, perhaps the most conservative of all belief systems. This can suffocate meaningful action, and it certainly doesn't inspire others to join the cause. "Liberals are good at criticism but often have no word of promise to speak," wrote the theologian Walter Brueggemann in 1978. But without that word of promise, we risk running adrift, cultivating an antipoverty identity that lacks an antipoverty politics. Even if effective policies fall well short of the mark, we should salute their effectiveness, because doing so affirms the concrete possibility of change. Even in the darkest moments, we should allow ourselves to imagine, to marvel over, a new social contract, because doing so expresses both our discontent with, and the impermanence of, the current one. "We need to ask not whether it is realistic or practical or viable but whether it is *imaginable,"* wrote Brueggemann. "We need to ask if our consciousness and imagination have been so assaulted and co-opted" by the established order "that we have been robbed of the courage or power to think an alternative thought."[32]

Things looked bleak in 1963, too, the year Lyndon Johnson assumed the presidency. John F. Kennedy had been assassinated. The country was embroiled in an unpopular war in Vietnam and deeply divided over the civil rights movement. The 1964 election handed Democrats majorities in both houses of Congress, but Washington was just as deadlocked as it is today, as southern Dixiecrats joined Republicans to block progressive reform. Some cities had experienced major riots and dozens more would burn before Johnson left office. In the midst of this political polarization and unease, the modern American welfare state was born. The War on Poverty and the Great Society constituted a bundle of domestic programs that included the Food Stamp Act, which made food aid permanent; the Economic Opportunity Act, which created Job Corps and Head Start; and the Social Security Amendments of 1965, which founded Medicare and Medicaid and expanded Social Security benefits. Nearly two hundred pieces of legislation were signed into law in Johnson's first five years in office, a breathtaking level of activity. And the result? Ten years after the first of these programs were rolled out in 1964, the share of Americans living in poverty was half what it was in 1960.[33]

In previous generations, and in recent memory, government investments have resulted in tremendous reductions in the number of Americans living in poverty. We can go further, and it wouldn't be hard to find the money to do so. By one estimate, simply collecting unpaid federal income taxes from the top 1 percent of households would bring in some $175 billion a year. We could just about fill the entire poverty gap in America if the richest among us simply paid all the taxes they owed.[34]

However impactful that would be—and it would be very impactful—we shouldn't stop there. The War on Poverty and the Great Society were launched during a time when organized labor was strong and incomes were climbing. In today's labor market, unions are weak and real wages are falling for far too many Americans. When the economy delivered for the average worker, and even those near the bottom of the pay scale, antipoverty programs were cures. Today, the labor market has turned those programs into something like dialysis, a treatment designed to make poverty less lethal, not to make it disappear.[35] Meanwhile, the housing market now recoups many of the gains workers make. After wages began to rise in 2021, following worker shortages, rents rose as well, and soon people found themselves back where they started or worse. It's an old pattern. Since 1985, rent prices have exceeded income gains by 325 percent.[36]

We can't just spend our way out of this. Over the past fifty years, we've tried that—doubling antipoverty aid per capita— and the poverty line hasn't meaningfully budged. A big reason why is that we insist on supporting policies that accommodate poverty, not ones that disrupt it. Our largest cash assistance program is the Earned Income Tax Credit, which props up corporate profits and depresses wages. Our biggest affordable housing initiative is the Housing Choice Voucher Program, which, by paying a portion of a family's rent, subsidizes private landlords and pushes up costs.[37] Do tax credits for low-income workers and housing vouchers for low-income renters make a difference? Unquestionably. Millions more families would be impoverished if these programs didn't exist. I have spent years advocating for more housing vouchers as a politically viable solution to the affordability crisis. But over the course of writing this book, I've been forced to face the fact that poverty has refused to decline significantly in the years since the Earned Income Tax Credit and the Housing Choice Voucher Program were rolled out and expanded. These policies are at once solutions to poverty and stanchions of it. They rescue millions of families from a social ill, but they do nothing to address its root causes.

We don't just need deeper antipoverty investments. We need different ones, policies that refuse to partner with poverty, policies that threaten its very survival. We need to ensure that aid directed at poor people stays in their pockets, instead of being captured by companies whose low wages are subsidized by government benefits, or by landlords who raise the rents as their tenants' wages rise, or by banks and payday loan outlets that issue exorbitant fines and fees. If we fail to address the many forms of exploitation at the bottom of the market, we risk increasing government spending only to experience another fifty years of sclerosis in the fight against poverty. We need to empower the poor.

CHAPTER 8

EMPOWER THE POOR

W E ALL DESERVE A FAIR DEAL, BUT THE POOR ARE TOO often denied one. Choice is the antidote for exploitation. So a crucial step toward ending poverty is giving more Americans the power to decide where to work, live, and bank, and when to start a family.

Let's start with jobs. In 2020, 1.1 million workers earned at or below the federal minimum wage of $7.25 an hour, a wage mandate that hasn't budged in over a decade. Most states still allow restaurant and other service workers to be paid a *subminimum* wage, which is a meager $2.13 an hour at the federal level, forcing nearly 5 million workers to survive on tips. (Where did the concept of subminimum wage come from? It's a vestige of slavery. After emancipation, restaurant owners hired formerly enslaved Black workers for free. They had to rely on customers' charity.) This is indefensible. Congress should raise the minimum wage and make sure all workers are paid it, ending subminimum pay. But it should do more than that. It should ensure that workers will never again have to fight to earn a living. At least eighty countries with minimum wage standards mandate that officials revisit them every year or so, but not us. The United States should require periodic (and humane) reviews of the minimum wage. It should also follow the lead of more than one hundred countries that empower the central government or an official (like the secretary of labor) to raise the minimum wage after consulting with businesses and worker organizations—or, better yet, allow minimum wages to be set through collective bargaining agreements between workers and employers. This would allow basic pay to increase in a timely fashion, not whenever Congress got around to it.[1]

Through the years, Congress has intervened when the labor market threatened people's health and freedom. It outlawed indentured servitude and child labor. It enforced measures of workplace safety and compensated those injured on the job. We are all better off with these protections. In the same way, Congress should outlaw undignified, even dangerous, poverty wages. According to a paper in *Preventive Medicine,* low wages "could be viewed as occupational hazards." From this perspective, there is no difference between substandard wages and workers being exposed to asbestos or harmful chemicals.[2] If companies are not allowed to place employees in unnecessary danger or degrade them via discrimination or harassment, why are they permitted to pay those workers dangerous and degrading wages?

The best way to address labor exploitation is to promote worker empowerment. Unions have an impressive track record of doing exactly that. But attempting to restore unions to their former glory would be a foolish exercise. Just as the

Gospel tells us that "new wine calls for new wineskins," a new economy calls for new labor law. What would that look like?

We might start with the recognition that Old Labor was exclusionary. The landmark National Labor Relations Act of 1935, which laid the foundation for the American labor movement, did not extend to sectors of the economy typically staffed by women and workers of color, such as domestic and agricultural work. And unions have a long history of withholding membership from Black workers, undercutting their own movement. New Labor must be inclusive and antiracist, empowering workers young and old, including those bending in our fields, waiting on our tables, cleaning our homes and offices, and caring for our old and sick.[3]

A renewed contract with American workers should make organizing easy. As things currently stand, unionizing a workplace is incredibly difficult. The laws regulating how to form a union are esoteric and baffling, and the federal government does a poor job of protecting workers who make the effort, leaving them exposed to firings and abuse. Small wonder that most union drives fail.[4] Under current labor law, workers who want to organize must do so one Amazon warehouse or one Starbucks location at a time. We have little chance of empowering the nation's warehouse workers and baristas this way.[5]

This is why many new labor movements are trying to organize entire sectors instead. The Fight for $15 campaign, led by the Service Employees International Union (SEIU), hasn't focused on a single franchise (a specific McDonald's store) or even a single company (McDonald's) but has brought together workers from several fast food chains. In Seattle, New York

City, and elsewhere, these workers successfully pressured elected officials to raise wages for all workers in their cities. Here is a new kind of labor power, one that strives to organize whole regions, and one that could be expanded: If enough workers in a specific economic sector—retail, hotel services, nursing—voted for the measure, the secretary of labor could establish a bargaining panel made up of representatives elected by the workers. The panel could negotiate with companies to secure the best terms for workers across the industry. This is a way to organize all Amazon warehouses and all Starbucks locations in a single go, and it's a way to empower all those independent contractors at Meta and Apple, too.[6]

Sectoral bargaining, as it's called, would impact tens of millions of Americans who have never benefitted from a union of their own, just as it has improved the lives of workers in Europe and Latin America. In Austria, for example, sector-by-sector collective bargaining established a countrywide minimum monthly wage of €1,500 in 2017.[7] Sectoral bargaining would even the playing field, not only between workers and bosses, but also between companies within the same sector that would no longer be locked into a race to the bottom, incentivized to shortchange their workforce to gain a competitive edge. Instead, the companies would be forced to compete over the quality of the goods and services they offer. Maybe we'd finally reap the benefits of all that economic productivity we were promised.[8]

These ideas for a new kind of labor law were the result of a two-year effort that brought together more than seventy union leaders, academics, advocates, and workers from around the world to sketch a blueprint for how to empower labor in the twenty-first century. The collective's 2020 report, *Clean Slate for Worker Power*, champions plenty of other solutions, too, including mandating that corporate boards have significant worker representation and levying heavy penalties on companies that thwart organizing efforts. These proposals are not anti-capitalist; they are anti-exploitation, anti-raw-deal, anti-purposeless-and-grotesque-inequality. (Orwell once said that "we could do with a little less talk of 'capitalist' and 'proletarian' and a little more about the robbers and the robbed.")[9] These are calls for a capitalism that serves the people, not the other way around.

WHAT ABOUT HOUSING? Poor families looking for a safe, affordable place to live in America usually have but one choice: to rent from private landlords and fork over at least half their income. Imagine if those families could choose between renting an apartment within reach on the private market, moving into public housing, owning their own home, or joining a housing cooperative collectively owned and managed by the tenants themselves. Under that scenario, poor families would have some leverage and a bit of market power, and they wouldn't have to settle for living in run-down, overpriced apartments. If we want to get rid of rent gouging and neglected properties, we need to expand housing opportunity for low-income families. There isn't a single right way to do this, but there is clearly a wrong way: the way we're doing it now.

One straightforward approach is to strengthen our commitment to the housing programs we already have. Public housing provides affordable homes to millions of Americans, but it's so underfunded relative to the need that the wait time to get into one of these units is often not counted in months or years but in decades.[10] The sky-high demand should tell us something: that affordable housing is a life changer, and families are desperate for it.

This may come as a surprise to those of us who consider America's experiment with public housing an abject failure, recalling those segregated, Soviet-style towers in cities like Chicago and St. Louis, towers that in the end had become so decrepit and violent that dynamiting them felt like a kindness. But I recommend withholding judgment until you visit Via Verde, a gorgeous affordable housing complex in the South Bronx, complete with a fitness center and a terraced roof planted with garden plots and trees. Or go see the Bent Tree Apartments in Austin, a 126-unit complex surrounded by mature oaks and even a swimming pool. Or check out the handsome duplexes scattered around Milwaukee or Pittsburgh or Washington, D.C., with tidy balconies and bright paint.[11] These are not your father's housing projects. The research affirms what parents on those long wait lists have already intuited: Children who grow up in subsidized housing are healthier, have lower exposure to lead poisoning, and do better in school than their peers living unassisted in the private rental market. As adults, they have lower rates of incarceration and higher incomes than their peers. Public housing works for the lucky minority of poor families who benefit from it. By extending its reach, we could provide permanent, affordable housing to many more—even all—low-income Americans.[12]

We could also pave the way for more Americans to become

homeowners, an initiative that could benefit poor, working-class, and middle-class families alike—as well as scores of young people. Families typically pay more as renters than they would as homeowners. For example, in 2019 the median renter in Louisville, Kentucky, paid $900 a month in rent and insurance, while housing costs for the median homeowner were only $573 a month, including mortgage payments, insurance, and property taxes. The problem is that banks have shown little interest in financing affordable homes. That year, roughly 27 percent of homes—2.1 million—were bought for less than $100,000, but only 23 percent of those homes were purchased with a mortgage. The rest were bought with cash by speculators and landlords. Paving the way for more renters to become homeowners would not only drastically lower housing costs; it could also provide a means of building wealth. This would be a step toward repairing historical injustices that excluded Black Americans from homeownership opportunities, particularly through redlining.[13]

Banks generally avoid issuing small-dollar mortgages, not because they're riskier—these mortgages have the same delinquency rates as larger mortgages—but because they're less profitable. There are fixed costs to initiating any mortgage, large or small, so from a bank's perspective, it makes the most sense to approve applications for expensive homes and deny applications for affordable ones. Over the life of a mortgage, interest on $1 million brings in a lot more coin than interest on $75,000. This is where the government could step in, providing extra financing to build on-ramps to first-time homeownership. In fact, it already does so in rural America through the 502 Direct Loan Program, which has moved over 2 million families into their own homes. These loans, fully guaranteed and serviced by the USDA, come with low interest rates and, for very poor families, cover the entire cost of the mortgage, nullifying the need for a down payment. Families can also apply for low-interest loans or grants to help with repairs. In 2021, the average 502 Direct Loan was for $187,181 but cost the government only $10,370 *in total,* chump change for such a durable intervention. Expanding this program into urban communities would provide even more low- and moderate-income families with homes of their own.[14]

If we want to imagine a post-poverty world, I find it instructive to pay attention to people who are already bringing it into being. A few years ago, I began spending time with Inquilinxs Unidxs por Justicia (United Renters for Justice), a tenants' rights organization in Minneapolis that goes by the abbreviation IX. The organization was made up of security guards, store clerks, night-shift custodians, immigrants, and young people. The members of IX didn't want to live in public housing or subsidized apartments. They didn't even want to own their own homes. What they wanted was to buy their apartment buildings from their landlord and turn them into a tenant-owned cooperative.[15]

"Commoning" is the term for the creation of homes that are collectively owned and controlled by the residents. There is a long tradition of this in urban America. Starting in the late 1960s, poor New Yorkers began rehabilitating apartment buildings abandoned by landlords, many damaged by fire and years of neglect. You could earn a spot through "sweat equity," pitching in with time and labor. The city got behind these efforts, transferring the titles of dozens of buildings to tenant organizations that created co-ops. Between late 1979 and late 1980, tenants led primarily by Black women created seventeen cooperatives in the nation's capital, comprising one thousand units, buying run-down properties and sprucing them up themselves.[16] A popular version of this model involves residents purchasing co-op shares and paying low monthly fees to cover the building's upkeep. If a family moves out, it can sell its share for slightly above the original purchase price, but only slightly. Bidding up the sale, even if there are plenty of takers, is seen as anathema to the co-op's social mission.[17]

The tenants in Minneapolis found their landlord to be neglectful—leaks were addressed with buckets, not patches; broken windows stayed broken—and began mobilizing against him. They banded together and convinced the city council to revoke the landlord's license, stripping him of his ability to collect rent. So, the tenants stopped paying it. He responded with eviction notices. IX members marched and protested, showing up at the landlord's house and even his church. They began raising money from local foundations and working with the Land Bank Twin Cities, a collection of real estate investors whose goal is not to maximize profit but to preserve affordable housing.

The final days of negotiation between the landlord and the IX tenants were intense, the outcome far from certain. The tenants had raised enough money to purchase their apartment buildings at a fair market price, but the landlord seemed intent on kicking everyone out. Chloé Jackson, a Black single mother who worked for $15.69 an hour at the airport iStore when she initially got involved with IX, volunteered to be the first tenant to have her eviction case heard by a jury. The lawyer for the landlord went first. He argued that his client simply wanted to clear out his buildings, renovate, and sell them on the free market. "That's not retaliation—that's a sound business decision," he said. "Make a little bit of money. Nothing wrong with that." Chloé's lawyer argued that the evictions were in fact retaliatory and illegal. "This case is about a tenant facing eviction because she stood up for herself," he said.

Around lunchtime, the jury walked out to deliberate. Chloé and her neighbors found an open space in the courtroom complex to await the verdict. I sat next to TeCara Ayler, one of Chloé's closest friends. TeCara had a small flower tattooed on her upper cheek and thick black hair dyed pink and yellow. She called the look the Phoenix and would bring it out whenever she felt self-doubt creeping in. "Phoenix coming back," she'd say, working the chemicals in. "Monster is coming back."

Hours passed, and it began to snow. Around four o'clock, the tenants learned that the jury had gone home for the day. They let out a collective sigh. As one tenant organizer jogged to the exit to pick up her son, she turned around. "When we fight?" she hollered to her friends, trying to sound optimistic. "We win," the tenants groaned in reply.

They did win. The following day, the jury ruled in Chloé's favor. When the verdict was announced, the tenants celebrated in the hallway, hugging one another.

Two months later, after years of struggle, the landlord finally agreed to sell five apartment buildings for around $7 million to Land Bank Twin Cities, which would sell the buildings back to the tenants at no interest. The tenants named their cooperative the Sky Without Limits Community.

Today, all five buildings are nearly filled to capacity, and maintenance calls get returned. Not everything is perfect—the hot water doesn't last long enough; the roof is still in rough shape—but their housing costs have dropped. Monthly rents in the cooperative fell by $100, even as rents nationwide were surging. Supporting tenant rights organizations like IX, both directly and by increasing funding to civic-minded land banks, is yet another way to fight exploitation in the rental market.[18]

Why did jury deliberation last two days? TeCara had a hunch. "You know what took them so long?" she asked me. "I bet the question they were held up on was: Why do the tenants want a raggedy building? People don't know how to dream."

It was the most American thing I had ever heard.

THE GOAL IS SINGULAR—to end the exploitation of the poor— but the means are many. We should empower American workers and expand housing access. We should also ensure fair access to capital. Banks should stop robbing the poor and near-poor of billions of dollars each year, immediately ending exorbitant overdraft fees. As the legal scholar Mehrsa Baradaran has pointed out, when someone overdraws their account, banks could simply freeze the transaction or could clear a check with insufficient funds, providing customers a kind of short-term loan with a low interest rate, say, 1 percent a day. The federal government could regulate bank fees, as in the United Kingdom and Israel, where overdraft fees are less than a tenth of what they are here.[19]

States should rein in payday lending institutions. For one,

they should insist that lenders make it crystal clear to potential
borrowers what a loan is likely to cost them. Just as fast food
restaurants must now publish calorie counts next to their
burgers and shakes, payday loan stores should publish the average overall cost of different loans. When Texas adopted disclosure rules mandating that potential borrowers be shown
payday loan costs compared to other forms of credit, residents
took out considerably fewer bad loans.[20] If Texas can do this,
why not California or Wisconsin?

Sixteen states, including Arkansas, Arizona, and New Jersey, along with the District of Columbia, prohibit high-cost
payday lending by capping interest rates or outlawing the
practice entirely. I would vote for these restrictions, but they
aren't enough. Studies have shown that when states prohibit
payday lending, low-income borrowers sometimes switch to
other forms of high-interest credit, like pawnshop loans.[21] To
stop financial exploitation, we need to expand, not limit, low-
income Americans' access to credit.

Some have suggested that the government get involved by
having the U.S. Postal Service or the Federal Reserve issue
small-dollar loans. Others have argued that we should revise
government regulations to entice commercial banks to pitch
in. Whatever our approach, solutions should offer low-income
Americans more choice, a way to end their reliance on predatory lending institutions that can get away with robbery because they are the only option available.[22]

AS LONG AS WE'RE considering ways to expand poor people's
choices, let's consider reproductive choice. The birth control

pill showed us that women's economic empowerment was tied to their reproductive empowerment. After the pill became widely available in the late 1960s, women's college enrollment and employment rates shot up, allowing them to gain more independence from men. Today as then, women with access to effective contraception go to school longer and participate in the job market at higher rates than women who don't. They have children later in life and have fewer of them. Yet the most reliable contraception remains out of reach for many poor women, and most of their pregnancies are unintended, meaning that the mother would have preferred getting pregnant later or not at all.[23]

In 2010, Delaware had the highest rate of unintended pregnancies in the country (57 percent). A collaboration between the state government and a nonprofit called Upstream USA sought to change that. Launched in 2014, their initiative, Delaware Contraceptive Access Now (Delaware CAN), set out to ensure that women of childbearing age could obtain the birth control method that best fit their needs. The approach was deceptively simple. When women saw a nurse or doctor, they were asked, in addition to the usual screening questions, "Do you want to get pregnant in the next year?" When women said no, health practitioners were enlisted to make sure they got the birth control of their choice before leaving. Women came for annual checkups and left with IUDs or pills—or nothing, if that was their preference.

The intervention worked. One evaluation credited the program for bringing about a 24 percent decline in unintended pregnancies among low-income and uninsured women between 2014 and 2017. When Delaware's healthcare workers made multiple kinds of birth control available to women, regardless of their income or insurance status, the women took them up on it. This approach could, and should, be replicated nationwide, providing all women with more power over when, how, and with whom to start a family.[24]

As the sociologist Dorothy Roberts has written, birth control has a dark side. In the not-too-distant past, states coerced women on probation into accepting long-acting contraceptives and even subjected some women to forced sterilization and unnecessary hysterectomies—the so-called Mississippi appendectomy. These vile practices disproportionately denied poor and Black women the right to have children.[25] Today, we are limiting low-income women's ability to have children when they want to, because top-shelf contraception is hard to come by. "Women should be able to access best-in-class contraceptive care as a primary thing, not a specialty thing," as Mark Edwards, CEO and cofounder of Upstream USA, told me. Edwards got into this work because he understood reproductive choice to be fundamental to economic uplift.

When women exercise control over family planning, including the ability to seek an abortion, they expand their educational and economic possibilities. And when reproductive choice is constricted, women and their children are often cast into poverty. The best evidence we have about the economic consequences of denying women abortions comes from the Turnaway Study, conducted by a team of researchers at the University of California, San Francisco. The study followed roughly one thousand women who had attempted to receive abortions at clinics across the country. Researchers compared women who were able to have abortions because they sought care just before the gestational deadline (typically ten weeks to the end of the second trimester, depending on the state) to those who were turned away because their pregnancy had advanced just beyond the deadline.

The study's design was groundbreaking and rigorous, and its findings were as unequivocal as they were unsettling. Compared to women who had had abortions, those forced to give birth were more likely to live below the poverty line four years later. The two groups of women were on similar paths at the time they got pregnant, but access to abortion caused their lives to diverge. Months and even years after receiving that consequential yes or no during their ultrasounds, women turned away at abortion clinics were less likely to hold down full-time jobs, less likely to be able to afford necessities, and more likely to be trapped in abusive relationships. Their children suffered, too. Many women who received abortions went on to have children later. When researchers compared those children to children born after women were denied abortions, they found that children in the latter group were far more likely to grow up poor.[26]

After combing through evidence from the Turnaway Study, I wanted to see a clinic for myself. So I spent a day at the Philadelphia Women's Center, an independent abortion provider located downtown. The center's walls are painted lavender and turquoise, and behind the bullet-proof-glass-encased front desk, someone had painted, "When you're here, bring only love." In the waiting room, the staff keep the lights low and the televisions off, creating a serene, even uplifting environment. It looks nothing like the dreary, fluorescent-lit waiting rooms in welfare offices or eviction court—except for the people waiting. The women who had scheduled abortions that day looked poor and weighed down. Some held babies. Some curled themselves in chairs and slept on their hands. Half of them, a lab tech told me, had low iron, a condition brought on by pregnancy as well as by poverty.

A first-trimester abortion at the Women's Center costs $445. Because Medicaid can't be used to cover the procedure except in cases of rape, incest, or life endangerment of the pregnant person, it was Ryan Bieber's job to help women cover the costs. As the financial intake advocate at the center, Ryan spent his mornings asking patients the same questions. *Can you pay anything? How much? Do you have a ride home?* The day I visited, Ryan helped around forty-five women find money for their abortions, drawing on aid from the National Abortion Federation and pinching additional funds from local organizations. He served women living in homeless shelters, women addicted to opioids, and working mothers who dedicate rent and food money to pay for abortions. Ryan also asked the women he saw: *Medicaid can be used to pay for an abortion in the case of rape or incest. Does this situation apply to you?* He estimated that 15 to 20 percent of the women he interviews say yes.

I find the abortion debate in America frustratingly abstract. *What are the limits of bodily integrity? When does life begin?* I don't know how to answer these questions. I do know, concretely, that the Supreme Court's decision to overturn *Roe v. Wade* and claw back the national right to abortion will have devastating consequences for poor women. We could, of course, ensure that no child in America is born into poverty. We could make sure all women have access to the best contra-

ception and healthcare, helping more pregnancies become intentional and safer. We could provide new mothers with
strong supports like paid parental leave and free childcare.
Which is all to say, a country as wealthy as ours could put our
money where our mouth is when it comes to supporting life.
But from the poor, we seem to just take and take.

THOSE WHO HAVE AMASSED the most power and capital bear
the most responsibility for America's vast poverty: political
elites who have utterly failed low-income Americans over the
past half century; corporate bosses who have spent and
schemed to prioritize profits over people; lobbyists blocking
the will of the American people with their self-serving interests; property owners who have exiled the poor from entire
cities and fueled the affordable housing crisis. Acknowledging
this is both crucial and deliciously absolving, directing our attention upward and distracting us from all the ways (many un-
intentional) we also contribute to the problem. Just as global
warming is not only caused by large industrial polluters and
multinational logging companies but also by the cars we choose
to drive and the energy we choose to buy, poverty in America is
not simply the result of actions taken by Congress and corporate boards but the millions of decisions we make each day
when going about our business.

To live and strive in modern America is to participate in a
series of morally fraught systems. If a family's entire financial
livelihood depends on the value of its home, it's not hard to
understand why that family would oppose anything that could
potentially lower its property values, like a proposal to develop

an affordable housing complex in the neighborhood. If an aging couple's nest egg depends on how the stock market performs, it's not hard to see why that couple would support legislation designed to yield higher returns, even if that means short-changing workers. Social ills—segregation, exploitation—can be motivated by bigotry and selfishness as well as by the best of intentions, such as protecting our children. Especially protecting our children.

These arrangements create what the postwar sociologist C. Wright Mills called "structural immorality" and what the political scientist Jamila Michener more recently labeled exploitation "on a societal level."[27] We are connected, members of a shared nation and a shared economy, where the advantages of the rich often come at the expense of the poor. But that arrangement is not inevitable or permanent. It was made by human hands and can be unmade by them. We can fashion a new society, starting with our own lives. Where we decide to work and live, what we buy, how we vote, and where we put our energies as citizens all have consequences for poor families. Becoming a poverty abolitionist, then, entails conducting an audit of our lives, personalizing poverty by examining all the ways we are connected to the problem—and to the solution.

We can vote with our wallets, reevaluating where we shop and what we buy. To the greatest extent possible, we should withdraw our support from corporations that exploit their workers. This requires doing our homework, looking into a company's track record. Trying to mail a package? UPS drivers are unionized, but FedEx drivers are not. Need a drink? Rolling Rock and Miller are union-made. Want some candy? The people who make Jolly Ranchers are unionized.[28] Increasingly, American consumers are considering the environmental impact of their purchases. We should consider their poverty impact, too.

From the Boston Tea Party to the campus anti-sweatshop movement, there is a long history of consumer activism in America. American revolutionaries proudly wore homespun clothes instead of importing them from Britain. During the 1960s, American households stopped buying grapes as a result of a national boycott led by farmworkers. More recently, Americans have refused to order cosmetics that rely on animal testing and chocolate from companies that use cocoa harvested by children in West Africa. Consumer activism recognizes that every purchase is an ethical choice. For poverty abolitionists, that means refusing to erase the people behind the products and endorsing companies that support their workforces.[29]

If a company has a record of tax evasion, union busting, and low pay, it is an exploitative company. Not everyone has much of a choice about where to shop, especially those of us cutting coupons and keeping a tight rein on our budgets, but those of us who do should avoid giving exploitative companies our dollars. We shouldn't be their customers or their shareholders. For those of us vested in the stock market, we should take another look at our portfolios with poverty abolitionism as our lodestar, examining not only our own personal investments but our state's pension funds as well. Many Americans have made it a priority to steer clear of "sin stocks" belonging to companies that manufacture weapons or promote gambling or drill for oil. What about companies that spread immiseration and despair or that cheat on their taxes, gutting public services? The returns we reap from those investments come at the expense of people directly and indirectly harmed in their making.

We can also look more closely at our own institutions. We can audit our alma maters or current universities, for example. Are they providing enough support to first-generation students? Are they fairly compensating their adjunct faculty, landscapers, and support staff? Are they responsible for gentrifying low-income neighborhoods? Are their endowments bankrolling exploitative corporations? We can evaluate our workplaces and industries, asking if they are in the business of exploiting their workers. For example, do their occupational licenses establish unnecessary entry barriers—in the form of hours of training and costly exams—that protect those with jobs but harm those trying to break in? Turning to our banks, we might ask: Are they charging exorbitantly high fees for overdrawing accounts? Are they bankrolling the payday loan industry? If so, might it be better to take our money elsewhere? Wherever we stand, we can leverage the specific influence we have—in our congregations and military units and companies and school boards—to instigate change.[30]

When poverty abolitionists shop and invest based on their commitments to human dignity and material well-being, they should brag about it, crafting an aesthetics and even a lifestyle around those decisions. There is considerable evidence that it's easier to change norms than beliefs. "You're wrong" is a less influential message than "Yeah, we're not really doing that anymore."[31] You might worry about climate change but install solar panels only after your neighbors do. You might acknowledge the impact of fast fashion but change your shopping habits only after your classmates do. We hold many ethical beliefs, but we tend to act on them only when we receive a social push. As the psychologist Betsy Levy Paluck put it to me once, "Norms license us to do things we already believe in." This is why it's important that we find ways to broadcast private acts of poverty abolitionism, bringing them into the light. If enough of us took some responsibility for this problem in our personal lives, and began mobilizing our workplaces and faith communities and schools to do likewise, a commitment to poverty abolition would spread, sparking a national moral reckoning and pressuring the most exploitative actors and agencies to divest.[32]

I would love to see companies market their antipoverty policies—collective bargaining agreements, a commitment to paying a living wage—just as they have promoted their commitment to climate justice and sustainability. Snapple has announced that its bottles are composed of 100 percent recycled plastic. I'd also like the company to tell us if they are union made. Most Americans approve of labor unions; so why not market them?[33] It's now common for local businesses to hang trans rights flags or BLACK LIVES MATTER signs in their store windows. How about also posting starting wages? Platforms such as DoneGood and Buycott steer customers toward businesses fairly compensating their workers. The nonprofit organization B Lab certifies companies that meet high social and environmental standards, scoring on the basis of worker compensation and benefits, job flexibility, potential for worker ownership, and a host of other criteria. If given the choice between a company that is B Lab certified and one that is not,

let's choose the businesses that are doing right by their workers and the planet.[34]

Consumer activism brought us cheap goods and services
borne on the backs of others, and consumer activism can help
reverse this trend, punishing poverty-creating companies and
sending a message that we will no longer support their exploitative ways. Since exploitation pays, this could dampen
our portfolios' stock performance. Banking and shopping in
ways that express solidarity with the poor could mean we pay
more. And by acknowledging those costs, we acknowledge
our complicity. When we cheat and rob one another, we lose
part of ourselves, too. Doing the right thing is often a highly
inconvenient, time-consuming, even costly process, I know. I
try, fail, and try again. But that's the price of our restored humanity.[35]

CHAPTER 9

TEAR DOWN THE WALLS

THERE IS ONE FINAL STEP WE MUST TAKE. OUR WALLS, THEY have to go. We have revised our textbooks and renamed our holidays to acknowledge the harms of colonization. We have begun the work of removing marble statues and changing street signs in recognition of the horrors of slavery. But do we not act as modern-day segregationists when we mobilize to block an affordable housing complex in our neighborhood? Do we not colonize the future when we reserve spaces there for our children while denying other children a fair shot?

By deconcentrating poverty in schools and communities, integration blunts its sting. Simply moving poor families to high-opportunity neighborhoods, without doing anything to increase their incomes, improves their lives tremendously. Even if they remain below the poverty line, they become less "poor" in the sense that their exposure to crime drops, and their mental health improves, and their children flourish in school. Studies have found that each year that poor children spend in a high-opportunity neighborhood increases their income in adulthood—so much so that younger siblings experi-

ence bigger gains than their older brothers and sisters because
of the additional years spent in a safer and more prosperous
place.[1]

Yet even the most ambitious antipoverty proposals in wide
circulation today, such as a universal basic income, often leave
segregation untouched. It's disappointing, like we've given up
on the problem, as if the best we can do is to create a nation
that is separate but a little less unequal. When the affluent and
poor live disparate lives, any institution or program on which
only the poor rely becomes vulnerable. It's easy to support
closing a public school that your kid doesn't attend or to approve aggressive policing tactics when you know it won't be
your nephew who gets patted down. But when families across
the class spectrum send their children to the same schools, pic-
nic in the same parks, and walk the same streets, those families
are equally invested in those schools, those parks, those streets.

Besides, let's admit it: Segregation poisons our minds and
souls. When affluents live, work, play, and worship mainly
alongside fellow affluents, they can grow insular, quite literally forgetting the poor. It brings out the worst in us, feeding
our prejudices and spreading moral decay. Engaging with one
another in integrated communities allows us to recognize our
blind spots, de-siloing our lives and causing families well above
the poverty line to become bothered by problems that affect
those below it. As Nietzsche wrote, "One must want to experience the great problems with one's body and one's soul."[2] And
I'd count poverty among the great problems. Integration
means we all have skin in the game. It not only disrupts poverty; on a spiritual level, over time it can foster empathy and

solidarity.[3] This is why opposing segregation is vital to poverty abolitionism.

If we lowered our walls and made it possible for poor families to move to high-opportunity neighborhoods, some would and some wouldn't. Poor neighborhoods, after all, are not *just* that. They are also the wellspring for family and familiarity, community and love, not to mention home to some of the best food in the nation. Black neighborhoods and ethnic enclaves can serve as a refuge for nonwhite Americans who work and study in predominately white institutions. I'm making an argument in favor of more neighborhood choice to ensure that the zip code where a child is born does not so powerfully predetermine the story of her life. Plus, I've never heard of an affordable housing development in an affluent community that had a difficult time filling up. Quite the opposite, in fact. When the wealthy township of Cherry Hill, New Jersey, opened applications for twenty-nine affordable apartments in 2021, 9,309 people applied.[4]

Integration works. That's the resounding conclusion from a half century of research. Consider the impact of school integration after the Supreme Court ruled in *Brown v. Board of Education* that laws upholding racial segregation in public schools were unconstitutional. In the years following the 1954 decision, desegregation orders were unevenly enforced throughout the nation, allowing social scientists to compare Black children who went to integrated schools with those who attended segregated ones. The economist Rucker Johnson did just that, finding that Black children who were enrolled in integrated schools performed better in the classroom, graduated at higher rates, and were more likely to go to college than their peers who experienced a segregated education. These educational gains had a real cash value, as Johnson's models showed that Black students who benefitted from court-ordered integration were significantly less likely to experience poverty as adults. Meanwhile, white children whose schools desegregated remained on track: Their academic achievement and later-life well-being did not suffer as a result of their new Black classmates.[5]

Increasing inequality has led to a rise in income segregation among school districts. Policymakers have passed education finance reforms that have helped to balance the scales, devoting more money to poorer schools. That's helped, but it's clearly not the solution. Consider what happened in Montgomery County, Maryland. In the early aughts, the housing authority there randomly assigned families to different public housing units, some of which were located in affluent neighborhoods with affluent schools. At the same time, the county made serious investments in its poorest schools, dedicating real money to pay for things like smaller class sizes and teacher training. This presented researchers with a chance to determine whether poor students fared better in low-poverty schools or in high-poverty schools with more resources. The results were striking. Students from poor families who attended low-poverty schools significantly outperformed those who attended high-poverty schools with "state-of-the-art educational interventions." Even when we expand the budgets of poor schools beyond those of rich ones, it does not make those schools anything close to equal.[6]

I feel a little stupid making the case that a child's environment matters. We know it does, which is why many of us expend so much energy and treasure fortifying our own schools and neighborhoods, hoarding the promise and security that come with them. What are we teaching our children when they plainly see us barring the doors of opportunity for other children—and doing it in their name?

America has backslid since *Brown,* so much so that our children's schools today are less economically diverse than their grandparents' schools were, and although we have taken baby steps toward racial integration, most of our communities remain sharply segregated by race as well. As our cities become more unaffordable, the sheer distance separating the haves and the have-nots will only grow wider. We used to gossip about poor families who lived on the other side of the tracks. Now we talk about those who live in the next county over.[7] We remain very separate and very unequal. But this corruption of opportunity can end with us.

HOW CAN WE, AT LAST, end our embrace of segregation? The most important thing we can do is to replace exclusionary zoning policies with inclusionary ordinances, tearing down our walls and using the rubble to build bridges. There are two parts to this. The first is to get rid of all the devious legal minutiae we've developed to keep low-income families out of high-opportunity neighborhoods, rules that make it illegal to build multifamily apartment complexes or smaller, more affordable homes. We cannot in good faith claim that our communities are antiracist or antipoverty if they continue to uphold exclusionary zoning—our politer, quieter means of promoting segregation.

Ending exclusionary zoning would make it legal for developers to build the kind of housing that low-income families need. But that's no guarantee they will do so. That's why the second part is necessary: passing inclusionary zoning mandates. Inclusionary zoning isn't just the passive absence of exclusionary ordinances but the proactive, insistent opposite of them. While exclusionary zoning makes it illegal to develop affordable housing, inclusionary zoning makes it illegal not to. That's the stronger version anyway, mandating that new developments set aside a percentage of their units for low-income families. The weaker version is voluntary, providing developers with incentives if they include affordable housing in their blueprints, usually in the form of tax relief or a "density bonus" that allows them to build more. A developer typically allowed to construct, say, a fifty-unit complex might be permitted to erect one with seventy-five units if she agrees to offer 15 percent of her apartments at below-market rates.[8]

Countries like Ireland and Spain have mandated inclusionary zoning as a solution to housing shortages. In the United States, the state leading the way on this is New Jersey. Nearly every suburban jurisdiction in the state has affordable housing. Why? Because in a series of landmark decisions, the New Jersey Supreme Court not only prohibited exclusionary zoning but also required all municipalities to provide their "fair share" of affordable housing, the fair share being calculated by the demographics of each town. If municipalities fail to do their part, courts can make them, redrawing the lines of a town's zoning map to allow affordable housing projects to move forward. Republican and Democratic jurisdictions have put up a fight, but the law's strong mandate has forced more than 340 towns to break ground on affordable housing developments. Once those plans are inked, it doesn't take long for developers to bid on the job because they can make more money on multifamily complexes than stand-alone homes, even when they rent out a share of their units to low-income families. This strategy has allowed New Jersey to create thousands of affordable units without a dime of state or federal money.[9]

Do affordable housing developments cause property values to decline? If they are built poorly and not maintained, then yes, just as any kind of neglected housing would. But studies have found that when affordable housing blends into the surrounding community, and when it is well managed and well distributed instead of being clustered in one place, it has zero effect on property values.[10] (In the years since New Jersey began economically integrating its communities more aggressively than any other state, its property values have remained among the highest in the nation, and it ranks first in public education.) Congress could incentivize more communities to invest in affordable housing with federal dollars that could be used to offset local property taxes or improve public services. What if homeowners enjoyed a bit more money in their pockets if they voted yes on affordable housing? What if the local elementary school was able to rehab its gymnasium or hire more teachers if its community welcomed more low-income families?

Carrots like this could be used to entice more communities

to share prosperity. Sticks could work, too. If localities refused to end exclusionary zoning, Congress could cut off their funding. Right now, whenever an exclusionary town or neighborhood receives federal dollars to repair sidewalks or update sewer systems or construct a public park, low-income taxpayers fund improvements in places actively rejecting them. Congress could end this warped arrangement by denying federal monies to jurisdictions with exclusionary zoning. Those who wish to remain behind their walls should get no help from the rest of us.

This wasn't my idea, by the way. It was George Romney's. The Republican politician and father of Utah senator Mitt Romney proposed it in 1970 when he was Nixon's secretary of the Department of Housing and Urban Development. Romney wanted the U.S. government to finally stop subsidizing segregation. His idea so enraged white suburbanites that Nixon smothered it and eventually forced Romney out of office.[11] Those white suburbanites picked up the phone. They showed up to political rallies, wrote letters.

If you have been to a meeting of your local planning board recently, you know that not much has changed. The people who follow the intrigues of zoning politics tend to be richer, older, and whiter than the surrounding community, and they are typically homeowners. This active voting bloc overwhelmingly and loudly opposes affordable housing, and often any new construction at all, contributing to the nation's painful rental crisis. Alexis de Tocqueville found that nineteenth-century Americans were only casual observers of politics until the town proposed to run a road through their property. Then they started showing up at public forums. In a similar way, twenty-first-century Americans don't typically read the minutes of the zoning board. But if someone proposes an affordable housing development near their home, you suddenly find them yelling at an alderman on a Tuesday evening.[12]

"These meetings are violent," Eric Dobson told me. Dobson is the deputy director of the Fair Share Housing Center, a public interest law firm devoted to expanding affordable housing in New Jersey, and he regularly attends community meetings where residents do their best to block court-ordered developments. Sometimes the meetings run until the wee hours of the morning. Dobson occasionally advises like-minded advocates not to speak, for fear of being accosted in the parking lot. At a recent meeting in the town of Old Bridge, New Jersey, a suburban enclave thirty-five miles from New York City, a white man turned to Dobson and barked, "Why don't you go build this stuff in your own neighborhood?" Dobson, a Black minister, replied that they already had.

Defenders of the status quo, this pro-segregationist propertied class, have shown themselves to be willing to do the tedious work of defending the wall. Their efforts have paid off in terms of delaying and killing proposals to build more housing, as local civil servants tend to respond to the voices they hear.[13] We need different voices in the room. We could especially use the voices of middle- and high-school students eager to welcome more young people into their classrooms, and it would be particularly powerful to hear from families planning on moving into proposed affordable housing developments.

I recognize that this is asking a lot. In 2022, I met Twinkle Borge, the leader of Puʻuhonua O Waiʻanae (POW), an unhoused community of 250 people on the Hawaiian island of

Oahu. In 2020, POW purchased twenty acres on the eastern side of the island, having raised funds from various sources, and began working with pro bono architects and developers to build permanent housing. But first, the POW families had to face their future neighbors at public hearings. "It was brutal," Borge told me. "They were saying things like, 'Our kids won't be able to play in the street!' They said that in front of us and our kids. It hurt."

The POW families persevered, but Borge's warm spirit still visibly dims when she remembers those meetings. She and her neighbors, and families in similar situations across the country, should not have to face the segregationists alone. Poverty abolitionists seeking a different kind of community, a more open, inclusive community, need to start showing up at Tuesday evening planning board sessions. We need to rise from our seats and tell our local officials: *This community's long-standing tradition of segregation stops with me. I refuse to deny other children opportunities my children enjoy by living here. Build it.*

THERE IS A MUSTARD yellow trifold brochure that I keep in my desk. It was published in 1953 by the state of Minnesota, through the governor's Human Rights Commission. It's about racial integration. Black families' incomes had been rising, and some were seeking to buy homes in middle-class neighborhoods, including in white sections of town. Acknowledging this trend, the brochure, addressed to white families, asked and answered some basic questions about what Black families wanted, which boiled down to the same things white families did: equal opportunity, a good home. In response to a question about why segregation persists, the pamphlet says that "many whites object [to Black neighbors] because they are unsure of their own social position."[14]

There is a serious sociological insight here. When the ground feels unsteady underfoot, we tend to hunker down and protect our own, growing less willing to consider what we have and more apt to pay mind to what we could lose. Stacks of social psychological evidence confirm that when we feel resources are scarce or could be, when we sense that our status (or that of our racial group) is slipping, we discard our commitments to equal opportunity.[15] If you survey the American public, you learn that most of us want less poverty and less inequality, at least in principle. But when you ask us about *specific* policies to accomplish those ends, we begin to equivocate, especially if we feel those policies could cost our families somehow.[16] The Minnesota brochure tries to temper this fear by asking white Americans to live up to their professed values. "The white American who acts to bar a [Black family] from his neighborhood is violating his own [American] creed," it reads, before ending on this note: "To many white persons these paragraphs may be disturbing. Candidly, the expression of these concepts in actual living will be difficult. Yet . . . American society improved only when citizens did the difficult thing."

Poverty abolitionists do the difficult thing. They donate to worthy organizations, yes, but they must do more. If charity were enough, well, it would be enough, and this book would be irrelevant. Giving money away is a beautiful act, and yet poverty persists. Rather than throwing money over the wall, let's tear the wall down. The evidence is in, and it's clear: We can integrate our communities without depressing property values, compromising school quality, or harming affluent children. So why do so many of us remain "unsure of our own social position"? Why do we scare so easily?

We have been taught this fear. Our institutions have socialized us to scarcity, creating artificial resource shortages and then normalizing them. For example, because the residents of affluent neighborhoods have been so successful at blocking the construction of new housing in their communities, developers have turned their sights on down-market neighborhoods, where they also meet resistance, often from struggling renters fretting about gentrification. As this dynamic has repeated itself in cities across America, the debate about addressing the affordable housing crisis and fostering inclusive communities has turned into a debate about gentrification, one pitting low-income families who have stable housing against low-income families who need it. But notice how contrived and weird this is, how our full range of action has been limited by rich homeowners essentially redlining their blocks.[17]

Or consider how a scarcity mindset frames so much of our politics, crippling our imaginations and stunting our moral ambitions. How many times have we all heard legislators and academics and pundits begin their remarks with the phrase "In a world of scarce resources . . . ," as if that state of affairs were self-evident, obvious, as unassailable as natural law, instead of something we've fashioned? The United States lags far behind other advanced countries when it comes to funding public services. In 2019, France, Germany, the Netherlands, Italy, and several other Western democracies each raised tax revenues equal to at least 38 percent of their GDPs, while the United States' total revenues languished at 25 percent.[18] Instead of catching up to our peer nations, we have lavished government benefits on affluent families and refused to prosecute tax dodgers. And then we cry poor when someone proposes a way to spur economic mobility or end hunger?

Significantly expanding our collective investment in fighting poverty will cost something. How much it will cost is not a trivial affair. But I would have more patience for concerns about the cost of ending family homelessness if we weren't spending billions of dollars each year on homeowner tax subsidies, just as I could better stomach concerns over the purported financial burden of establishing a living wage if our largest corporations weren't pocketing billions each year through tax avoidance. The scarcity mindset shrinks and contorts poverty abolitionism, forcing it to operate within fictitious fiscal constraints.

It also pits economic justice against climate justice. When lawmakers have tried to curb pollution and traffic gridlock through congestion pricing, for instance, charging vehicles a fee if they enter busy urban neighborhoods during peak hours, critics have shot down the proposal by claiming it would hit low-income workers in transit deserts the hardest. In many cases, this is true. But it doesn't have to be. We allow millions to live paycheck to paycheck, then leverage their predicament to justify inaction on other social and environmental issues. Politicians and pundits inform us, using their grown-up voice, that unfortunately we can't tax gas-guzzling vehicles or transition to green energy or increase the cost of beef because it

would harm poor and working-class families. My point isn't
that these tradeoffs aren't pertinent but that they aren't inescapable. They are by-products of fabricated scarcity.

Scarcity pits issue against issue, and neighbor against
neighbor. Since the nation's founding, the story of class politics in America has been a story of white worker against Black,
native against newcomer. Racism thwarted the rise of a multiracial mass labor movement, which could have brought about
sweeping economic reforms—including the establishment of
a Labor Party—like the kind adopted in nineteenth-century
France and Britain. And racism spoiled the creation of integrated communities and schools, ghettoizing poverty, and
urban Black poverty in particular, aggravating and intensify-
ing its miseries. Manufactured scarcity empowers and justifies
racism, so much so that the historical sociologist Oliver Cromwell Cox once speculated that without capitalism "the world
might never have experienced race prejudice."[19]

Let's call it the *scarcity diversion*. Here's the playbook. First,
allow elites to hoard a resource like money or land. Second,
pretend that arrangement is natural, unavoidable—or better
yet, ignore it altogether. Third, attempt to address social problems caused by the resource hoarding only with the scarce resources left over. So instead of making the rich pay all their
taxes, for instance, design a welfare state around the paltry
budget you are left with when they don't. Fourth, fail. Fail to
drive down the poverty rate. Fail to build more affordable
housing. Fifth, claim this is the best we can do. Preface your
comments by saying, "In a world of scarce resources . . ."
Blame government programs. Blame capitalism. Blame the
other political party. Blame immigrants. Blame anyone you

can except those who most deserve it. "Gaslighting" is not too strong a phrase to describe such pretense.

The opposite of the scarcity diversion is a recognition of the nation's bounty. The ecologist Robin Wall Kimmerer has recently advocated for "an economy of abundance."[20] Choosing abundance, at once a perspective and a legislative platform, a shift in vision and in policy design, means recognizing that this country has a profusion of resources—enough land and capital to go around—and that pretending otherwise is a farce. "I want to be part of a system in which wealth means having enough to share," Kimmerer writes, "and where the gratification of meeting your family needs is not poisoned by destroying that possibility for someone else." Unrealistic? Perhaps, but then again, who gets to decide what is workable and what is not? Don't we have to admit that the dreams of the rich often become realities (carried interest, unlimited incomes) while the dreams of the poor are dismissed as outlandish? Have we forgotten that there was a time, as E. P. Thompson has shown, when people found it immoral, even unnatural, to "profit from the necessities of others" even during seasons of drought and famine, and instead held up a "moral economy of provision"?[21]

Why do we continue to accept scarcity as given, treating it as the central organizing principle of our economics, policymaking, city planning, and personal ethics? Why do we continue to act like the farmer who, upon learning that his dog is lying on a pile of hay meant for cattle to eat and baring his teeth when the cows come near, chooses to drop their rations, feeding them with what scraps he can snatch from the edge of the pile? Why don't we just move the dog?

———

LIFT THE FLOOR BY rebalancing our social safety net; empower the poor by reining in exploitation; and invest in broad
prosperity by turning away from segregation. That's how we
end poverty in America. And if we do, what will it look like?

Things would change, and sometimes that change would
be uncomfortable or even painful—for all of us. It would be
dishonest to suggest otherwise. There are costs to the status
quo, terrible costs, and there would be costs to weaning ourselves off our addiction to poverty and segregation. There
would be political costs, for one thing: vitriolic backlash by
homeowners and parents who view integration as a menace.
There would be challenges for schools that previously didn't
have to think much about providing free lunch or counseling
students through trauma. Neighborhoods previously insu-
lated from anything close to poverty might have to install a
bus stop or boost social services or find a way to deal with
public disorder. At first, everyone would encounter more fric-
tion in their daily life: more slights, missteps, and awkward
moments of misunderstanding that arise when not everyone
in your community has gone to college or to the ballet or to
St. Barts.

"Any real change," writes James Baldwin, "implies the
breakup of the world as one has always known it, the loss of all
that gave one an identity, the end of safety. And at such a mo-
ment, unable to see and not daring to imagine what the future
will now bring forth, one clings to what one knew, or thought
one knew; to what one possessed or dreamed that one possessed." Ending segregation, at last, would require affluent

families to give up some things, but what we'd gain in return would be more valuable. We would have to give up the ways we hoard opportunity and public safety, but in doing so we'd also give up the shame that haunts us when we participate in the evil business of exclusion and poverty creation. We'd have to give up some comforts and familiarities of life behind the wall and give up the stories we've told ourselves about that place and our role in it, but we'd also be giving up the loneliness and empty materialism that have come to characterize much of upper-class life, allowing ourselves, in Baldwin's words, to reach "for higher dreams, for greater privileges."[22]

The best place I ever lived was a neighborhood in Madison, Wisconsin. It was a mixed-race, mixed-income community on the South Side called Bram's Addition. My neighbors across the street were a couple who had migrated from South America. A neighbor a house over was an older Black veteran who wore copper bracelets around his wrists. You could find him at the local farmers market, playing a drum for tips. The neighborhood definitely had issues, including some open-air drug dealing. I remember a police column in a community newsletter that read something to the effect of: *Some people use Penn Park to play and exercise. Unfortunately, other people use the park for shooting.* True enough.

But these issues didn't define the neighborhood. What defined us, I think, was the community garden, where Hmong and Hispanic and white and Black neighbors grew beans and peppers and collards and hosted potlucks; and Jada's, a soul food spot with church-basement folding chairs and sweetened yams that I still think about; and Taqueria Guadalajara with its pink sign and the best *mole de panza* this California native has

ever had. When the snow fell hard and heavy, some of us
would reach for our shovels—no one had a snowblower—and
clear the driveways and sidewalks, not just our own but the
entire street's. While this was happening, others cooked breakfast, and when the work was done, we'd all pile into someone's house to eat and warm up.

When my family moved to East Arlington, a suburb of
Boston, after taking new jobs, we landed in a neighborhood
with far fewer issues and far less joy. When the snow fell there,
the neighbors cleared only their own walks, stopping abruptly
at the property line. I remember a blizzard hit when I was
stuck in L.A. My wife was visibly pregnant, but as she cleared
the sidewalk that evening, no one came to her aid. She still
gets angry when remembering how the twentysomething son
of our downstairs neighbor, the one who tended a pristine
New England garden, silently watched her shovel from his
window. What irked her wasn't the physical labor exactly
(she's now a farmer), but that she would never have had to
shovel alone in Bram's Addition. Had we been able to afford to
buy a home in East Arlington, our property's value would
have grown exponentially faster than it would have had we
stayed on Madison's South Side. But in exchange, we'd have
had to give up love for a community and trade a feeling of
being known and held for the anomie of wealth. To us, that
was a bad bargain.

An America without poverty would be neither a utopia nor
a land of gray uniformity. Look around: There are plenty of
capitalist countries with far less poverty than us. Walt Disney
World would still exist in a poverty-free America. There would
still be markets and private property rights. Hermès handbags,

Tesla cars, Levi's jeans, and Nike shoes would still be allowed. You could still strike it rich. Ending poverty wouldn't lead to social collapse, nor would it erase income inequality. There is so much of that in America today that we could make meaningful gains in equality, certainly enough to abolish poverty, and still have miles and miles of separation between the top and bottom. Conservatives like to say they are not for equality of conditions (everyone gets the same thing) but equality of opportunity (everyone gets the same shot). Fine by me—but only if we actually work to make equality of opportunity a reality.

It is hard to put into words what the end of poverty would mean for millions of workers and parents and tenants and children below the line. It would mean a wholly different existence, a life marked by more safety and health, by more fairness and security. It would mean lives directed not by the scramble of survival but by passions and aspirations. It would mean finally being able to breathe. It would mean an opening up of the nation, the full embrace of the poor into the Union—to the benefit of the Union as a whole. Ending poverty would not solve all our problems. But since poverty is a catalyst and cause of an untold number of social ills, finally cutting the cancer out would lead to enormous improvements in many aspects of American life.

The end of poverty would bring a net gain in broad prosperity. In today's America, we can ascend to incredible heights and amass great fortunes, and yet poverty surrounds us. It's there in the morning paper, on our commute to work, in our public parks, dragging us all down, making even those quite secure in their money feel diminished and depressed. From his

Birmingham jail cell, Martin Luther King, Jr., wrote that "injustice anywhere is a threat to justice everywhere" because "we are caught up in an inescapable network of mutuality, tied in a single garment of destiny."[23] These words are so well known to us that we can be forgiven for failing to pause over the profundity of that word, "threat." Injustice isn't just an "affront" or "mockery" to justice but a *threat* to it, a danger, a predation. King was making an empirical point as much as a moral one. Allowed to fester, injustice tends to test its boundaries, creeping along. It menaces even lives not caught in its grasp. This is certainly the case when it comes to economic injustice. Poverty infringes on American prosperity, making it a barricaded, stingy, frightened kind of affluence.

Prosperity without poverty would carry a different feeling. Imagine what your life would be like if we abolished poverty. You'd go to bed at night worrying far less about being victimized by crime, for a country that shares its wealth is a much safer country. You'd check the news in the morning, and the top stories of the day would not be about a spike in evictions or hours-long lines at the food bank or the latest exploitative escapade of some corporation. You'd walk out your door and feel lighter, more secure, as you wouldn't see sprawling tent encampments or the exhausted faces of the working poor commuting to their jobs. You wouldn't be one of those faces, as we'd all go to work knowing that we'd be earning a living wage. You'd go out to a restaurant or spend the night in a hotel, knowing that the people who were cooking your food and changing your sheets would be well compensated. Local and national elections would command higher rates of civic participation and voting. And whatever your lot in life, you'd know that a sudden change in fortune wouldn't tip your family into destitution.

If we had to boil it down to a single concept, we might just say that without poverty, we'd be more free. A nation invested in ending poverty is a nation that is truly, obsessively committed to freedom. Franklin Roosevelt was right: "True individual freedom cannot exist without economic security and independence. Necessitous men are not free men," and a country besieged by poverty is not a free country. Compared to a freedom that is contingent on our bank accounts—rich people's freedom—a freedom that comes from shared responsibility, shared purpose and gain, and shared abundance and commitment strikes me as a different sort of human liberation altogether: deeper, warmer, more lush. This kind of freedom "makes you happy—and it makes you accountable," as Robin Wall Kimmerer has put it. "All flourishing is mutual." Why? Because poverty anywhere is a threat to prosperity everywhere.[24]

We can feel it, the emotional violence we inflict upon ourselves, knowing that our abundance causes others' misery. It's there in that residue of shame and malaise coating our insular lives; that loss of joy, the emptiness; our boring satiation, our guilt and nausea. Our disfigured humanity. In 2020, public opinion data showed, to quote a report from the University of Chicago, "an all-time low in people saying they are very happy (14%), combined with an all-time high in people saying they are satisfied with their family's financial situation (80%)."[25]

And consider all the raw talent and beauty and brilliance that we squander by requiring that tens of millions of Americans expend so much energy just trying to make it from one day to the next. A 2019 study published in *The Quarterly Journal of Economics* found that children from rich families were ten times as likely to become inventors than children from families in the bottom half of the income distribution. The researchers attributed this gap to environmental factors, not to differences in innate abilities, by showing that young children from low-income families who scored high in math, which turns out to be very predictive of inventing something later in life, were still much less likely to become inventors than wealthier children with similar math scores. What conclusion did the researchers draw from this? That "there are many 'lost Einsteins'" who would have made enormous contributions had they been allowed to reach their full potential. Poverty reduces people born for better things.[26]

How many artists and poets has poverty denied us? How many diplomats and visionaries? How many political and spiritual leaders? How many nurses and engineers and scientists? Think of how many more of us would be empowered to thrive if we tore down the walls, how much more vibrant and forward-moving our country would be.[27]

EPILOGUE

POVERTY ABOLITION IS A PERSONAL AND POLITICAL PROJECT. Those of us who embrace this project seek to divest from poverty in our consumer choices, investment decisions, and jobs. We support a government actively striving to end scarcity by rebalancing the nation's safety net and expanding policies that empower the poor. We detest all forms of exploitation, whether it is carried out by corporations, property owners, or financial institutions, even if—especially if—it benefits us. We oppose racism, segregation, and opportunity hoarding in our communities, and stand for shared prosperity. Poverty abolitionists are solutionists, doers, prioritizing plan over critique, tangible wins over rhetorical ones, usefulness over purity—and we must organize.[1]

Behind every great blow dealt to the scourge of poverty, there have been ordinary Americans who have bound themselves to one another to accomplish extraordinary things. Social movements spark ideas, providing the blueprint for reform, as when the unemployed workers' movement of the late nineteenth century called for a public works program decades before the New Deal. And they make sure that rights on paper become rights in practice, as when unions during the twentieth century demanded that their employers honor new labor laws.[2]

Most important, movements apply the heat. The American labor movement was the dominant force behind the New Deal. The tenants' movement that rose up during the Depression provoked Congress to establish our public housing system. How was President Johnson able to break through congressional gridlock to deliver the civil rights acts, the Great Society, and the War on Poverty? The civil rights movement forced his hand by putting unrelenting pressure on lawmakers. Johnson admitted as much in 1965, telling Congress that the actions of Black Americans who had joined the civil rights movement "called upon us to make good the promise of America. And who among us can say that we would have made the same progress were it not for [their] persistent bravery, and [their] faith in American democracy?" When Johnson uttered these words, Congress was polarized; the Democratic Party was coming apart at the seams; and the country, by denying Black citizens access to the ballot box, was undemocratic in fact. In other words, the Washington that passed transformational legislation outlawing racial discrimination, expanding access to healthcare, food, and education, and slashing the poverty rate was just as broken as the Washington of today. Ordinary Americans still found a way to win, as we now must.[3]

Poverty will be abolished in America only when a mass movement demands it so. And today, such a movement stirs. American labor is once again on the move, growing more boisterous and feistier by the day, organizing workplaces once thought untouchable. A renewed movement for housing justice is gaining steam. In a resurgence of tenant power, renters have formed eviction blockades and chained themselves to the entrances of housing court, meeting the violence of displacement with a force of their own. The Poor People's Campaign has elevated the voices of low-income Americans around the country, voices challenging "the lie of scarcity in the midst of abundance" and mobilizing for things like educational equity and a reinvestment in public housing.[4] They march under different banners—workers' unions and tenants' unions; movements for racial justice and economic justice—but they share a commitment to ending poverty in America.

All of us can learn from, support, and join movements led by those who have intimate knowledge of poverty's many slights and humiliations: attending meetings, signing petitions, donating time and money, amplifying social media messages, working the phone banks, adding our voices to public protests, and running supplies to the picket line.

"Get into relationship." That's the clear advice of Deepak Bhargava, former president and executive director of the Center for Community Change, to those seeking to be allies in the movement to abolish poverty. "Find some way in your life to be in relationship with working class and poor people." Deepak wasn't speaking about charity, where a person of means serves someone in need, but about genuine connection, one built on mutual respect and understanding, where Americans across the class spectrum join low-income Americans in a political struggle for more dignity and more power.

You might not think of yourself as the protesting type. I'm

not either. But mass movements are composed of scores of
people finding their own way to pitch in. Some abolitionists
participated in slave revolts and sheltered runaways; others
gave fiery sermons and refused to buy goods made by enslaved
hands. Movements need people to march, but they also need
graphic designers and cooks and marketing professionals and
teachers and faith leaders and lawyers. We can all direct our
obsessions and talents toward abolishing poverty. How could
we resist joining this fight? Americans organizing against exploitation are the spiritual descendants of the best of the
American labor movement and the modern-day realization of
King's multiracial antipoverty crusade. In defying economic
injustice and unfair taxes, they are the true heirs of 1776.[5]

When your power comes from people, you need a lot of
them. The movement must grow, which means we can't afford to write anyone off. As Alicia Garza, co-creator of the
Black Lives Matter Global Network, has put it, "To build the
kind of movement that we need to get the things that we deserve, we can't be afraid to establish a base that is larger than
the people we feel comfortable with." That is, "We have to
reach beyond the choir."

Antipoverty movements are doing just that. People's Action (whose tagline is "Join our joyous rebellion") has brought
rural and urban poor and working-class families together to
campaign for housing justice and healthcare for all. Co-chair
of the Poor People's Campaign, Reverend William Barber—
who has found receptive audiences among struggling Black
families in deep-blue cities and struggling white families in
deep-red rural counties—advocates for "fusion coalitions"
made up of people of different faiths, ethnicities, and political

identities joining together and demanding change "from a moral perspective." Poverty abolitionism transcends partisan divides because, frankly, poor and working-class people deserve more than either party has delivered for them over the past fifty years. Visionary organizers don't view "those people"—liberals or conservatives, the young or the old, undocumented immigrants or citizens—as adversaries but as potential allies in the fight against poverty. They ascribe to the old political wisdom that there are no permanent friends or enemies, only permanent issues. This can be slow, fraught work, and also electrifying and invigorating work, much like democracy itself. Perhaps the reason protestors often chant "This is what democracy looks like" is because we can so easily forget.[6]

In May 2022, Saru Jayaraman, president of One Fair Wage, joined three other workers in a shopping mall in western Michigan, Republican country, to collect signatures supporting a higher minimum wage. "I really thought we were going to be punched or something was going to happen," Saru told me. She and her team stood out. They were all women of color, including two wearing hijabs, in a place where nearly all the shoppers were white. "But we'd walk up to them and say, 'Do you want to sign a petition for 15 [dollars an hour]?' Ninety-nine percent of people said, 'I already signed it,' or 'Where can I sign?'" It reminded Saru of what had happened almost two years before, in November 2020. One Fair Wage workers were gathered outside the statehouse in Albany, New York, to call for a $15-an-hour minimum wage for tipped workers. The crowd of mostly Black and Hispanic New Yorkers had brought with them a twenty-four-foot-high statue of a flexing

and aproned Black woman nicknamed Elena the Essential
Worker. As the workers were chanting and cheering on speak-
ers, a group of white men and women in red MAKE AMERICA
GREAT AGAIN hats approached. Unbeknownst to One Fair
Wage, the day of their rally was also the day the state legislature had scheduled to certify the results of the presidential
election, and MAGA protestors had gathered earlier to challenge the count. When the pro-Trump crowd learned that the
workers were there to push for higher wages, they shook
hands and joined their protest.

It makes you wonder: Is all the rhetoric around political
polarization just another kind of scarcity diversion, just another way to narrow our vision so that an emancipated future
remains outside of our field of view? "The conversation is,
'Oh, this issue is so polarizing. We're so polarized. We think so
differently,'" Saru told me. "And it's just such bullshit. We are
not polarized from each other. We are polarized from our
electeds." The majority of Americans believe the economy is
benefitting the rich and harming the poor. The majority believe the rich aren't paying their fair share in taxes. The majority support a $15 federal minimum wage.[7] Why, then, aren't
our elected officials representing the will of the people? This
we must demand of them.

Whose fight is this? If you are homeless or unemployed, a
person with disabilities on a fixed income, if you have been
exploited and excluded, incarcerated or evicted, this is your
fight. If you are an undocumented immigrant, giving this
country your sweat, your very body, but receiving few rights
in return, or a worker shortchanged and kicked around by
your company, this is your fight. If you are one of the tens of

millions of Americans scraping, pinching, living paycheck to paycheck, floating somewhere between poverty and security, this is your fight.[8] If you are a young person fed up not only with impossibly expensive cities and $100,000 college degrees but also with polite excuses and insipid justifications for why things are the way they are, this is your fight. If you have found security and prosperity and wish the same for your neighbors, if you demand a dignified life for all people in America, if you love fairness and justice and want no part in exploitation for personal gain, if all the hardship in your country violates your sense of decency, this is your fight, too.

There are a good many challenges facing this big, wide country, but near the top of the list must be concerns about basic needs. We must ask ourselves—and then ask our community organizations, our employers, our places of worship, our schools, our political parties, our courts, our towns, our families: What are we doing to divest from poverty? Every person, every company, every institution that has a role in perpetuating poverty also has a role in ameliorating it. The end of poverty is something to stand for, to march for, to sacrifice for. Because poverty is the dream killer, the capability destroyer, the great waster of human potential. It is a misery and a national disgrace, one that belies any claim to our greatness. The citizens of the richest nation in the world can and should finally put an end to it.[9]

We don't need to outsmart this problem. We need to outhate it.

ACKNOWLEDGMENTS

Tecara Ayler, Chloé Jackson, and everyone at Inquilinxs Unidxs por Justicia; Deepak Bhargava, Susanna Blankley, Twinkle Borge, Eric Dobson, Adam Gordon, Peter O'Connor, and the whole Fair Share Housing Center crew; Mark Edwards, George Goehl, Lakia Higbee, Saru Jayaraman, Julio Payes, Crystal Mayberry, Arleen, Vanetta, Woo, and all my friends in Milwaukee; Lyndsey Peck; Roxanne Sutocky along with the staff at the Philadelphia Women's Center; and Vanessa Solivan—thank you for your generosity and camaraderie and confidences, and for showing me.

This book began to take shape through a series of conversations with Jill Kneerim, my singular, fiercely intelligent literary agent. By the time the manuscript was finished, Jill was dying. I remember her sunbathed hospice room and what she told me after I laid the manuscript on the blanket. There was someone beautiful among us—someone who marveled at this world, believed in it—and now she is gone. I miss and love you, Jill.

Thank you, Amanda Cook, for demanding more of me, for

finding this book's heart, and for hating poverty. To the world-class team at Crown—especially Craig Adams, Katie Berry, Gillian Blake, Chris Brand, Julie Cepler, David Drake, Mason Eng, Annsley Rosner, Penny Simon, and Stacey Stein—thank you for rallying around this cause.

To Phoebe Anderson-Dana, Miriam Feuerle, Hannah Scott, and the Lyceum team, thank you for believing in the power of ideas and for helping me get the word out. To Katherine Flynn, Sarah Khalil, and the Kneerim & Williams agency, thank you for seeing it through.

Xavier Briggs, Dalton Conley, Tressie McMillan Cottom, Jason DeParle, Tessa Lowinske Desmond, Mitch Duneier, Kathy Edin, Filiz Garip, Katharine Huffman, Harvey Molotch, Tim Nelson, Betsy Levy Paluck, John Robinson, Luke Shaefer, Eldar Shafir, Patrick Sharkey, Paul Starr, Sarah Stillman, Keeanga-Yamahtta Taylor, Bruce Western, and Frederick Wherry all read an early version of this book and participated in a series of workshops which were among the most intellectually thrilling and politically motivating experiences of my life. Thank you all for your critical feedback and your mandates. My shortcomings and failures, of course, remain mine alone.

Jacob Haas at Princeton's Eviction Lab was the lead researcher for this book. Thank you, Jacob, for your obsession with the fine print and for your tirelessness and unflappability. Also at the Eviction Lab, I thank Adam Chapnik, Bria Dixon, Kathryn Doyle, Joe Fish, Danny Grubbs-Donovan, Amber Jackson, Olivia Jin, Jasmine Rangel, and Tasneem Yusufali for organizing book workshops, synthesizing research, and especially for those long weeks of fact-checking. The exacting, meticulous Riley Blanton was the lead fact-checker for this book.

In recent years, I've had the privilege of collaborating with several students, postdoctoral fellows, and colleagues on several projects that informed this work. Thank you Anne Kat Alexander, Monica Bell, Emily Benfer, Alieza Durana, Lavar Edmonds, Ian Fellows, Juan Pablo Garnham, Carl Gershenson, Madeleine Gilson, Henry Gomory, Nick Graetz, Ashley Gromis, James Hendrickson, Peter Hepburn, Gracie Himmelstein, Katie Krywokulski, Emily Lemmerman, Lillian Leung, Renee Louis, James Minton and the team at Hyperøbjekt, Matt Mleczko, Helena Najm, Zachary Parolin, Adam Porton, Devin Rutan, Gillian Slee, Tim Thomas, Adam Travis, Nathan Wilmers, and Chris Wimer for your brilliant insights and hard work.

To my students and colleagues at Princeton University, who never cease to inspire and challenge me, thank you. And thanks to my team at *The New York Times Magazine,* especially Claire Gutierrez, Jake Silverstein, and Bill Wasik, for backing slowly reported stories about American poverty.

Heartfelt thanks to the following people who answered questions, shared data, recommended studies, and aided me along my journey in countless other ways: Robert Allen, Lonnie Berger, Claire Brown, Philip Cohen, Robert Doar, Peter Edelman, Kevin Fagan, Phil Garboden, Lily Geismer, Larry Glickman, Meghan Greene, Bilal Habib, Alex Horowitz, Hilary Hoynes, Jennifer Jennings, Shamus Khan, James Koshiba, Kevin Kruse, Angela Li, Elizabeth Linos, Evie Lopoo, Kimberley Lufkin, Ian Lundberg, Darren Lutz, Kate Manne, Doug Massey, Suzanne Mettler, Robert Moffitt, Sanyu Mojola, Kelly

Musick, Laura Nolan, Amanda Nothaft, Alice O'Connor, Ann Owens, Joshua Page, Gwyn Pauley, Sheila Reynertson, Ryan Rippel, Eva Rosen, Jake Rosenfeld, Ali Safawi, Matt Salganik, Rob Sampson, Isabel Sawhill, Diane Whitmore Schanzenbach, Juliet Schor, Liz Schott, Zachariah Sippy, Maura Smyth, Carol Stack, Kirk Stark, Tom Sugrue, Laura Tach, Sehrish Taqweem, Ruth López Turley, Lawrence Vale, Wendy Wang, Brad Wilcox, Robb Willer, Yu Xie, Diane Yentel, and the good spokespeople at the U.S. Department of Agriculture and the Congressional Budget Office who wish to remain anonymous.

Support from Princeton University, the Bill & Melinda Gates Foundation, and the William T. Grant Scholars Program funded a sabbatical that allowed me to write this book. I'd also like to thank the Ford Foundation, the JPB Foundation, the John D. and Catherine T. MacArthur Foundation, and the Russell Sage Foundation, along with the Chan Zuckerberg Initiative and Funders for Housing and Opportunity, for supporting the Eviction Lab and research cited in these pages. Thank you, Robin Pispecky and the team at Princeton's Office of Population Research, for grant support.

Thanks to the Bassoonists, the Diggers, and all my friends. Thank you, Mom and Dad, Michelle, Dave, Cedar, and Maegan, for your unconditional love and support. Thank you, Sterling and Walter, for filling my life with laughter and hope. Tessa—thank you for your vision and courage, for your steadfastness and love, and for holding me through it all.

Devah Pager, you were the best of us. This one's for you.

NOTES

PROLOGUE

1. Matthew Desmond, "Severe Deprivation in America: An Introduction," *RSF: The Russell Sage Foundation Journal of the Social Sciences* 1 (2015): 1–11; Liana Fox, *The Supplemental Poverty Measure, 2019* (Washington, D.C.: U.S. Bureau of the Census, 2020), figure 2, appendix table 1; Organisation for Economic Co-operation and Development (OECD) Data, "Poverty Rate (indicator)," Organisation for Economic Co-operation and Development, 2022; U.S. Census Bureau, Current Population Survey, 2021 Annual Social and Economic Supplement, HINC-01; U.S. Census Bureau, Table B-1. People in Poverty by Selected Characteristics: 2019 and 2020. See also PolicyLink, *100 Million and Counting: A Portrait of Economic Insecurity in the United States* (Oakland, Calif.: PolicyLink, 2018).

2. DigDeep and the U.S. Water Alliance, *Closing the Water Access Gap in the United States: A National Action Plan* (Los Angeles: DigDeep, 2019), 8, 12; Megan McKenna et al., "Human Intestinal Parasite Burden and Poor Sanitation in Rural Alabama," *The American Journal of Tropical Medicine and Hygiene* 97 (2017): 1623–28; National Center for Homeless Education, *Student Homelessness in America: School Years 2017–18 to 2019–20* (Greensboro, N.C.: National Center for Homeless Education, 2021), 1; Monica Parise et al., "Neglected Parasitic Infections in the United States: Needs and Opportunities," *The American Journal of Tropical Medicine and Hygiene* 90 (2014): 783–85.

Of course, over the long run other aspects of incarceration—

particularly isolation and exposure to violence—compromise health. See Bruce Western, "Inside the Box: Safety, Health, and Isolation in Prison," *Journal of Economic Perspectives* 35 (2021): 97–122, 109; David Rosen, David Wohl, and Victor Schoenbach, "All-Cause and Cause-Specific Mortality Among Black and White North Carolina State Prisoners, 1995–2005," *Annals of Epidemiology* 21 (2011): 719–26; Christopher Wildeman and Christopher Muller, "Mass Imprisonment and Inequality in Health and Family Life," *Annual Review of Law and Social Science* 8 (2012): 11–30.

3. U.S. Bureau of Economic Analysis, *GDP Summary, Annual by State* (Washington, D.C.: U.S. Department of Commerce, 2022); The World Bank, *GDP (Current US$)* (Washington, D.C.: World Bank Group, 2022).

4. Jane Addams, "Jane Addams's Own Story of Her Work: The First Fifteen Years at Hull-House," *Ladies' Home Journal*, April 1906, 11–12; Jane Addams, *Twenty Years at Hull-House with Autobiographical Notes* (New York: Macmillan, 1912), 175–76; James Agee and Walker Evans, *Let Us Now Praise Famous Men: Three Tenant Families* (New York: Mariner Books, 1941); Michael Harrington, *The Other America: Poverty in the United States* (New York: Penguin Books, 1962), 170; Jacob Riis, *How the Other Half Lives: Studies Among the Tenements of New York* (New York: Penguin, 1997 [1890]).

CHAPTER 1

1. Carmen DeNavas-Walt and Bernadette Proctor, "Income and Poverty in the United States" (Washington, D.C.: U.S. Bureau of the Census, 2015), 44, table B-1; Bruce Meyer and James Sullivan, "Identifying the Disadvantaged: Official Poverty, Consumption Poverty, and the New Supplemental Poverty Measure," *Journal of Economic Perspectives* 26 (2012): 111–36; National Academies of Sciences, Engineering, and Medicine, *A Roadmap to Reducing Child Poverty* (Washington, D.C.: National Academies Press, 2019), 291–92; National Research Council, *Measuring Poverty: A New Approach* (Washington, D.C.: National Academies Press, 1995); Alice O'Connor, "Poverty Knowledge and the History of Poverty Research," in *The Oxford History of the Social Science of Poverty*, eds. David Brady and Linda Burton (New York: Oxford University Press, 2016), 169–92; Alice O'Connor, "When Measurements Matter: Poverty, Wealth, and the Politics of Inequality in the United States,"

History of Political Economy 52 (2020): 589–607; Mollie Orshansky, "Counting the Poor: Another Look at the Poverty Profile," *Social Security Administration Bulletin*, January 1965, 4; James Scott, *Seeing Like a State: How Certain Schemes to Improve the Human Condition Have Failed* (New Haven, Conn.: Yale University Press, 1998); Office of the Assistant Secretary for Planning and Evaluation, *2020 Poverty Guidelines* (Washington, D.C.: U.S. Department of Health and Human Services, 2020).

2. Layli Long Soldier, *Whereas* (Minneapolis: Graywolf Press, 2017), 44; Office of the Assistant Secretary for Planning and Evaluation, *2022 Poverty Guidelines* (Washington, D.C.: U.S. Department of Health and Human Services, 2022).

3. Crystal Mayberry is a pseudonym. Desmond, "Severe Deprivation"; Matthew Desmond, *Evicted: Poverty and Profit in the American City* (New York: Crown, 2016).

4. Robert Bullard, *Dumping in Dixie: Race, Class, and Environmental Equality* (New York: Westview Press, 2009); National Center for Health Statistics, *Health, United States, 2019*, Centers for Disease Control and Prevention, "Table 28: Untreated Dental Caries, by Selected Characteristics: United States, Selected Years 1988–1994 Through 2015–2018"; Robin Cohen et al., "Health Insurance Coverage: Early Release of Estimates from the National Health Interview Survey, 2021," National Center for Health Statistics, Centers for Disease Control and Prevention, 2022; Bhargavi Ganesh et al., "The Relationship Between Housing and Asthma Among School-Age Children," Urban Institute, October 2017; Emily Guendelsberger, *On the Clock: What Low-Wage Work Did to Me and How It Drives America Insane* (New York: Little, Brown, 2019); Helen Hughes et al., "Pediatric Asthma Health Disparities: Race, Hardship, Housing, and Asthma in a National Survey," *Academic Pediatrics* 17 (2017): 127–34; Gerald Markowitz and David Rosner, *Deceit and Denial: The Deadly Politics of Industrial Pollution* (Berkeley: University of California Press, 2013); Christopher Muller, Robert Sampson, and Alix Winter, "Environmental Inequality: The Social Causes and Consequences of Lead Exposure," *Annual Review of Sociology* 44 (2018): 263–82; Kamyar Nasseh, Marko Vujicic, and Cassandra Yarbrough, *A Ten-Year, State-by-State Analysis of Medicare Fee-for-Service Reimbursement Rates for Dental Care Services* (Chicago: Health Policy Institute, American Dental Association, 2014); Leah Rosenbaum, "Tooth Decay: An Epidemic in America's Poorest Children," *Science in the News*, Harvard University, June 22,

2017; Andrew Wasley, Christopher Cook, and Natalie Jones, "Two Amputations a Week: The Cost of Working in a US Meat Plant," *The Guardian*, July 5, 2018.

5. Anthony Braga and Philip Cook, "The Association of Firearm Caliber with Likelihood of Death from Gunshot Injury in Criminal Assaults," *JAMA Network Open* 1 (2018): 1–10; Jooyoung Lee, "Wounded: Life After the Shooting," *Annals of the American Academy of Political and Social Science* 642 (2012): 244–57; Laurence Ralph, *Renegade Dreams: Living Through Injury in Gangland Chicago* (Chicago: University of Chicago Press, 2014); Rosenbaum, "Tooth Decay"; Gillian Slee and Matthew Desmond, "Resignation without Relief: Democratic Governance and the Relinquishing of Parental Rights," Working Paper, Princeton University, 2022; Bruce Western, "Lifetimes of Violence in a Sample of Released Prisoners," *RSF: The Russell Sage Foundation Journal of the Social Sciences* 1 (2015): 14–30. Chicago gun violence statistics come from Patrick Sharkey, personal communication, March 2, 2021.

6. I met Scott (a pseudonym) while conducting research in Milwaukee for my book *Evicted*.

7. CoreLogic, "United States Residential Foreclosure Crisis: Ten Years Later," 2017; Desmond, *Evicted*, part 2; Matthew Desmond, "Unaffordable America: Poverty, Housing, and Eviction," Institute for Research on Poverty, *Fast Focus* 22 (2015): 1–6; Will Fischer, "President's Budget Would Provide More Vouchers to Help Families with Rising Housing Costs," Center on Budget and Policy Priorities, April 20, 2022; Ashley Gromis et al., "Estimating Eviction Prevalence Across the United States," *Proceedings of the National Academy of Sciences* 119 (2022): e2116169119; Dowell Myers and JungHo Park, "A Constant Quartile Mismatch Indicator of Changing Rental Affordability in U.S. Metropolitan Areas, 2000 to 2016," *Cityscape* 21 (2019): 163–200; RealtyTrac, "Record 2.9 Million U.S. Properties Receive Foreclosure Filing in 2010 Despite 30-Month Low in December," 2011; U.S. Census Bureau, American Community Survey, 1985–2022; U.S. Census Bureau, Current Population Survey/Housing Vacancy Survey, April 27, 2022, table 11A; U.S. Department of Housing and Urban Development, "40th Percentile Fair Market Rent, 1985–2022"; U.S. Census Bureau, American Housing Survey, 2019, table 10. Estimates of housing cost burden exclude renters reporting no cash rent as well as those spending over 100 percent of their household income on housing costs.

8. U.S. Bureau of Labor Statistics, "Table 16. Annual Total Separations Rates by Industry and Region, Not Seasonally Adjusted," March 10, 2022; Business Wire, "Temporary Employment in the U.S. to Grow Faster Than All Jobs Through 2025, According to New Job Forecast from TrueBlue and Emsi," November 1, 2019; Matthew Desmond, "Americans Want to Believe Jobs Are the Solution to Poverty. They're Not," *The New York Times Magazine,* September 11, 2018; Henry Farber, "Job Loss and the Decline in Job Security in the United States," in *Labor in the New Economy,* eds. Katharine Abraham, James Spletzer, and Michael Harper (Chicago: University of Chicago Press, 2010), 223–62; Jacob Hacker and Elisabeth Jacobs, "The Rising Instability of American Family Incomes, 1969–2004: Evidence from the Panel Study of Income Dynamics," Economic Policy Institute, May 29, 2008; Erin Hatton, *The Temp Economy: From Kelly Girls to Permatemps in Postwar America* (Philadelphia: Temple University Press, 2011); Wojciech Kopczuk, Emmanuel Saez, and Jae Song, "Earnings Inequality and Mobility in the United States: Evidence from Social Security Data Since 1937," *The Quarterly Journal of Economics* 125 (2010): 91–128; Jake Rosenfeld, *You're Paid What You're Worth: And Other Myths of the Modern Economy* (Cambridge, Mass.: Harvard University Press, 2021), 158, 173; U.S. Bureau of Labor Statistics, Temporary Help Services, 1991–2021, source code CES605613200.

9. PolicyLink, *100 Million and Counting;* Ann Huff Stevens, "The Dynamics of Poverty Spells: Updating Bane and Ellwood," *American Economic Review* 84 (1994): 34–37; U.S. Census Bureau, Current Population Survey, 2021 Annual Social and Economic Supplement, HINC-01.

10. Karl Marx, "The Eighteenth Brumaire of Louis Bonaparte," in *The Marx-Engels Reader,* 2nd ed., ed. Robert Tucker (New York: Norton, 1978 [1852]), 594–617.

11. National Academies of Sciences, Engineering, and Medicine, *Roadmap to Reducing Child Poverty,* 62; Office of the Assistant Secretary for Planning and Evaluation, *2020 Poverty Guidelines* (Washington, D.C.: U.S. Department of Health and Human Services, 2020); U.S. Census Bureau, Current Population Survey, 2021 Annual Social and Economic Supplement (CPS ASEC), POV-01: Age and Sex of All People, Family Members and Unrelated Individuals: 2020, Below 50% of Poverty.

12. Robert Allen, "Absolute Poverty: When Necessity Displaces Desire," *American Economic Review* 107 (2017): 3690–721; Robert Allen, "Poverty and the Labor Market: Today and Yesterday," *Annual Review of*

Economics 12 (2020): 107–34, 113–15; Angus Deaton, "Price Indexes, Inequality, and the Measurement of World Poverty," *American Economic Review* 100 (2010): 5–34; Angus Deaton, "The U.S. Can No Longer Hide from Its Deep Poverty Problem," *The New York Times,* January 24, 2018. More recent international poverty estimates have been made more difficult by the fact that the World Bank's International Comparison Program stopped reporting prices for cheap millets and sorghum, units of measurement essential to calculate basic food costs.

13. Jason DeParle and Robert Gebeloff, "Living on Nothing but Food Stamps," *The New York Times,* January 2, 2010; Poverty Solutions, *Markers of Extreme Poverty* (Ann Arbor: University of Michigan, 2021); National Center for Homeless Education, *Federal Data Summary, School Years 2016–17 Through 2018–19* (Browns Summit, N.C.: National Center for Homeless Education, 2021); National Center for Homeless Education, *Analysis of Data, from the 2007–08 Federally Required State Data Collection for the McKinney-Vento Education Assistance Improvements Act of 2001* (Browns Summit, N.C.: National Center for Homeless Education, 2009); H. Luke Shaefer and Kathryn Edin, "Extreme Poverty Among Households with Children Since the 1996 Welfare Law," in *Social Stratification,* 5th ed., eds. David Grusky, Nima Dahir, and Claire Daviss (New York: Routledge, 2022); H. Luke Shaefer and Kathryn Edin, *Extreme Poverty in the United States, 1996 to 2011* (Ann Arbor, Mich.: National Poverty Center, 2012), table 1; H. Luke Shaefer et al., "The Decline of Cash Assistance and the Well-Being of Poor Households with Children," *Social Forces* 98 (2020): 1000–25. For a debate about extreme poverty counts, see Bruce Meyer et al., "The Use and Misuse of Income Data and Extreme Poverty in the United States," National Bureau of Economic Research, Working Paper 25907, May 2019; and H. Luke Shaefer, "Critique of *$2.00 a Day,* or New Evidence of Need Among America's Poor?" at twodollarsaday.com.

14. Deborah Johnson, "Connections Among Poverty, Incarceration, and Inequality," Institute for Research on Poverty, *Fast Focus* 48 (May 2020); Melissa Kearney et al., "Ten Economic Facts About Crime and Incarceration in the United States," Policy Memo, Brookings Institution, May 2014; Becky Pettit, *Invisible Men: Mass Incarceration and the Myth of Black Progress* (New York: Russell Sage Foundation, 2012); Pew Charitable Trusts, "Probation and Parole Systems Marked by High Stakes, Missed Opportunities," September 25, 2018; Wendy Sawyer,

"How Much Do Incarcerated People Earn in Each State?," Prison Policy Initiative, April 10, 2017; Wendy Sawyer and Peter Wagner, "Mass Incarceration: The Whole Pie 2022," Prison Policy Initiative, March 14, 2022; U.S. Census Bureau, "Fact Sheet: Differences Between the American Community Survey (ACS) and the Annual Social and Economic Supplement to the Current Population Survey (CPS ASEC)" (Washington, D.C.: U.S. Bureau of the Census, 2021); Bruce Western, *Punishment and Inequality in America* (New York: Russell Sage Foundation, 2006), 98.

15. Katherine Beckett and Steve Herbert, *Banished: The New Social Control in Urban America* (New York: Oxford University Press, 2010); Gun Violence Archive 2021, verified August 28, 2022; Sheila Harris, "More Than Three-Quarters of Black Mothers Worry Their Children Will Be Victims of Police Brutality, *Essence* Survey Finds," *Essence,* June 15, 2020; Christopher Ingraham, "1 in 13 People Killed by Guns Are Killed by Police," *The Washington Post,* June 1, 2015; Susan Schweik, *The Ugly Laws* (New York: New York University Press, 2009). Gun death statistics pertain to nonsuicide deaths.

16. Alexes Harris, Heather Evans, and Katherine Beckett, "Drawing Blood from Stones: Legal Debt and Social Inequality in the Contemporary U.S.," *American Journal of Sociology* 115 (2010): 1755–99; Alexes Harris, Mary Pattillo, and Bryan Sykes, "Studying the System of Monetary Sanctions," *RSF: The Russell Sage Foundation Journal of the Social Sciences* 8 (2022): 1–34; Issa Kohler-Hausmann, *Misdemeanorland: Criminal Courts and Social Control in an Age of Broken Windows Policing* (Princeton, N.J.: Princeton University Press, 2018); Joshua Page and Joe Soss, "Preying on the Poor: Criminal Justice as Revenue Racket" in *Money and Punishment, Circa 2020,* ed. Anna VanCleave et al. (New Haven, Conn.: Yale Law School, 2020), 15; Devah Pager et al., "Criminalizing Poverty: The Consequences of Court Fees in a Randomized Experiment," *American Sociological Review* 87 (2022): 529–53; Vesla Weaver, "The Only Government I Know," *Boston Review,* June 10, 2014; Vesla Weaver and Amy Lerman, "Political Consequences of the Carceral State," *American Political Science Review* 104 (2010): 817–33.

17. Dean Herd, Andrew Mitchell, and Ernie Lightman, "Rituals of Degradation: Administration as Policy in the Ontario Works Programme," *Social Policy and Administration* 39 (2005): 65–79; Linda Nochlin, *Misère: The Visual Representation of Misery in the 19th Century* (London: Thames and Hudson, 2018), 8; Celeste Watkins-Hayes, *The New Welfare*

Bureaucrats: Entanglements of Race, Class, and Policy Reform (Chicago: University of Chicago Press, 2009).

18. Patrick Sharkey, "The Acute Effect of Local Homicides on Children's Cognitive Performance," *Proceedings of the National Academy of Sciences* 107 (2010): 11733–38.

19. Sendhil Mullainathan and Eldar Shafir, *Scarcity: Why Having Too Little Means So Much* (New York: Times Books, 2013), 13, 54, 161; Baba Shiv and Alexander Fedorikhin, "Heart and Mind in Conflict: The Interplay of Affect and Cognition in Consumer Decision Making," *Journal of Consumer Research* 26 (1999): 278–92.

20. John Creamer, "Poverty Rates for Blacks and Hispanics Reached Historic Lows in 2019," U.S. Bureau of the Census, September 15, 2020; Lincoln Quillian et al., "Meta-Analysis of Field Experiments Shows No Change in Racial Discrimination in Hiring over Time," *Proceedings of the National Academy of Sciences* 114 (2017): 10870–75; H. Luke Shaefer, Pinghui Wu, and Kathryn Edin, "Can Poverty in America Be Compared to Conditions in the World's Poorest Countries?," *American Journal of Medical Research* 4 (2017): 84–92; U.S. Bureau of Labor Statistics, "Labor Force Statistics from the Current Population Survey" (Washington, D.C.: Bureau of Labor Statistics, 2021).

21. Douglas Massey, "Still the Linchpin: Segregation and Stratification in the USA," *Race and Social Problems* 12 (2020): 1–12; Douglas Massey and Nancy Denton, *American Apartheid: Segregation and the Making of the Underclass* (Cambridge, Mass.: Harvard University Press, 1993); Robert Sampson, *Great American City: Chicago and the Enduring Neighborhood Effect* (Chicago: University of Chicago Press, 2012); William Julius Wilson, *The Truly Disadvantaged: The Inner City, the Underclass, and Public Policy* (Chicago: University of Chicago Press, 1987).

22. The owner-renter divide is as salient as any other in this nation, and this divide is a historical result of statecraft designed to protect and promote racial inequality. Ours was not always a nation of homeowners; the New Deal fashioned it so, particularly through the GI Bill of Rights. The GI Bill was enormous, consuming 15 percent of the federal budget in 1948, and remains unmatched by any other single social policy in the scope and depth of its provisions. The GI Bill brought a rollout of veterans' mortgages, padded with modest interest rates and down payments waived for loans up to thirty years. Returning soldiers lined up and bought new homes by the millions. In the years immedi-

ately following World War II, veterans' mortgages accounted for more than 40 percent of home loans. But both in its design and its application, the GI Bill excluded a large number of citizens. To get the New Deal through Congress, President Roosevelt needed to appease the southern arm of the Democratic Party. So he acquiesced when Congress blocked many nonwhites, particularly African Americans, from accessing his newly created ladders of opportunity. Farmwork, housekeeping, and other jobs disproportionately staffed by African Americans were omitted from programs like Social Security and unemployment insurance. Local Veterans Administration (VA) centers and other entities loyal to Jim Crow did their parts as well, systematically denying nonwhite veterans access to the GI Bill. If those veterans got past the VA, they still had to contend with the banks, which denied loan applications in nonwhite neighborhoods because the Federal Housing Administration refused to insure mortgages there. "The consequences proved profound," writes the historian Ira Katznelson in his perfectly titled book, *When Affirmative Action Was White: An Untold History of Racial Inequality in Twentieth-Century America* (New York: Norton, 2005), 16–23, 55, 116, 122–28, 170. "By 1984, when G.I. Bill mortgages had mainly matured, the median white household had a net worth of $39,135; the comparable figure for Black households was only $3,397, or just 9 percent of white holdings. Most of this difference was accounted for by the absence of homeownership." See also Matthew Desmond, "House Rules," *The New York Times Magazine,* May 9, 2017.

23. Mehrsa Baradaran, *The Color of Money: Black Banks and the Racial Wealth Gap* (Cambridge, Mass.: Harvard University Press, 2017); Neil Bhutta et al., "Disparities in Wealth by Race and Ethnicity in the 2019 Survey of Consumer Finances," Board of Governors of the Federal Reserve System, September 28, 2020; Desmond, "House Rules"; Heather Long and Andrew Van Dam, "The Black-White Economic Divide Is as Wide as It Was in 1968," *The Washington Post,* June 4, 2020.

24. A multidimensional approach to poverty measurement was pioneered in the field of development economics. For quantitative approaches to the American context, see Udaya Waglé, "Multidimensional Poverty: An Alternative Measurement Approach for the United States?," *Social Science Research* 37 (2008): 559–80; Roger White, *Multidimensional Poverty in America* (New York: Springer Books, 2020). For reviews, see Sudhir Anand and Amartya Sen, "Concepts of Human Development and Poverty: A Multidimensional Perspective," in *United Nations Development Programme, Poverty and Human Development: Human Development Papers* (1997): 1–20; Matthew Desmond and Bruce Western, "Poverty in America: New Directions and Debates," *Annual Review of Sociology* 44 (2018): 305–18.

CHAPTER 2

1. Centers for Disease Control and Prevention, "History of Smallpox," February 20, 2021; GSM Arena, "Apple iPhone 12," May 10, 2021; Lauren Medina, Shannon Sabo, and Jonathan Vespa, "Living Longer: Historical and Projected Life Expectancy in the United States, 1960 to 2060" (Washington, D.C.: U.S. Bureau of the Census, 2020), figure 1; National Center for Health Statistics, *Health, United States, 2019* (Hyattsville, Md.: Centers for Disease Control and Prevention, 2021), table 5; Emily Shrider et al., "Income and Poverty in the United States: 2020" (Washington, D.C.: U.S. Bureau of the Census, 2021), 56, table B-4; The World Bank, "Mortality Rate, Infant (Per 1,000 Live Births)—United States," May 10, 2021; "Infant Mortality Rate for the United States," FRED, Federal Reserve Bank of St. Louis, February 16, 2022; The World Bank, "Individuals Using the Internet (% of Population)—United States," May 10, 2021.

2. Critics (including Mollie Orshansky herself) have long pointed out the flaws of the Official Poverty Measure. For one, the measure doesn't count as income certain kinds of public aid, including housing assistance and Medicaid, or refundable tax credits like the Earned Income Tax Credit. Imagine two families, each made up of two parents and two children. Family A makes $26,000 a year and receives a housing voucher worth $5,000 in rent as well as an annual Earned Income Tax Credit of $2,000, giving it an effective annual income of $33,000. Family B makes $28,000 a year but does not benefit from these programs. Although Family A is better off, that family would be officially classified as poor—and eligible for certain kinds of government assistance—while Family B would not, its income being just above the poverty line. The Official Poverty Measure also ignores regional differences in the cost of living, which are substantial. And it narrowly defines a "family," so if the parents in Family A were not married, only one adult's income

(typically the mother's) would be counted, while both would be counted if the parents were married.

With these limitations in mind, researchers developed another measure, the Supplemental Poverty Measure (SPM). It accounted for regional differences in costs of living and counted government benefits and taxes as well as major expenses, like medical and childcare costs, as well as household expenses and contributions of children and adults the Official Poverty Measure ignored. When the SPM was released, the United States officially gained 3 million more poor people. Possible reductions in poverty from counting government aid like food stamps, housing assistance, and tax benefits were more than offset by recognizing how low-income people were burdened by rising housing and healthcare costs. Researchers have developed a way to estimate what the Supplemental Poverty Measure was in years prior to its adoption. Going back to 1967, the researchers found, first, that the SPM rate was consistently higher than the federal poverty line and, second, that since the early 1970s, its rate was generally constant, fluctuating between 14 and 17 percent a year, except for a ten-year dip between 1997 and 2006 when the SPM rate remained under 14 percent. We're still in rolling hills territory.

The Supplemental Poverty Measure is not a flawless measure, either. Because it places so much weight on regional variation in living costs—which also are connected to strong public services, like schools and transportation—the measure ranks California as the poorest state in the union, worse off than Mississippi or West Virginia, which is absurd.

Researchers have also developed an *anchored* Supplemental Poverty Measure. Using this measure, they found that the poverty rate has fallen by roughly 40 percent over the past fifty years. In 2022, Child Trends, a nonpartisan research organization, used an anchored poverty measure in a widely cited report claiming that child poverty fell by 59 percent between 1993 and 2019. How can this be? Because the anchor is doing a lot of the work.

Anchoring is a popular statistical method that allows researchers to assess well-being over time by assuming that standards of well-being don't change. But that can produce questionable estimates of the depths of poverty in any given year because, well, standards of well-being do change. If we anchored the poverty rate to today's standards of living and ran the clock back to 1800, then plantation owners who lived on giant estates and enslaved hundreds of Black workers would be reduced to peasants, and we would all be transformed into royalty, as most of us have electricity in our homes and cars in our driveways, luxuries the upper crust of the nineteenth century couldn't have dreamed of. For the same reason, if we anchored the poverty rate in 1800, there would be no "poverty" to speak of in America today.

So, when researchers find that the poverty rate has fallen dramatically in recent decades, they don't mean that the share of people in 1980 who lived below the 1980 poverty line was larger than the share of people today who live below today's poverty line. They mean, technically, that the share of people in 1980 who lived below the 2012 poverty line (the poor's standard of living for that year, their anchor) was larger than the share of people today who live below the 2012 poverty line, as measured by the Supplemental Poverty Measure. As such, if researchers using an anchored measure have estimated sizable declines in poverty, it is because they have pushed up the poverty line in decades past to create a downward slope. (In this vein, the Child Trends report estimates such a large decline in child poverty because their anchoring methodology adds roughly 3 million more children to the poverty rolls in 1993 than are counted using the conventional unanchored Supplemental Poverty Measure.) There are good reasons for doing this—it shows that investments in government programs have borne fruit—but it's always struck me as something akin to making a patient sicker so you can marvel at his progress.

Even if we use the anchored Supplemental Poverty Measure, it remains the case that most of the poverty reductions observed by this indicator took place over two periods: between 1970 and 1980 and between 1995 and 2000. In other words, according to the measure some scholars prefer to use to show that the country has made significant headway in lifting families out of poverty, momentum has stalled since 2000. In fact, urban poverty has increased since that time, and hardship measures, from the number of homeless schoolchildren to the number of families in extreme poverty, are up. *This,* I feel, is the lede that studies are burying in their effort to show that government programs help. They do—but they're clearly not enough.

On the Official Poverty Measure, see DeNavas-Walt and Proctor, "Income and Poverty in the United States," 44, table B-1; Bruce Meyer and James Sullivan, "Identifying the Disadvantaged: Official Poverty, Consumption Poverty, and the New Supplemental Poverty Measure," *Journal of Economic Perspectives* 26 (2012): 111–36; National Academies of Sciences, Engineering, and Medicine, *Roadmap to Reducing Child Poverty*, 291–92; National Research Council, *Measuring Poverty: A New Approach* (Washington, D.C.: National Academies Press, 1995); O'Connor, "Poverty Knowledge and the History of Poverty Research," 169–92; O'Connor, "When Measurements Matter"; Lawrence Vale, *From the Puritans to the Projects: Public Housing and Public Neighbors* (Cambridge, Mass.: Harvard University Press, 2009), 68; Office of the Assistant Secretary for Planning and Evaluation, *2020 Poverty Guidelines* (Washington, D.C.: U.S. Department of Health and Human Services, 2020).

On the Supplemental Poverty Measure, see Fox, *Supplemental Poverty Measure: 2019*, 16–21, figure 3; National Academies of Sciences, Engineering, and Medicine, *Roadmap to Reducing Child Poverty;* National Research Council, *Measuring Poverty;* Kathleen Short, "The Research Supplemental Poverty Measure: 2011" (Washington, D.C.: U.S. Bureau of the Census, 2012), table 1; Shrider et al., "Income and Poverty in the United States"; and Christopher Wimer et al., "Progress on Poverty? New Estimates of Historical Trends Using an Anchored Supplemental Poverty Measure," *Demography* 53 (2016): 1207–18.

On anchored poverty measures, see Center on Poverty and Social Policy, *Historical Supplemental Poverty Measure Data* (New York: Columbia University, 2021); Jason DeParle, "Expanded Safety Net Drives Sharp Drop in Child Poverty," *The New York Times,* September 11, 2022; Fox, "Supplemental Poverty Measure: 2019," figure 4; Laura Nolan, Jane Waldfogel, and Christopher Wimer, "Long-Term Trends in Rural and Urban Poverty: New Insights Using a Historical Supplemental Poverty Measure," *The Annals of the American Academy of Political and Social Science* 672 (2017): 123–42; Jessica Semega et al., "Income and Poverty in the United States: 2019" (Washington, D.C.: U.S. Bureau of the Census, 2020), 12, 61; H. Luke Shaefer and Pat Cooney, "How Much Did Child Poverty Fall Between 1993 and 2019?," Working Paper, University of Michigan, Poverty Solutions, September 2022; Shaefer and Edin, "Extreme Poverty Among Households with Children Since the 1996 Welfare Law"; Dana Thomson et al., *Lessons from a Historic Decline in Child Poverty* (Bethesda, Md.: Child Trends, 2022); and Wimer et al., "Progress on Poverty," 1207–18.

3. Daniel Bell, *The End of Ideology: On the Exhaustion of Political Ideas in the Fifties* (New York: Free Press, 1965), 283; George Orwell, *The Road to Wigan Pier* (New York: Harvest Books, 1958 [1937]), 88–90.

4. Ron Haskins and Isabel Sawhill, *Creating an Opportunity Society* (Washington, D.C.: Brookings Institution Press, 2009), 39.

5. U.S. Bureau of Labor Statistics, *Consumer Price Index Databases for All Urban Consumers*, 2022. Overall, the cost of all goods and services tracked by the Consumer Price Index increased by 69.3 percent between 2000 and 2022. Nonessential goods like microwaves and televisions have become much cheaper in recent years, but more essential human needs such as the cost of rent, utilities, and healthcare have become more expensive. Monica Prasad, *The Trade-Off Between Social Insurance and Financialization: Is There a Better Way?* (Washington, D.C.: Niskanen Center, 2019), figure 2.

6. Harrington, *Other America*, 12.

7. Paul Pierson, *Dismantling the Welfare State? Reagan, Thatcher and the Politics of Retrenchment* (New York: Cambridge University Press, 1994).

8. Figures are in 2009 dollars. These data were compiled by Robert Moffitt of Johns Hopkins University and Gwyn Pauley of the University of Wisconsin–Madison and were generously shared with me via personal communication, August 12, 2021. The thirteen means-tested transfer programs they included were Medicaid; the Children's Health Insurance Program; Supplemental Security Income; cash welfare (AFDC/TANF); the Earned Income Tax Credit; the Child Tax Credit; the Additional Child Tax Credit; food stamps; housing assistance; school food programs; Special Supplemental Nutrition for Women, Infants, and Children; and Head Start. When Moffitt and Pauley included the largest social insurance programs—Social Security's Old Age and Survivors Insurance, Medicare, Unemployment Insurance, Workers' Compensation, and Disability Insurance—in addition to these means-tested transfers, they found that federal spending rose from $3,780 a person in 1980 to $9,457 a person in 2018 (in 2009 dollars), a 150 percent increase.

9. Office of Management and Budget, "Historical Tables," table 11.3;

H. Luke Shaefer, Kate Naranjo, and David Harris, "Spending on Government Anti-Poverty Efforts: Healthcare Expenditures Vastly Outstrip Income Transfers," Poverty Solutions, University of Michigan, September 2019. See also Office of Management and Budget, *Appendix, Budget of the U.S. Government, Fiscal Year 2023* (Washington, D.C.: Government Printing Office, 2022), 164, 450, 1021.

10. Figures are in 2009 dollars. Robert Moffitt and Gwyn Pauley, personal communication, August 12, 2021; Shaefer et al., "Spending on Government Anti-Poverty Efforts." In other work, Moffitt has shown that the significant expansion of government spending, largely directed at poor Americans, is not explained by the growth of a small set of programs, like Medicaid or Social Security. Although the number of retired workers drawing Social Security began to climb in the early aughts after decades of stability (baby boomers), growth in per capita spending predates this surge. Robert Moffitt, "The Deserving Poor, the Family, and the U.S. Welfare System," *Demography* 52 (2015): 729–49; Social Security, *Fast Facts and Figures: About Social Security, 2020* (Washington, D.C.: Social Security Administration, July 2020), 14.

11. As Suzanne Mettler observes in *The Submerged State: How Invisible Government Policies Undermine American Democracy* (Chicago: University of Chicago Press, 2011), 6, 16, visible social programs (like public housing) have diminished as more hidden government benefits (like tax credits) have grown. If some have documented welfare retrenchment, it's because it has happened in a conspicuous way, even as the overall size of the country's welfare state has grown through programs designed not to look like public aid. See also Aaron Rosenthal, "Submerged for Some? Government Visibility, Race, and American Political Trust," *Perspectives on Politics* 19 (2020): 1098–114.

12. Jana Parsons, "To Target Aid to the Neediest Families, We Need to Strengthen TANF," Brookings Institution, June 10, 2020.

13. Center on Budget and Policy Priorities, on "State Fact Sheets: How States Spend Funds Under the TANF Block Grant," January 12, 2022; Diana Azevedo-McCaffrey and Ali Safawi, "To Promote Equity, States Should Invest More TANF Dollars in Basic Assistance," Center for Budget and Policy Priorities, January 12, 2022; U.S. Department of Health and Human Services, *TANF Financial Data—FY 2020* (Washington, D.C.: Office of Family Assistance, 2021).

States with large Black populations were less likely to turn TANF funds into cash assistance and more likely to funnel those dollars into programs that discouraged single motherhood. Parolin estimated that getting rid of racial inequalities in TANF spending would increase direct aid to poor families and narrow the Black-white child poverty gap by 15 percent. Zachary Parolin, "Temporary Assistance for Needy Families and the Black-White Child Poverty Gap," *Socio-Economic Review* 19 (2019): 1–31.

14. Trevor Brown, "State Ends Marriage Initiative as Part of Budget Cuts," *Oklahoma Watch*, August 3, 2016; Krissy Clark, "Oh My God— We're on Welfare?!," *Slate*, June 2, 2016; Jenifer McKenna and Tara Murtha, *Designed to Deceive: A Study of the Crisis Pregnancy Center Industry in Nine States* (Allentown, Pa.: The Alliance, State Advocates for Women's Rights and Gender Equality, 2021), 58; Zach Parolin, "Welfare Money Is Paying for a Lot of Things Besides Welfare," *The Atlantic*, June 13, 2019; Mississippi Department of Human Services, *Mississippi State Plan for Temporary Assistance for Needy Families*, reauthorized by the Deficit Reduction Act of 2005; State of Arizona, *State Plan for Temporary Assistance for Needy Families (TANF)*, effective October 1, 2020; Texas Health and Human Services, *Texas State Plan for Temporary Assistance for Needy Families*, October 1, 2019; State of Washington, *State Plan for Temporary Assistance for Needy Families (TANF)*, effective January 28, 2020, attachment B11.

15. The U.S. government is prohibited from monitoring how states spend federal TANF dollars. Cindy Boren and Des Bieler, "Brett Favre to Repay Welfare Money for Appearances He Didn't Make, Mississippi Auditor Says," *The Washington Post*, May 7, 2020; Steve Rabey, "How Mississippi Turned Your Tax Dollars into Welfare for the Rich," Ministry Watch, May 7, 2020; Luke Ramseth, "MS Welfare Scandal Audit," *The Clarion Ledger*, May 6, 2020; Shad White et al., *Single Audit Report* (Jackson: State of Mississippi, Office of the State Auditor, 2020).

16. Azevedo-McCaffrey and Safawi, *To Promote Equity*, 14; Organisation for Economic Co-operation and Development (OECD), "CO2.2: Child Poverty," OECD Family Database, August, 2021, 1; Talk Poverty, "Child Poverty—2020"; U.S. Census Bureau, American Community Survey 2019, 1-Year Estimates, table S1701.

17. Center on Budget and Policy Priorities, "Chart Book: Social Security Disability Insurance," February 12, 2021; Social Security Administration, *Annual Statistical Supplement to the Social Security Bulletin, 2019,*

SSA Publication No. 13-11700 (Washington, D.C.: Social Security Office of Retirement and Disability Policy, 2020), table 6.C7. Applications for Supplemental Security Income also surged during this time, rising from 1.92 million in 1996 to roughly 3.15 million in 2010. After that year, the number of applications began to decline, returning to mid-1990s levels by 2018. Social Security Administration, *SSI Annual Statistical Report, 2019, SSA Publication No. 13-11827* (Washington, D.C.: Social Security Office of Retirement and Disability Policy, 2020).

18. Social Security Administration, "How You Earn Credits"; Social Security Administration, *SSI Annual Statistical Report, 2019.*

19. By "disability and other benefits," I mean Title II Social Security programs, which along with SSDI encompass old-age and survivors' insurance. In 2016, the Social Security Administration issued an additional $214 million to claimant representatives processing SSI applications, the money drawn from a different funding stream.

Michael J. Astrue, Commissioner of Social Security, "Maximum Dollar Limit in the Fee Agreement Process," *Federal Register* 74 (2009): 6080; Social Security Administration, *Representation of Claimants*, Sec. 206 [42 U.S.C. 406]; Office of the Inspector General, *The Cost of Administering Claimant Representative Fees* (Woodlawn, Md.: Social Security Administration, 2018), B2; Social Security Administration, *Statistics on Title II Direct Payments to Claimant Representatives* (Washington, D.C.: Social Security Office of Retirement and Disability Policy, 2020). See also Hilary Hoynes, Nicole Maestas, and Alexander Strand, "The Effect of Attorney and Non-Attorney Representation on the Initial Disability Determination Process," National Bureau of Economic Research, Working Paper DRC NB16-15, September 2016.

20. Market actors siphon off federal dollars allocated to other major antipoverty programs as well. For example, in some cities, housing low-income families using the Low-Income Housing Tax Credit (LIHTC)—the nation's largest source of government-subsidized low-income housing construction—would be twice as expensive as doing so through housing vouchers, because of building and regulatory costs associated with housing construction. Studies have also shown that Community Development Block Grants (CDBGs), often cities' largest source of federal funding, are regularly used to support housing, infrastructure, and economic development projects in high-income communities. On LIHTC, see Lan Deng, "The Cost-effectiveness of the Low-Income

Housing Tax Credit Relative to Vouchers: Evidence from Six Metro-politan Areas," *Housing Policy Debate* 16 (2005): 469–511; Michael Eriksen, "The Market Price of Low-Income Housing Tax Credits," *Journal of Urban Economics* 66 (2009): 141–49; Edward Glaeser and Joseph Gyourko, *Rethinking Federal Housing Policy: How to Make Housing Plentiful and Affordable* (Washington, D.C.: AEI Press, 2008). On CDBGs, see Leah Brooks and Maxim Sinitsyn, "Where Does the Bucket Leak? Sending Money to the Poor via the Community Development Block Grant Program," *Housing Policy Debate* 24 (2014): 119–71; Robert Collinson, "Assessing the Allocation of CDBG to Community Development Need," *Housing Policy Debate* 24 (2014): 91–118; Michael Rich, *Federal Policymaking and the Poor* (Princeton, N.J.: Princeton University Press, 1993).

21. Arthur Okun, *Equality and Efficiency: The Big Tradeoff* (Washington, D.C.: Brookings Institution Press, 2005 [1975]).

22. Centers for Medicare and Medicaid Services, *Financial Management Report for FY 2019* (Woodlawn, Md.: Centers for Medicare and Medicaid Services, 2020); Robert Greenstein and CBPP Staff, "Romney's Charge That Most Federal Low-Income Spending Goes for 'Overhead' and 'Bureaucrats' Is False," Center on Budget and Policy Priorities, January 23, 2012; Social Security Administration, *FY 2021 Congressional Justification* (Woodlawn, Md.: Social Security Administration, 2021), 40, 44, 138; Social Security Administration Office of Retirement and Disability Policy, *Annual Statistical Supplement to the Social Security Bulletin, 2020* (Washington, D.C.: Social Security Administration, 2021), table 4, A3; U.S. Department of Agriculture, *2021 USDA Explanatory Notes—Food and Nutrition Service* (Washington, D.C.: USDA, 2021), 34–60, 34–65.

23. Josh Boak, "AP Fact Check: Trump Plays on Immigration Myths," *PBS News Hour,* February 8, 2019; Matthew Desmond and Mustafa Emirbayer, *Race in America* (New York: Norton, 2015), 76; Alan Gauthreaux, "An Inhospitable Land: Anti-Italian Sentiment and Violence in Louisiana, 1891–1924," in *Louisiana History: The Journal of the Louisiana Historical Association* 51 (2010): 41–68; Jessica Barbata Jackson, *Dixie's Italians: Sicilians, Race, and Citizenship in the Jim Crow Gulf South* (Baton Rouge: Louisiana State University Press, 2020).

24. Abby Budiman, "Key Findings About U.S. Immigrants," Pew Research Center, August 20, 2020; U.S. Census Bureau, America's Foreign Born in the Last 50 Years, 2021.

25. U.S. Census Bureau, 1970 Census: Count 4Pa—Sample-Based Population Data, tables NT23, NT126; U.S. Census Bureau, American Community Survey 2019 1-Year Estimates, table B05012; U.S. Census Bureau, 1970 Census: Count 4Pa—Sample-Based Population Data, tables NT18, NT83, NT89; U.S. Census Bureau, American Community Survey 2019 1-Year Estimates, table S1701. See also Jeff Chapman and Jared Bernstein, "Immigration and Poverty: How Are They Linked?," *Monthly Labor Review,* April 2003.

26. Ran Abramitzky and Leah Boustan, *Streets of Gold: America's Untold Story of Immigrant Success* (New York: PublicAffairs, 2022).

27. Francine Blau and Christopher Mackie, eds., *The Economic and Fiscal Consequences of Immigration* (Washington, D.C.: National Academies Press, 2017), 5, chap. 5.

28. When the United States limited immigration from Europe in the 1920s by imposing strict quotas on certain countries, the foreign-born population shrank dramatically. In response, landowners bought tractors. It wasn't the invention of the tractor itself that ushered in the age of automated agriculture. That happened when adopting the new technology made the most business sense given the reduced immigrant labor pool. The same pattern is repeating itself today in large farms across America, where owners facing dwindling numbers of undocumented workers have purchased machines to harvest everything from salad mix to tree nuts. A century ago, many European immigrants found work as miners. When immigration quotas caused their numbers to plummet, the mining companies could neither attract native-born workers—who, said one commentator at the time, did "not care to go back to the track, the pickaxe, and the shovel"—nor take refuge in machines because the technology didn't exist at that time. As a result, one mining operation after another went under. Today, farms are going the way of the mines. In 2000, workers in California harvested 37,000 acres of asparagus, which cannot be mechanically picked. In 2020, they harvested only 4,000 acres. See Ran Abramitzky et al., "The Effect of Immigration Restrictions on Local Labor Markets: Lessons from the 1920s Border Closure," *American Economic Journal,* forthcoming (2022); Eduardo Porter, "Farming Transformation in the Fields of California," *The New York Times,* May 28, 2022.

29. Blau and Mackie, eds., *Economic and Fiscal Consequences of Immigration,* 11.

30. U.S. Census Bureau, Current Population Survey, Historical Poverty Tables: People and Families—1959 to 2020, tables 4 and 10; Vee Burke, Thomas Gabe, and Gene Falk, *Children in Poverty: Profile, Trends, and Issues* (Washington, D.C.: Congressional Research Service, 2008), 17.

31. David Brady and Rebekah Burroway, "Targeting, Universalism, and Single-Mother Poverty: A Multilevel Analysis Across 18 Affluent Democracies," *Demography* 49 (2012): 719–46; David Cooper, *Raising the Federal Minimum Wage to $15 by 2024 Would Lift Pay for Nearly 40 Million Workers* (Washington, D.C.: Economic Policy Institute, 2019); Organisation for Economic Co-operation and Development (OECD), *Hours of Work Needed to Escape Poverty for Workless Families* (Paris: OECD.Stat, 2021). See also Laurie Maldonado and Rense Nieuwenhuis, "Family Policies and Single Parent Poverty in 18 OECD Countries, 1978–2008," *Community, Work and Family* 18 (2015): 395–415; Joya Misra, Stephanie Moller, and Michelle Budig, "Work-Family Policies and Poverty for Partnered and Single Women in Europe and North America," *Gender and Society* 21 (2007): 804–27.

32. Andrew Cherlin, *Labor's Love Lost: The Rise and Fall of the Working-Class Family in America* (New York: Russell Sage Foundation, 2014), 2; Kathryn Edin and Maria Kefalas, *Promises I Can Keep: Why Poor Women Put Motherhood Before Marriage* (Berkeley: University of California Press, 2011); Christina Gibson-Davis, Anna Gassman-Pines, and Rebecca Lehrman, "'His' and 'Hers': Meeting the Economic Bar to Marriage," *Demography* 55 (2018): 2321–43.

33. If poor couples are choosing to put off marriage until the time is right, why aren't they choosing to put off having babies? Limited access to the most effective contraception is one answer. The fact that we no longer force couples to marry when a woman gets pregnant is another. But it's also important that we recognize that a baby can bring joy and honor, identity and purpose to lives where such things are in short supply, as the work of Kathryn Edin and others have so powerfully shown. Children born poor will be exposed to hardship, but they'll also be exposed to recycled jokes and passed-down recipes and soft-sung songs. See George Akerlof and Janet Yellen, "An Analysis of Out-of-Wedlock Births in the United States," Brookings Institution, August 1, 1996; Suzanne Bianchi, John Robinson, and Melissa Milke, *Changing Rhythms of American Family Life* (New York: Russell Sage Foundation, 2006); Stephanie Coontz, *The Way We Never Were: American Families and the Nostalgia Trap* (New York: Basic Books, 2016 [1992]), xxvii, 25, 33, 43–44, 392, 402;

Edin and Kefalas, *Promises I Can Keep;* Dorothy Roberts, *Killing the Black Body: Race, Reproduction, and the Meaning of Liberty* (New York: Vintage, 2014).

In *The Cultural Contradictions of Capitalism* (New York: Basic Books, 1996 [1976], 18), Daniel Bell remarked that the bourgeois class embraced radicalism in economics, "a willingness to tear up all traditional social relations in the process," but adopted conservatism in the realms of culture and sex. The excesses of the American rich were material, not spiritual or carnal. This helps explain, perhaps, why some of us consider having a child outside of wedlock more scandalous than clear-cutting a forest or destroying a rival company for profit.

34. Anna Gassman-Pines and Hirokazu Yoshikawa, "Five-Year Effects of an Anti-Poverty Program on Marriage Among Never-Married Mothers," *Journal of Policy Analysis and Management* 25 (2006): 11–30; Lisa Gennetian, *The Long-Term Effects of the Minnesota Family Investment Program on Marriage and Divorce Among Two-Parent Families* (New York: MDRC, 2003); Daniel Schneider, "Lessons Learned from Non-Marriage Experiments," *The Future of Children* 25 (2015): 155–78.

35. Laura Maruschak and Todd Minton, "Correctional Populations in the United States, 2017–2018," U.S. Department of Justice, Bureau of Justice Statistics, 2020; Pew Charitable Trusts, "One in 100: Behind Bars in America 2008," February 28, 2008; Becky Pettit and Bruce Western, "Mass Imprisonment and the Life Course: Race and Class Inequality in US Incarceration," *American Sociological Review* 69 (2004): 151–69; Jeremy Travis, Bruce Western, and F. Stevens Redburn, *The Growth of Incarceration in the United States: Exploring Causes and Consequences* (Washington, D.C.: National Academies Press, 2014); Bruce Western and Becky Pettit, "Incarceration and Social Inequality," *Daedalus* 139 (2010): 8–19; Western, *Punishment and Inequality in America.*

36. Maurice Chammah, "Can German Prisons Teach America How to Handle Its Most Violent Criminals?," The Marshall Project, 2015; Travis et al., *Growth of Incarceration in the United States,* 260–67. See also Daniel Schneider, Kristen Harknett, and Matthew Stimpson, "What Explains the Decline in First Marriage in the United States? Evidence from the Panel Study of Income Dynamics, 1969 to 2013," *Journal of Marriage and Family* 80 (2018): 791–811; Western, *Punishment and Inequality in America,* 155.

37. Center on Budget and Policy Priorities, *A Quick Guide to SNAP Eli-*

gibility and Benefits (Washington, D.C.: CBPP, 2020); Rahim Kurwa, "The New 'Man in the House' Rules: How the Regulation of Housing Vouchers Turns Personal Bonds into Eviction Liabilities," *Housing Policy Debate* 30 (2020): 926–49; SSI Spotlights, *Understanding Supplemental Security Income—Spotlight on Living Arrangements* (Washington, D.C.: Social Security Administration, 2021); Robert Stalker, "Protecting Subsidized Housing for Families of Released Prisoners," *Clearinghouse Review* 41 (2007): 198–201.

On the mismatch between family policy and the realities of modern families, see Lawrence Berger and Marcia Carlson, "Family Policy and Complex Contemporary Families: A Decade in Review and Implications for the Next Decade of Research and Policy Practice," *Journal of Marriage and Family* 82 (2020): 478–507.

38. Congressional Research Service, *The Earned Income Tax Credit (EITC): How It Works and Who Receives It* (Washington, D.C.: U.S. Government Printing Office, 2021).

39. Marianne Bitler et al., "The Impact of Welfare Reform on Marriage and Divorce," *Demography* 41 (2004): 213–36; Sarah Halpern-Meekin et al., *It's Not Like I'm Poor: How Working Families Make Ends Meet in a Post-Welfare World* (Berkeley: University of California Press, 2015); Robert Moffitt, *The Effect of Welfare on Marriage and Fertility* (Washington, D.C.: National Academies Press, 1998).

40. Wendy Wang and W. Bradford Wilcox, "The Millennial Success Sequence: Marriage, Kids, and the 'Success Sequence' Among Young Adults," AEI Institute for Family Studies, 2017; George Will, "Listen Up, Millennials. There's a Sequence to Success," *The Washington Post,* July 5, 2017. I asked Wang and Wilcox, the authors of the American Enterprise Institute report, to run additional analyses for me, and they kindly agreed, showing that obtaining a full-time job was by far the most important step in the success sequence.

41. See Matt Bruenig, "The Success Sequence Is About Cultural Beefs, Not Poverty," People's Policy Project, August 5, 2017; Philip Cohen, "The Failure of the Success Sequence," Cato Institute, May 16, 2018; Ashley Fetters, "The Working-to-Afford-Child-Care Conundrum," *The Atlantic,* January 18, 2020; Haskins and Sawhill, *Creating an Opportunity Society,* 69–74; Dylan Matthews, "Conservatives Love This Deeply Misleading Factoid About Poverty in America," *Vox,* July 24, 2015; Richard Reeves, Edward Rodrigue, and Alex Gold, "Following the Success Sequence? Success Is More Likely If You're White," Brookings Institution, August 6, 2015.

42. The children of poor single mothers grow up to be poor themselves at high rates, but research by the sociologist Regina Baker has shown that since the mid-1970s, marriage has become a weaker rampart against child poverty while work has become a stronger one. Marriage's influence on child poverty dipped sharply in the mid-1990s. This indicates that massive policy reforms that occurred during that time— namely, the end of cash welfare and the rise of the employment-based safety net that ties government aid to having a job—are behind this trend. Regina Baker, "The Changing Association Among Marriage, Work, and Child Poverty in the United States, 1974–2010," *Journal of Marriage and Family* 77 (2015): 1166–78.

CHAPTER 3

1. When William Julius Wilson published *The Truly Disadvantaged* in 1987, it changed the poverty debate. A 2001 review of the literature called the book "the most important publication in urban poverty over the past twenty-five years." Concerned with extremely poor Black men disconnected from the labor market, Wilson argued that concentrated poverty in urban centers was the result of increasing Black male joblessness owing to deindustrialization. As factories shuttered in cities like Chicago and Buffalo, Black communities lost their economic base, giving rise to a group of prime-age men who were out of work. Wilson laid out a strong argument that identified the drivers of poverty, but his theory did not subscribe to the notion that the rich strive to keep the poor down for their own benefit. For Wilson, urban poverty stemmed from the hard stumble of American industrialism and the systematic exclusion of the Black poor from gainful employment. In his view, urban poverty was caused not by unfair work conditions but by no work at all.

Mario Luis Small and Katherine Newman, "Urban Poverty After *The Truly Disadvantaged:* The Rediscovery of the Family, the Neighborhood, and Culture," *Annual Review of Sociology* 27 (2001): 23–45, 23; Arthur Stinchcombe, "The Social Determinants of Success," *Science* 178 (1972): 603–4; Donald Tomaskovic-Devey and Dustin Avent-Holt, "Observing Organizational Inequality Regimes," *Research in the Sociology of*

Work 28 (2016): 187–212; Wilson, *Truly Disadvantaged;* Erik Olin Wright, *Interrogating Inequality* (London: Verso, 1994), 36.

2. Matthew Desmond, "Capitalism," in *The 1619 Project: A New Origin Story,* ed. Nikole Hannah-Jones (New York: One World, 2021), 165–85; Sven Beckert and Seth Rockman, eds., *Slavery's Capitalism: A New History of American Economic Development* (Philadelphia: University of Pennsylvania Press, 2016); "A Little Priest," *Sweeney Todd, the Demon Barber of Fleet Street,* music and lyrics by Stephen Sondheim, book by Hugh Wheeler, based on Christopher Bond's *Sweeney Todd,* directed by Hal Prince, opened at the Uris Theatre March 1, 1979.

3. Richeson has conducted several studies documenting a widespread belief in racial progress that far outpaces actual progress. A 2019 paper showed that Americans underestimated what the Black-white wealth gap was in 1963 by roughly 40 percentage points but underestimated what it was in 2016 by roughly 80 percentage points. The wealth gap in 2016 was as wide as it was in the 1960s, but the average American assumed it had shrunk dramatically. Summing up the findings, Richeson wrote, "People are willing to assume that things were at least somewhat bad 50 years ago, but they also assume that things have gotten substantially better." Michael Kraus et al., "The Misperception of Racial Economic Inequality," *Perspectives on Psychological Science* 14 (2019): 899–921; Jennifer Richeson, "Americans Are Determined to Believe in Black Progress," *The Atlantic,* September 2020.

4. For sociological explanations of exploitation, see David Brady, Monica Biradavolu, and Kim Blankenship, "Brokers and the Earnings of Female Sex Workers in India," *American Sociological Review* 80 (2015): 1123–49; Arthur Sakamoto and ChangHwan Kim, "Is Rising Earnings Inequality Associated with Increased Exploitation? Evidence for U.S. Manufacturing Industries, 1971–1996," *Sociological Perspectives* 53 (2012): 19–44; Aage Sørensen, "Toward a Sounder Basis for Class Analysis," *American Journal of Sociology* 105 (2000): 1523–58; Erik Olin Wright, *Class Counts: Comparative Studies in Class Analysis* (New York: Cambridge University Press, 1997).

5. Annette Bernhardt et al., *Broken Laws, Unprotected Workers: Violations of Employment and Labor Laws in America's Cities* (Chicago: Center for Economic Development, 2009), 42, 44; Reuben Miller, *Halfway Home: Race, Punishment, and the Afterlife of Mass Incarceration* (New York: Little, Brown, 2021); Peter Wagner and Alexi Jones, "State of Phone

Justice: Local Jails, State Prisons and Private Phone Providers," Prison Policy Initiative, 2019.

6. Brady, Biradavolu, and Blankenship, "Brokers and the Earnings of Female Sex Workers in India," 1127; John Steinbeck, *The Grapes of Wrath* (New York: Penguin Classics, 2006 [1939]), 38.

7. Matthew Desmond, "Dollars on the Margins," *The New York Times Magazine,* February 23, 2019.

8. George Stigler, "The Economics of Minimum Wage Legislation," *American Economic Review* 36 (1946): 358–65.

9. Charles Brown, Curtis Gilroy, and Andrew Kohen, "The Effect of the Minimum Wage on Employment and Unemployment," *Journal of Economic Literature* 20 (1982): 487–528; Richard Posner, *Economic Analysis of Law,* 9th ed. (New York: Wolters Kluwer, 2014).

10. David Card and Alan Krueger, "Minimum Wages and Employment: A Case Study of the Fast-Food Industry in New Jersey and Pennsylvania," *American Economic Review* 84 (1994): 772–93.

11. For meta studies and reviews of the literature, I recommend Hristos Doucouliagos and Tom Stanley, "Publication Selection Bias in Minimum-Wage Research? A Meta-Regression Analysis," *British Journal of Industrial Relations* 47 (2009): 406–42; David Neumark and Peter Shirley, "Myth or Measurement: What Does the New Minimum Wage Research Say About Minimum Wages and Job Loss in the United States?," National Bureau of Economic Research, Working Paper 28388, May 2021; David Neumark and William Wascher, "Minimum Wages and Employment," *Foundations and Trends in Microeconomics* 3 (2007): 1–182; John Schmitt, *Why Does the Minimum Wage Have No Discernible Effect on Employment?* (Washington, D.C.: Center for Economic and Policy Research, 2013).

12. There's not much evidence that employers cut back hours when the government makes them raise the wages of their worst-paid workers. Businesses seem to make up the loss by raising prices. For example, when San Jose increased its minimum wage by 10 percent, restaurants raised their menu prices by 0.58 percent. A comprehensive review of the evidence found that a 10 percent increase to the minimum wage raised food prices by less than 4 percent and overall prices by less than 0.4 percent. Sylvia Allegretto and Michael Reich, "Are Local Minimum Wages Absorbed by Price Increases? Estimates from Internet-based Restaurant Menus," Institute for Research on Labor and Employment,

Working Paper 124-15, November 21, 2016; Sara Lemos, "A Survey of the Effects of the Minimum Wage on Prices," *Journal of Economic Surveys* 22 (2008): 187–212.

13. Rosenfeld, *You're Paid What You're Worth,* 5. This pay discrepancy exists across multiple sectors. For example, after adjusting for purchasing power, in 2018 clerical workers in Germany took home 23 percent more than those in the United States; service and sales workers took home 13 percent more; and agricultural workers 17 percent more. International Labour Organization, "Average Monthly Earnings of Employees by Sex and Occupation—Annual," ILOSTAT, 2020.

14. Jefferson Cowie, *Stayin' Alive: The 1970s and the Last Days of the Working Class* (New York: New Press, 2010), 2; Philip Dray, *There Is Power in a Union: The Epic Story of Labor in America* (New York: Anchor Books, 2010); Melvyn Dubofsky and Foster Rhea Dulles, *Labor in America: A History,* 8th ed. (Malden, Mass.: Wiley, 2010), 337–38; Henry Farber et al., "Unions and Inequality over the Twentieth Century: New Evidence from Survey Data," National Bureau of Economic Research, Working Paper 24587, May 2018 (updated April 2021); Barry Hirsch, David Macpherson, and Wayne Vroman, "Estimates of Union Density by State," *Monthly Labor Review* 124 (2001): 51–55; Lawrence Mishel et al., *The State of Working America,* 12th ed. (Ithaca, N.Y.: Cornell University Press, 2012), 26–27, 184–85, 289–91.

15. "Discrimination by Labor Union Bargaining Representatives Against Racial Minorities," *The Yale Law Journal* 56 (1947): 731–37; Dray, *There Is Power in a Union,* 482–83; Desmond, "Capitalism," 183; Robin Kelley, "Building Bridges: The Challenge of Organized Labor in Communities of Color," *New Labor Forum* 5 (1999): 42–58, 46–48; H. Luke Shaefer and Elizabeth Sammons, "The Development of an Unequal Social Safety Net: A Case Study of the Employer-Based Health Insurance (Non)System," *Journal of Sociology and Social Welfare* 36 (2009): 177–97, 190–91.

16. Cowie, *Stayin' Alive,* 222, 229–33, 246; Dubofsky and Dulles, *Labor in America,* 385–86.

17. Dray, *There Is Power in a Union,* 627, 636, 644–49; Andrew Glass, "Reagan Fires 11,000 Striking Air Traffic Controllers, Aug. 5, 1981," *Politico,* August 5, 2017; Joseph McCartin, *Collision Course: Ronald Reagan, the Air Traffic Controllers, and the Strike That Changed America* (New York: Oxford University Press, 2011), 295, 301.

18. The National Labor Relations Act permits employers to *predict* a shutdown if workers organize—*If you unionize, the factory could close*—but forbids them from *threatening* one: *If you unionize, we'll padlock the factory.* Employers do both. In 1995, managers at Michigan's ITT Automotive plant parked thirteen tractor-trailers loaded with shrink-wrapped equipment for the duration of its workers' union drive, signaling that the company would pack up and leave after a yes vote. Bosses at a Texas Fruit of the Loom plant once hung a sign during an organizing drive that read: "WEAR THE UNION LABEL. UNEMPLOYED." Kate Bronfenbrenner, "We'll Close! Plant Closings, Plant-Closing Threats, Union Organizing and NAFTA," *Multinational Monitor* 18 (1997): 8–14, 8; Kate Boo, "The Churn," *The New Yorker,* March 21, 2004; Thomas Kochan et al., "Worker Voice in America: Is There a Gap Between What Workers Expect and What They Experience?," *ILR Review* 72 (2019): 3–38, 4–5, 7–8, 19–21, 30; Gordon Lafer and Lola Loustaunau, *Fear at Work* (Washington, D.C.: Economic Policy Institute, 2020), 3–7; Celine McNicholas et al., *Unlawful: U.S. Employers Are Charged with Violating Federal Law in 41.5% of All Union Election Campaigns* (Washington, D.C.: Economic Policy Institute, 2019); David Streitfeld, "How Amazon Crushes Unions," *The New York Times Magazine,* March 16, 2021; U.S. Bureau of Labor Statistics, "Union Members Summary" (Economic News Release), January 20, 2022.

19. A 2017 meta-analysis of the research on unions found slight positive effects of American unions on productivity in construction and education sectors but no statistically significant effect in manufacturing. Hristos Doucouliagos, Richard Freeman, and Patrice Laroche, *The Economics of Trade Unions: A Study of a Research Field and Its Findings* (London: Routledge, 2017), 56–59, 67–69, 89, 104–5. See also John Addison's insightful review of *The Economics of Trade Unions* published in *ILR Review* 71 (2018): 273–76.

A 2004 review found that unions have larger positive effects on productivity in relatively competitive, cost-conscious sectors, where managers respond to union efforts by increasing efficiency. Studies have found that unions were associated with higher productivity in construction companies, private hospitals, and nursing homes; other studies reported null or negative effects of unions on productivity in other sectors such as sawmills and manufacturing, findings attributed in part to the fact that nonunionized firms often adopted management techniques that boosted productivity. In other words, negative associations between unions and productivity might reflect the fact that unionized firms are not optimally productive for reasons that don't have to do with labor organizing. Barry Hirsch, "What Do Unions Do for Economic Performance?," *Journal of Labor Research* 25 (2004): 415–55.

See also Richard Freeman and James Medoff's classic book, *What Do Unions Do?* (New York: Basic Books, 1984), as well as John DiNardo and David Lee, "Economic Impacts of New Unionization on Private Sector Employers: 1984–2001," *Quarterly Journal of Economics* 119 (2004): 1383–441; and Brigham Frandsen, "The Surprising Impacts of Unionization: Evidence from Matched Employer-Employee Data," *Journal of Labor Economics* 39 (2021): 861–94.

20. Eric Posner and E. Glen Weyl, *Radical Markets: Uprooting Capitalism and Democracy for a Just Society* (Princeton, N.J.: Princeton University Press, 2018), 11. See also Chad Syverson, "Challenges to Mismeasurement Explanations for the US Productivity Slowdown," *Journal of Economic Perspectives* 31 (2017): 165–86.

21. By "ordinary workers" I am referring to the "production and non-supervisory workers," as classified by the U.S. Bureau of Labor Statistics, which represent 80 percent of the workforce and typically exclude managers and high earners. Drew Desilver, "For Most U.S. Workers, Real Wages Have Barely Budged in Decades," Pew Research Center, August 7, 2018; John Schmitt, Elise Gould, and Josh Bivens, "America's Slow-Motion Wage Crisis: Four Decades of Slow and Unequal Growth," Economic Policy Institute, 2–3. See also U.S. Bureau of Labor Statistics, "Union Members Summary" (Economic News Release), January 20, 2022; Congressional Research Service, *Real Wage Trends, 1979 to 2019* (Washington, D.C.: Congressional Research Service, 2020).

22. Raj Chetty et al., "The Fading American Dream: Trends in Absolute Income Mobility Since 1940," *Science* 356 (2017): 398–406; Thomas DiPrete, "The Impact of Inequality on Intergenerational Mobility," *Annual Review of Sociology* 46 (2020): 379–98; Michael Hout, "Americans' Occupational Status Reflects the Status of Both of Their Parents," *Proceedings of the National Academy of Sciences* 115 (2018): 9527–32; Xi Song et al., "Long-Term Decline in Intergenerational Mobility in the United States Since the 1850s," *Proceedings of the National Academy of Sciences* 117 (2020): 251–58.

23. The U.S. Bureau of Labor Statistics defines a working poor person as someone below the poverty line who spent at least half the year either working or looking for employment. In 2018, there were roughly 7 million Americans who fell into this category. U.S. Bureau of Labor Statistics, "A Profile of the Working Poor, 2019," May 2021; Matthew Desmond, "Why Work Doesn't Work Anymore," *The New York Times Magazine,* September 11, 2018; Schmitt et al., *America's Slow-Motion Wage Crisis,* figure D.

24. The Pell Grant program for low-income college students was a $7.5 billion program during the 1980–81 academic year; its budget for the 2020–21 academic year was $26 billion (in 2020 dollars). Margaret Cahalan et al., *Indicators of Higher Education Equity in the United States: 2020 Historical Trend Report* (Washington, D.C.: The Pell Institute for the Study of Opportunity in Higher Education, Council for Opportunity in Education, and Alliance for Higher Education and Democracy of the University of Pennsylvania, 2020), 40, 43, 216; Richard Fry and Anthony Cilluffo, "A Rising Share of Undergraduates Are from Poor Families, Especially at Less Selective Colleges," Pew Research Center, May 22, 2019, 3–4; U.S. Census Bureau, Current Population Survey, 2021 Annual Social and Economic Supplement, tables PINC-03 and HINC-01; U.S. Department of Education, National Center for Education Statistics, Integrated Postsecondary Education Data System, Fall 2021, table E12. See also Stijn Broecke, Glenda Quintini, and Marieke Vandeweyer, "Wage Inequality and Cognitive Skills: Reopening the Debate," in *Education, Skills, and Technical Change: Implications for Future US GDP Growth,* eds. Charles Hulten and Valerie Ramey (Chicago: University of Chicago Press, 2018), 251–86. On international education and poverty data, see National Center for Education Statistics, "International Educational Attainment," May 2022; OECD Data, "Poverty Rate."

25. Thomas Frank, *Listen, Liberal; or, Whatever Happened to the Party of the People?* (New York: Metropolitan Books, 2016), 85–89; David Howell, "Low Pay in Rich Countries: Institutions, Bargaining Power, and Earnings Inequality in the U.S., U.K., Canada, Australia and France," Washington Center for Equitable Growth, December 2021; David Howell and Arne Kalleberg, "Declining Job Quality in the United States: Explanations and Evidence," *RSF: The Russell Sage Foundation Journal of the Social Sciences* 5 (2019): 1–53, 42.

26. Geoffrey Gilbert, "Adam Smith on the Nature and Causes of Poverty," *Review of Social Economy* 55 (1997): 273–91; John Stuart Mill, *Prin-*

ciples of Political Economy, vol. 1 (New York: Appleton, 1877), bk. 2, chap. 1.

27. Gerald Davis, *The Vanishing American Corporation: Navigating the Hazards of a New Economy* (Oakland, Calif.: Berrett-Koehler, 2016), 144. See also Howell and Kalleberg, "Declining Job Quality in the United States," 10, 22; Steven Vallas, "Platform Capitalism: What's at Stake for Workers?," *New Labor Forum* 28 (2019): 48–59.

28. Desmond, "Why Work Doesn't Work Anymore"; Howell and Kalleberg, "Declining Job Quality in the United States," 14; Rosenfeld, *You're Paid What You're Worth,* 234–37; Daisuke Wakabayashi, "Google's Shadow Work Force: Temps Who Outnumber Full-Time Employees," *The New York Times,* May 28, 2019; David Weil, *The Fissured Workplace* (Cambridge, Mass.: Harvard University Press, 2014); David Weil, "Mending the Fissured Workplace," in *What Works for Workers? Public Policies and Innovative Strategies for Low-Wage Workers,* ed. Stephanie Luce et al. (New York: Russell Sage Foundation, 2014), 108–33, 109, 111.

29. Peter Coy, "Why Are Fast Food Workers Signing Noncompete Agreements?," *The New York Times,* September 29, 2021; Rosenfeld, *You're Paid What You're Worth,* 57–67, 74–82; Alan Krueger and Orley Ashenfelter, "Theory and Evidence on Employer Collusion in the Franchise Sector," *Journal of Human Resources* (2021): 1–33; Evan Starr, J. J. Prescott, and Norman Bishara, "Noncompete Agreements in the US Labor Force," *The Journal of Law and Economics* 64 (2021): 53–84.

30. Natasha Bernal, "Uber Has Lost in the Supreme Court. Here's What Happens Next," *Wired,* February 19, 2021; The Center for European Policy Analysis (CEPA), "Gig Workers or Full Timers—Europe's Balancing Act," June 24, 2022; Pieter Haeck, "Uber Drivers Are Employees, Dutch Judge Rules," *Politico,* September 13, 2021; Len Sherman, "Why Can't Uber Make Money?," *Forbes,* December 14, 2017; Vallas, "Platform Capitalism," 48; Steven Vallas and Juliet Schor, "What Do Platforms Do? Understanding the Gig Economy," *Annual Review of Sociology* 46 (2020): 273–94. On the growth of gig work, see Lawrence Katz and Alan Krueger, "The Rise and Nature of Alternative Work Arrangements in the United States, 1995–2015," *ILR Review* 72 (2019): 382–416.

31. Lobbying totals come from Open Secrets, a nonpartisan research group tracking money in politics. See Neil Bradley, "U.S. Chamber Letter on H.R. 582, the 'Raise the Wage Act,'" U.S. Chamber of Commerce, July 11, 2019; Lee Drutman, *The Business of America Is Lobbying:*

How Corporations Became Politicized and Politics Became More Corporate (New York: Oxford University Press, 2015); Lee Drutman, "How Corporate Lobbyists Conquered American Democracy," *The Atlantic*, April 20, 2015; Sean Redmond, "Union Membership Drops to Previous Low in 2021," U.S. Chamber of Commerce, January 26, 2022; Vallas, "Platform Capitalism," 54.

32. Desmond, "Capitalism"; Jodi Kantor and Arya Sundaram, "The Rise of the Worker Productivity Score," *The New York Times*, August 14, 2022; Lamar Pierce, Daniel Snow, and Andrew McAfee, "Cleaning House: The Impact of Information Technology Monitoring on Employee Theft and Productivity," *Management Science* 61 (2015): 2299–319; Steven Vallas, Hannah Johnston, and Yana Mommadova, "Prime Suspect: Mechanisms of Labor Control at Amazon's Warehouses," *Work and Occupations* 49 (2022): 421–56; Alex Wood, *Despotism on Demand: How Power Operates in the Flexible Workplace* (Ithaca, N.Y.: Cornell University Press, 2020).

33. Suresh Naidu, Eric Posner, and Glen Weyl, "Antitrust Remedies for Labor Market Power," *Harvard Law Review* 132 (2018): 536–601; Suresh Naidu, Eric Posner, and Glen Weyl, "More and More Companies Have Monopoly Power over Workers' Wages. That's Killing the Economy," *Vox*, April 6, 2018.

34. U.S. Government Accountability Office, *Federal Social Safety Net Programs: Millions of Full-Time Workers Rely on Federal Health Care and Food Assistance Programs*, GAO-21-45 (Washington, D.C.: Government Accountability Office, 2020), 9–10.

35. SNAP data are as of February 2020 and include working adults between nineteen and sixty-four years old. Medicaid enrollment numbers include nondisabled, nonelderly adults between nineteen and sixty-four years old. U.S. Government Accountability Office, *Federal Social Safety Net Programs*, 38, 41, 59, 65; Jane Little, "Largest N.C. Employers," *Triad Business Journal*, July 30, 2020; Sean McFadden and Hilary Burns, "The Largest Employers in Massachusetts," *Boston Business Journal*, July 30, 2020; Oklahoma Department of Commerce Policy, Research and Economic Analysis Division, *Oklahoma's Largest Employers* (Oklahoma City, Okla.: Oklahoma Department of Commerce, 2020), 1.

36. The EITC is emblematic of a transformation of the American welfare state that has taken place over recent decades, with support being extended to the near and working poor and withdrawn from the deeply poor and jobless. Families just above and just below the poverty threshold today receive significantly more government aid than they did twenty years ago, but those far below the poverty line receive significantly less (Moffitt, "Deserving Poor," 741). See Center on Budget and Policy Priorities, "Policy Basics: The Earned Income Tax Credit," December 10, 2019; Congressional Research Service, *Earned Income Tax Credit (EITC)*; Zachary Parolin, Matthew Desmond, and Christopher Wimer, "Inequality Below the Poverty Line Since 1967: The Role of U.S. Welfare Policy," Princeton University, Working Paper, March 2022.

37. "Brown Introduces Bill to Boost Free Tax Preparation and Filing Services to Help Ohioans Get Full Return," Office of U.S. Senator Sherrod Brown, January 27, 2017; The Institute for a Competitive Workforce, *Community Building Through the Earned Income Tax Credit (EITC)* (Washington, D.C.: U.S. Chamber of Commerce, 2007); Steven Greenhouse, "How Walmart Persuades Its Workers Not to Unionize," *The Atlantic*, June 8, 2015; Robert Greenstein, "Greenstein: Assessing the Tax Provisions of the Bipartisan Budget and Tax Deals," Center on Budget and Policy Priorities, December 16, 2015; Pamela Herd and Donald Moynihan, *Administrative Burden: Policymaking by Other Means* (New York: Russell Sage Foundation, 2019), 205; National Restaurant Association, "Statement on the Introduction of the Raise the Wage Act of 2021," January 26, 2021; National Restaurant Association, "How to Help the Working Poor; and Problems of the Working Poor," hearings before the Subcommittee on Human Resources, 101st Congress (1989); National Restaurant Association, "National Restaurant Association Statement on Today's Labor Activities," Restaurant News Resource, September 4, 2014; Rosenfeld, *You're Paid What You're Worth*, 249; Walmart, "Walmart Foundation Teams Up with United Way and One Economy to Provide Free Tax Preparation and Filing Services," February 10, 2009.

38. Rosenfeld, *You're Paid What You're Worth*, 117, 143; Hiroko Tabuchi, "Walmart Stock Sinks After a Warning on Sales," *The New York Times*, October 14, 2015; Phil Wahba, "Walmart Takes $20 Billion Hit as Weak Forecast Scares Investors," *Fortune*, October 14, 2015. On the link between labor costs and firm profit, see John Abowd, "The Effect of Wage Bargains on the Stock Market Value of the Firm," *American Economic Review* 79 (1989): 774–800; Mirko Draca, Stephen Machin, and John Van

Reenen, "Minimum Wages and Firm Profitability," *American Economic Journal: Applied Economics* 3 (2011): 129–51.

39. Neil Bhutta et al., *Changes in U.S. Family Finances from 2016 to 2019: Evidence from the Survey of Consumer Finances* (Washington, D.C.: Board of Governors of the Federal Reserve System, 2020), 18, 40; Thorstein Veblen, *Absentee Ownership: Business Enterprise in Recent Times: The Case of America* (New Brunswick, N.J.: Transaction Publishers, 2009 [1923]); Edward Wolff, "Household Wealth Trends in the United States, 1962 to 2016: Has Middle Class Wealth Recovered?," National Bureau of Economic Research, Working Paper 24085, November 2017.

40. Juliet Schor and William Attwood-Charles, "The 'Sharing' Economy: Labor, Inequality, and Social Connections on For-Profit Platforms," *Sociology Compass* 11 (2017): 1–16, 9; Kaitlyn Tiffany, "In Amazon We Trust—But Why?," *Vox*, October 25, 2018.

41. Accountable.US, "Corporate Donations Tracker"; Valerie Wilson and William Darity, Jr., "Understanding Black-White Disparities in Labor Market Outcomes Requires Models That Account for Persistent Discrimination and Unequal Bargaining Power," Economic Policy Institute, March 25, 2022, 10.

42. Lindsey Rose Bullinger, "The Effect of Minimum Wages on Adolescent Fertility: A Nationwide Analysis," *American Journal of Public Health* 107 (2017): 447–52; Ellora Derenoncourt and Claire Montialoux, "Minimum Wages and Racial Inequality," *The Quarterly Journal of Economics* 136 (2021): 169–228; Kelli Komro et al., "The Effect of an Increased Minimum Wage on Infant Mortality and Birth Weight," *American Journal of Public Health* 106 (2016): 1514–16; Paul Leigh, Wesley Leigh, and Juan Du, "Minimum Wages and Public Health: A Literature Review," *Preventive Medicine* 118 (2019): 122–34; Kerri Raissian and Lindsey Rose Bullinger, "Money Matters: Does the Minimum Wage Affect Child Maltreatment Rates?," *Children and Youth Services Review* 72 (2017): 60–70; Joseph Sabia, M. Melinda Pitts, and Laura Argys, "Are Minimum Wages a Silent Killer? New Evidence on Drunk Driving Fatalities," *Review of Economics and Statistics* 101 (2019): 192–99; Tsu-Yu Tsao et al., "Estimating Potential Reductions in Premature Mortality in New York City from Raising the Minimum Wage to $15," *American Journal of Public Health* 106 (2016): 1036–41.

43. "Tobacco Industry Marketing," American Lung Association, December 10, 2020; Leigh et al., "Minimum Wages and Public Health"; Kelly McCarrier et al., "Associations Between Minimum Wage Policy and Access to Health Care: Evidence from the Behavioral Risk Factor Surveillance System, 1996–2007," *American Journal of Public Health* 101 (2011): 359–67; Tsao et al., "Estimating Potential Reductions in Premature Mortality in New York City from Raising the Minimum Wage to $15."

CHAPTER 4

1. Charles Tilly, *Durable Inequality* (Berkeley: University of California Press, 1998); Wright, *Class Counts,* chap. 1. The belief that we should have choices, and that when we don't, we can expect a raw deal, is anything but a radical or polarizing insight. When George Orwell, a socialist, described a poor person as someone who does not act but is acted upon, and when Friedrich Hayek, decidedly not a socialist, remarked that "nothing makes conditions more unbearable than the knowledge that no effort of ours can change them," they were essentially saying the same thing. Friedrich Hayek, *The Road to Serfdom* (New York: Routledge, 2005 [1944]), 98; Orwell, *Road to Wigan Pier,* 49.

2. Elizabeth Blackmar, *Manhattan for Rent, 1785–1850* (Ithaca, N.Y.: Cornell University Press, 1989), 199; Matthew Desmond and Nathan Wilmers, "Do the Poor Pay More for Housing? Exploitation, Profit, and Risk in Rental Markets," *American Journal of Sociology* 124 (2019): 1090–1124; Lewis Mumford, *The Culture of Cities* (New York: Harcourt, Brace, 1938), 82–86; Lewis Mumford, *The City in History: Its Origins, Its Transformations, and Its Prospects* (New York: MJF Books, 1961), 417; Riis, *How the Other Half Lives,* 11.

3. Arnold Hirsch, *Making the Second Ghetto: Race and Housing in Chicago, 1940–1960* (New York: Cambridge University Press, 1983), 29; Beryl Satter, *Family Properties: How the Struggle over Race and Real Estate Transformed Chicago and Urban America* (New York: Metropolitan Books, 2009), 5; Allan Spear, *Black Chicago: The Making of a Negro Ghetto, 1890–1920* (Chicago: University of Chicago Press, 1967), 148; Thomas Sugrue, *The Origins of the Urban Crisis: Race and Inequality in Postwar Detroit* (Princeton, N.J.: Princeton University Press, 2005 [1996]), 54; Isabel Wilkerson, *The Warmth of Other Suns: The Epic Story of America's Great Migration* (New York: Vintage, 2010), 270–71.

4. Marx, "The Eighteenth Brumaire of Louis Bonaparte"; Wright, *Interrogating Inequality,* 49.

5. U.S. Census Bureau, American Community Survey, 1985–2022; U.S. Department of Housing and Urban Development, "40th Percentile Fair Market Rent, 1985–2022."

6. Abha Bhattarai, Chris Alcantara, and Andrew Van Dam, "Rents Are Rising Everywhere. See How Much Prices Are Up in Your Area," *The Washington Post,* April 21, 2022; U.S. Census Bureau, "Housing Vacancies and Homeownership (CPS/HVS)," table 4.

7. Between 2011 and 2017, owners of multifamily properties (with five or more units) saw their rental revenues increase by 24 percent, but their expenses increased by only 18 percent. Landlords who owned properties with market valuations in the bottom twenty-fifth percentile, properties located primarily in poor neighborhoods, saw their rental revenues increase by 47 percent between 2012 and 2018, but their operating expenses increased by only 14 percent. Author's calculations, U.S. Census Bureau, Rental Housing Finance Survey, 2012 and 2018.

8. Desmond and Wilmers, "Do the Poor Pay More for Housing?" The version of the Rental Housing Finance Survey (RHFS) we used excluded single-unit rental properties. The most recent version of the RHFS (2018) includes these properties and still shows higher landlord profit margins in poor neighborhoods.

9. Here, a poor neighborhood is a census tract with poverty rates in excess of 27 percent. A rich neighborhood is one with poverty rates below 8 percent, and a middle-class neighborhood has poverty rates in between.

10. Landlords in distressed neighborhoods face higher repair costs and more missed payments than their peers in more affluent areas. Those anticipating risk may price up their housing units, just as landlords who have themselves incurred losses may recoup by asking future renters to pay for the misfortunes of past tenants, socializing risk. Perceived market risk and consumer exploitation have long gone hand in hand. When the Federal Housing Administration redlined Black neighborhoods, it justified the decision by claiming that insuring mortgages in those communities was too risky. You see the same pattern in pawnshops, check cashing stations, payday lenders, and rent-to-own businesses that cater to low-income consumers and justify high-interest charges by pointing to anticipated risk. Consumer exploitation is made

possible when a disadvantaged group is deemed risky and forced to pay a social price. David Caplovitz, *The Poor Pay More: Consumer Practices of Low-Income Families* (New York: Free Press, 1967 [1963]); Satter, *Family Properties;* Sugrue, *Origins of the Urban Crisis.*

The perceived risk that helps drive higher rental profits in poor neighborhoods may also help ensure they remain high by preventing investors from flocking to this market segment. Typically, when there are higher profits to be had in a marketplace with low barriers to entry, entrepreneurs find their way to it. With time, this can erase the lucrative advantage on which they originally sought to capitalize. However, it may be the case that new entrants to the rental market, and even experienced investors operating in nonpoor sectors of the city, are generally unaware of the higher profits that can be extracted from tenants in disadvantaged communities. Conventional wisdom about renting in poor communities may emphasize the risk and not the reward, a misrepresentation that those profiting most from the situation have no incentive to correct. Poor neighborhoods also possess strong profit-making capacity precisely because they lack amenity value. Even if investors sense the opportunity, many have no desire to participate in this challenging and morally ambiguous business. As one real estate investor bluntly put it, "Yes, you can make money in a bad neighborhood, but you also can face some problems no civilized person should have to face. You're better off looking for the worst house in the best neighborhood." Carleton Sheets, *Real Estate: The World's Greatest Wealth Builder* (Chicago: Bonus Books, 1998), 232.

11. U.S. Census Bureau, American Community Survey 2019 5-Year Estimates, tables B25031 and B17020. See also Geoff Boeing and Paul Waddell, "New Insights into Rental Housing Markets Across the United States: Web Scraping and Analyzing Craigslist Rental Listings," *Journal of Planning Education and Research* 37 (2017): 457–76.

12. Philip Garboden, "Amateur Real Estate Investing," *Journal of Urban Affairs* (2021): 1–20; Devin Rutan and Matthew Desmond, "The Concentrated Geography of Eviction," *The Annals of the American Academy of Political and Social Science* 693 (2021): 64–81.

13. Desmond, *Evicted,* part 3. Hope Harvey et al., "Forever Homes and Temporary Stops: Housing Search Logics and Residential Selection," *Social Forces* 98 (2020): 1498–523.

14. Lincoln Quillian, John Lee, and Brandon Honoré, "Racial Dis-

crimination in the US Housing and Mortgage Lending Markets: A Quantitative Review of Trends, 1976–2016," *Race and Social Problems* 12 (2020): 13–28. See also Maria Krysan and Kyle Crowder, *Cycle of Segregation: Social Processes and Residential Stratification* (New York: Russell Sage Foundation, 2017); Douglas Massey, "Racial Discrimination in Housing: A Moving Target," *Social Problems* 52 (2005): 148–51.

15. In the fall of 2021, Lakia Higbee's home had an estimated value of $93,900, according to realtor.com. To estimate her monthly mortgage payment, inclusive of taxes and fees, I made the following assumptions: that Lakia would have put down 7 percent for the down payment for a thirty-year fixed mortgage at 3.5 percent interest, which was based on a credit score between 700 and 719. I didn't ask Lakia to provide her credit score. But even if it was much lower (620–639), her estimated monthly mortgage payment ($622), inclusive of taxes and fees, would still have been considerably lower than her rent. Matthew Desmond, " 'The Moratorium Saved Us. It Really Did,' " *The New York Times*, September 30, 2021.

16. Jacob Faber, "Segregation and the Geography of Creditworthiness: Racial Inequality in a Recovered Mortgage Market," *Housing Policy Debate* 28 (2018): 215–47; Desmond, "House Rules"; Baradaran, *Color of Money*, 106–9; Matthew Goldstein, "Where a Little Mortgage Goes a Long Way," *The New York Times*, August 2, 2020; Linna Zhu and Rita Ballesteros, "Making FHA Small-Dollar Mortgages More Accessible Could Make Homeownership More Equitable," *Urban Wire*, Urban Institute, April 22, 2021.

17. Mehrsa Baradaran, *How the Other Half Banks* (Cambridge, Mass.: Harvard University Press, 2015), 103–7; Caplovitz, *The Poor Pay More*, xv; John Caskey, *Fringe Banking: Check-Cashing Outlets, Pawnshops, and the Poor* (New York: Russell Sage Foundation, 1994), 13; Rudolf Goldscheid, "A Sociological Approach to Problems of Public Finance," in *Classics in the Theory of Public Finance*, eds. Richard Musgrave and Alan Peacock (London: Macmillan, 1958), 202–13; Melanie Tebbutt, *Making Ends Meet: Pawnbroking and Working-Class Credit* (New York: St. Martin's Press, 1983), 2.

18. Caskey, *Fringe Banking*, 87–89; Peter Smith, Shezal Babar, and Rebecca Borné, *Banks Must Stop Gouging Consumers During the COVID-19 Crisis* (Washington, D.C.: Center for Responsible Lending, 2020).

19. Baradaran, *How the Other Half Banks*, 141–43; Matthew Goldberg,

"Survey: Free Checking Accounts on the Rise as Total ATM Fees Fall," Bankrate, October 20, 2021.

20. Baradaran, *How the Other Half Banks,* 5–12; Emily Flitter, "'Banking While Black': How Cashing a Check Can Be a Minefield," *The New York Times,* June 18, 2020; Laurie Goodman and Bing Bai, "Traditional Mortgage Denial Metrics May Misrepresent Racial and Ethnic Discrimination," *Urban Wire: Housing and Housing Finance,* Urban Institute, August 23, 2018; Raheem Hanifa, "High-Income Black Homeowners Receive Higher Interest Rates Than Low-Income White Homeowners," Harvard Joint Center for Housing Studies, February 16, 2021; Jacob Rugh and Douglas Massey, "Racial Segregation and the American Foreclosure Crisis," *American Sociological Review* 75 (2010): 629–51.

21. Federal Deposit Insurance Corporation, *How America Banks: Household Use of Banking and Financial Services,* 2019 FDIC Survey, October 2020, 12–13. See also Lisa Servon, *The Unbanking of America: How the New Middle Class Survives* (New York: Houghton Mifflin Harcourt, 2017).

22. Mario Small et al., "Banks, Alternative Institutions and the Spatial-Temporal Ecology of Racial Inequality in US Cities," *Nature Human Behaviour* (2021): 1–7; Frederick Wherry and Parijat Chakrabarti, "Accounting for Credit," *Annual Review of Sociology* 48 (2022): 131–47.

23. Tony Armstrong, "The Cost of Being Unbanked: Hundreds of Dollars a Year, Always One Step Behind," NerdWallet, September 13, 2016; Baradaran, *How the Other Half Banks,* 1, 138–39; Caskey, *Fringe Banking;* Meghan Greene et al., *The FinHealth Spend Report 2021: What Financially Coping and Vulnerable Americans Pay for Everyday Financial Services* (Chicago: Financial Health Network, 2021), table 6; Lisa Servon, "RiteCheck 12," Public Books, July 10, 2013; Walmart, "Check Cashing," Walmart.com. Owing to the pandemic, 2020 was an unusual year, but the revenue from check cashing was roughly equivalent to what it was the year prior ($1.66 billion). People spent $1.73 billion cashing checks in 2018. Personal correspondence, Meghan Greene, director of Research for Financial Health Network, November 11, 2021.

24. Tara Siegel Bernard, "Apps Will Get You Paid Early, for a Price," *The New York Times,* October 2, 2020; Laurence Darmiento, "The Hidden Costs Behind the Cash Advance App Dave," *Los Angeles Times,* May 19, 2022; Emily Stewart, "Buy Now, Pay Later Sounds Too Good to Be True Because It Is," *Vox,* August 11, 2022; Evan Weinberger, "Earned-

Wage Access Products Face Fresh Scrutiny from CFPB, States," *Bloomberg Law*, February 3, 2022.

25. The estimate for the number of consumers who are either credit invisible or who have unscored credit records—45 million in total—comes from Kenneth Brevoort, Philipp Grimm, and Michelle Kambara, *Data Point: Credit Invisibles* (Washington, D.C.: Consumer Financial Protection Bureau, May 2015). More recently, the credit reporting company Experian published a study (using a different method) that put the number at 49 million. See Experian, *2022 State of Alternative Credit Data* (Costa Mesa, Calif.: Experian, 2022).

How is it possible that so many Americans lack a credit score? Because many of the bills poor people pay aren't tracked by credit rating agencies. If you pay your mortgage bill on time, that can improve your credit score, but making consistent rent payments typically does nothing to build credit. Car loans? Reported to credit bureaus. Credit card payments? Reported. Utility bills? Usually not reported. Cell phone bills? Usually not. That is, unless you miss a payment. Then your landlord, utility company, or cell phone provider may refer your case to a debt collection agency, which does affect your credit. Credit bureaus seem to notice the poor only when they fall short. See Consumer Financial Protection Bureau, "Your Tenant and Debt Collection Rights," September 23, 2021; Consumer Financial Protection Bureau, "CFPB Study Shows Financial Product Could Help Consumers Build Credit," July 13, 2020; Caroline Ratcliffe et al., "Delinquent Debt in America," Urban Institute, July 30, 2014, 1–2, 4, 7–8; Michele Scarbrough, "Who Are the Credit Invisible?," Consumer Financial Protection Bureau, December 12, 2016; Lisa Stifler and Leslie Parrish, "Debt Collection and Debt Buying" in *The State of Lending in America and Its Impact on Households* (Durham, N.C.: Center for Responsible Lending, 2014), 2–4, 6; Frederick Wherry, Kristin Seefeldt, and Anthony Alvarez, *Credit Where It's Due: Rethinking Financial Citizenship* (New York: Russell Sage Foundation, 2019), 2, 25.

26. Barbara Kiviat, "The Art of Deciding with Data: Evidence from How Employers Translate Credit Reports into Hiring Decisions," *Socio-Economic Review* 17 (2019): 283–309; Barbara Kiviat, "The Moral Limits of Predictive Practices: The Case of Credit-Based Insurance Scores," *American Sociological Review* 84 (2019): 1134–58; Marion Fourcade, "Ordinal Citizenship," *The British Journal of Sociology* 72 (2021): 154–73.

27. Baradaran, *How the Other Half Banks,* 109; Center for Responsible Lending, "Map of U.S. Payday Interest Rates," March 23, 2021. As payday lending has migrated online—roughly half of all such loans are now executed over the Internet—and some states have beefed up regulations, the number of payday loan stores has declined from around 24,000 at its peak in the mid-2000s to roughly 13,700. That number still exceeds the combined number of branch locations for Wells Fargo and Bank of America. An additional 4,000 or so stores offer auto title loans but not payday loans. Bureau of Consumer Financial Protection, "Payday Vehicle Title, and Certain High-Cost Installment Loans," 12 CFR Part 1041, Docket No. CFPB-2019-0006, July 2020, 8; Pew Charitable Trusts, "Auto Title Loans: Market Practices and Borrowers' Experiences," March 2015; Statista, "Leading Banks in the United States in 2021, by Number of Branches," May 2022.

28. Consumer Financial Protection Bureau, "What Are the Costs and Fees for a Payday Loan?," last reviewed January 17, 2022; Consumer Financial Protection Bureau, "What Is a Payday Loan?," June 2, 2017; Pew Charitable Trusts, "Payday Loan Facts and the CFPB's Impact," May 2016.

29. Kathleen Burke et al., "Data Point: Payday Lending," CFPB Office of Research, 2014; Pew Charitable Trusts, "Payday Loan Facts." See also Baradaran, *How the Other Half Banks,* 101–12; Jeannette Bennett, "Fast Cash and Payday Loans," Economic Research, FRED, Federal Reserve Bank of St. Louis, April 2019; Consumer Financial Protection Bureau, "Consumer Use of Payday, Auto Title, and Pawn Loans," May 5, 2021; Pew Charitable Trusts, "Payday Lending in America: Who Borrows, Where They Borrow, and Why," 2021; Susan Urahn et al., "Fraud and Abuse Online: Harmful Practices in Internet Payday Lending," Pew Charitable Trusts, 2014.

30. Nick Bourke, "Momentum Is Building for Small-Dollar Loans," Pew Charitable Trusts, September 12, 2018; Pew Charitable Trusts, "Standards Needed for Safe Small Installment Loans from Banks, Credit Unions," February 15, 2018.

31. Personal communication, Alex Horowitz, principal officer, Consumer Finance Project, Pew Charitable Trusts, November 9, 2021; Pew Charitable Trusts, "Payday Lending in America: Policy Solutions," October 30, 2013, 18, 28; Pew Charitable Trusts, "Trial, Error, and Success in Colorado's Payday Lending Reforms," December 2014, tables 1 and 3.

32. Here I say "up to $9.8 billion" because that figure combines the estimated revenues from single-payment payday loans ($4.5 billion) with revenue from installment loans to "financially vulnerable" households ($5.3 billion). This assumes that all installment lending to those households involves payday lending, which is untenable. The true number likely lies somewhere between $4.5 and $9.8 billion, likely closer to the larger end of the scale, since so much of the payday lending business relies on multiple payments. The Financial Health Network, which reported these figures, uses its own methodology to identify "financially vulnerable" households based on eight indicators, such as having a prime credit score, paying bills on time, and carrying manageable debt. These indicators sum up to 100 possible points; those with scores below 40 are considered financially vulnerable. See Greene et al., *The FinHealth Spend Report 2021,* table A1. See also Bennett, "Fast Cash and Payday Loans"; Pew Charitable Trusts, "Payday Loan Facts and the CFPB's Impact: Fact Sheet," January 14, 2016; Peter Smith, Shezal Babar, and Rebecca Borné, *Banks Must Stop Gouging Consumers During the COVID-19 Crisis;* James Baldwin, *Nobody Knows My Name* (New York: Dial Press, 1961), 59.

33. Keeanga-Yamahtta Taylor, *Race for Profit: How Banks and the Real Estate Industry Undermined Black Homeownership* (Chapel Hill: University of North Carolina Press, 2019). See also Baradaran, *How the Other Half Banks,* 3; Tressie McMillan Cottom, "Where Platform Capitalism and Racial Capitalism Meet: The Sociology of Race and Racism in the Digital Society," *Sociology of Race and Ethnicity* 6 (2020): 441–49; Nathaniel Popper, "Big Banks Play Key Role in Financing Payday Lenders," *Los Angeles Times,* September 15, 2010; Wherry et al., *Credit Where It's Due,* 102.

34. While a graduate student at Princeton, Gillian Slee used the phrase "the best bad option" in a paper we wrote together. I appropriate it here with her permission.

35. Sumit Agarwal, Brent Ambrose, and Moussa Diop, "Do Minimum Wage Increases Benefit Intended Households? Evidence from the Performance of Residential Leases," Federal Reserve Bank of Philadelphia, Working Paper 19-28, July 2019. See also Atsushi Yamagishi, "Minimum Wages and Housing Rents: Theory and Evidence," *Regional Science and Urban Economics* 87 (2021): 1–13. On the history of landlords raising rents following wage increases, see Blackmar, *Manhattan for Rent;* Mumford, *City in History.*

36. Tommy Orange, *There There* (New York: Alfred A. Knopf, 2018), 104.

37. Social science is not innocent here. For far too long, the poverty research industrial complex, and much of public policy along with it, has focused on collecting individual-level data about the poor, particularly through massive, multiyear surveys. From those one-sided data, we have built an evidence base about inequality devoid of serious empirical treatments of power and exploitation. The individual-level data simply don't think in those terms. For example, if you asked me to explain someone's risk of eviction, I could draw on the best social-scientific data we have, databases that cost tens of millions of dollars, and answer that question by referencing people's race and gender and family status—as if the person evicted herself. Yale Law professor Harold Koh once said, "When you cannot measure what is important, you tend to make important what you can measure." Social science has measured individual variables of vulnerable populations, making this information paramount. I hope the next generation of inequality scholars makes data about power, ownership, and exploitation more central. See Harold Koh, "The Just, Speedy, and Inexpensive Determination of Every Action?," *University of Pennsylvania Law Review* 162 (2014): 1525–42.

CHAPTER 5

1. Matthew Desmond, "Can America's Middle Class Be Saved from a New Depression?," *The New York Times Magazine,* May 26, 2020; Dylan Matthews, "The Coronavirus Unemployment Insurance Plan, Explained," *Vox,* March 29, 2020.

2. Peter Ganong, Pascal Noel, and Joseph Vavra, "US Unemployment Insurance Replacement Rates During the Pandemic," *Journal of Public Economics* 191 (2020): 1–12; U.S. Chamber of Commerce, "U.S. Chamber Calls for Ending $300 Weekly Supplemental Unemployment Benefits to Address Labor Shortages," May 7, 2021; Matthews, "Coronavirus Unemployment Insurance Plan, Explained."

3. Patrick Cooney and H. Luke Shaefer, "Material Hardship and Mental Health Following the COVID-19 Relief Bill and American Rescue Plan Act," Poverty Solutions, University of Michigan, May 2021; John Creamer et al., "Poverty in the United States: 2021" (Washington: U.S. Bureau of the Census, 2022), table B-2; Jason DeParle, "Pandemic

Aid Programs Spur a Record Drop in Poverty," *The New York Times,* July 28, 2021; Dylan Matthews, "How the US Won the Economic Recovery," *Vox,* April 30, 2021; Laura Wheaton, Linda Giannarelli, and Ilham Dehry, "2021 Poverty Projections: Assessing the Impact of Benefits and Stimulus Measures," Urban Institute, July 28, 2021.

4. Adam Chandler, "No, Unemployment Benefits Don't Stop People from Returning to Work," *The Washington Post,* May 13, 2021; "Stories from the Great American Labor Shortage," *The New York Times, The Daily,* August 3, 2021; Jillian Kay Melchior, "Covid Unemployment Relief Makes Help Impossible to Find," *The Wall Street Journal,* April 23, 2021.

5. These figures pertain to nonfarm work. Alaska ended the $300 weekly unemployment insurance in June 2021 but retained other enhanced benefits. Sarah Chaney Cambon and Danny Dougherty, "States That Cut Unemployment Benefits Saw Limited Impact on Job Growth," *The Wall Street Journal,* September 1, 2021; Ben Casselman, "Cutoff of Jobless Benefits Is Found to Get Few Back to Work," *The New York Times,* August 20, 2021; Kyle Coombs et al., "Early Withdrawal of Pandemic Unemployment Insurance: Effects on Earnings, Employment and Consumption," Columbia University, Working Paper, August 2021; U.S. Bureau of Labor Statistics, "State Employment and Unemployment Summary," August 20, 2021.

6. One study did find that throughout the summer of 2021, employment rates rose faster in states that cut benefits, but the effect was small. Joseph Altonji et al., "Employment Effects of Unemployment Insurance Generosity During the Pandemic," Yale University, July 14, 2020; David Autor, "Good News: There's a Labor Shortage," *The New York Times,* September 4, 2021; Alexander Bartik et al., "Measuring the Labor Market at the Onset of the COVID-19 Crisis," National Bureau of Economic Research, Working Paper 27613, July 2020; Arindrajit Dube, "The Impact of the Federal Pandemic Unemployment Compensation on Employment: Evidence from the Household Pulse Survey," University of Massachusetts, Amherst, Working Paper, July 31, 2020; Michele Evermore and Marokey Sawo, "Unemployed Workers and Benefit 'Replacement Rate': An Expanded Analysis," National Employment Law Project and Groundwork Collaborative, August 2020.

7. Joseph Townsend, *A Dissertation on the Poor Laws, By a Well-Wisher of Mankind* (Berkeley: University of California Press, 1971 [1786]), 13–14.

8. Karl Polanyi, *The Great Transformation: The Political and Economic Origins of Our Time* (Boston: Beacon Press, 2001 [1944]), 81, 114, 147. See also Desmond, "Capitalism"; Robin Einhorn, "Slavery and the Politics of Taxation in the Early United States," *Studies in American Political Development* 14 (2000): 156–83; Paul Finkelman, *Supreme Injustice: Slavery in the Nation's Highest Court* (Cambridge, Mass.: Harvard University Press, 2018); Mark Graber, *Dred Scott and the Problem of Constitutional Evil* (New York: Cambridge University Press, 2006); Thomas Malthus, *An Essay on the Principle of Population,* McMaster University Archive for the History of Economic Thought, 1798; Paul Starr, *Entrenchment: Wealth, Power, and the Constitution of Democratic Societies* (New Haven, Conn.: Yale University Press, 2019).

9. "Text of President Clinton's Announcement on Welfare Legislation," *The New York Times,* August 1, 1996; Council of Economic Advisers, *Expanding Work Requirements in Non-Cash Welfare Programs* (Washington, D.C.: The White House, July 2018); Dray, *There Is Power in a Union*; University of Chicago, General Social Survey, NORC, 2018; Martin Gilens, *Why Americans Hate Welfare: Race, Media, and the Politics of Antipoverty Policy* (Chicago: University of Chicago Press, 1999), 8; Nancy Fraser and Linda Gordon, "A Genealogy of Dependency: Tracing a Keyword of the U.S. Welfare State," *Signs: Journal of Women in Culture and Society* 19 (1994): 309–36; Josh Levin, *The Queen: The Forgotten Life Behind an American Myth* (New York: Back Bay Books, 2019), 85, 87; Charles Murray, *Losing Ground: American Social Policy, 1950–1980* (New York: Basic Books, 1985), 9; Margaret Somers and Fred Block, "From Poverty to Perversity: Ideas, Markets, and Institutions over 200 Years of Welfare Debate," *American Sociological Review* 70 (2005): 260–87.

10. Jazmin Brown-Iannuzzi et al., "Wealthy Whites and Poor Blacks: Implicit Associations Between Racial Groups and Wealth Predict Explicit Opposition Toward Helping the Poor," *Journal of Experimental Social Psychology* 82 (2019): 26–34; General Social Survey, "Hard Working—Lazy," 2021; Gilens, *Why Americans Hate Welfare;* John Levi Martin and Matthew Desmond, "Political Position and Social Knowledge," *Sociological Forum* 25 (2010): 1–26; University of Chicago, General Social Survey, NORC, 1990–2018; Suzanne Mettler, *The Government-Citizen Disconnect* (New York: Russell Sage Foundation, 2018), 76; Rosenthal, "Submerged for Some?," 4.

11. Malthus, quoted in Somers and Block, "From Poverty to Perversity," 273; *The New Yorker, Politics and More Podcast*, "The Child Tax Credit: One Small Step Toward Universal Basic Income?" September 6, 2021.

12. Arcenis Rojas and Ann Foster, "Program Participation and Spending Patterns of Families Receiving Government Means-Tested Assistance," *Monthly Labor Review*, U.S. Bureau of Labor Statistics, January 2018; U.S. Bureau of Labor Statistics, "Table 1101. Quintiles of Income Before Taxes: Annual Expenditure Means, Shares, Standard Errors, and Coefficients of Variation, Consumer Expenditure Surveys, 2020," September 2021; Thorstein Veblen, *The Theory of the Leisure Class* (London: Macmillan, 1912 [1899]), 44.

13. Stacia West et al., *Preliminary Analysis: SEED's First Year* (Stockton, Calif.: Stockton Economic Empowerment Demonstration, 2021). In April 2009 the federal government expanded the Supplemental Nutrition Assistance Program as part of the American Recovery and Reinvestment Act, motivated by the Great Recession. On average, SNAP recipients saw their per-person food stamp benefits increase to $125 from around $100 a month, which amounted to the largest onetime increase in the history of the program. Overnight, a family of four suddenly had $100 more in food stamps each month. How'd they spend it? They used increased aid primarily to buy more groceries, and with their freed-up income, they tended to upgrade their housing and invest in social mobility opportunities (by enrolling in community college, for example). There was no evidence that raising SNAP benefits led people to increase tobacco or alcohol consumption. Jiyoon Kim, "Do SNAP Participants Expand Non-Food Spending When They Receive More SNAP Benefits?—Evidence from the 2009 SNAP Benefits Increase," *Food Policy* 65 (2016): 9–20. Other studies have found that when EITC stipends increase, low-income working parents tend to respond by saving more and paying off debt. Lauren Jones and Katherine Michelmore, "The Impact of the Earned Income Tax Credit on Household Finances," *Journal of Policy Analysis and Management* 37 (2018): 521–45; H. Luke Shaefer, Xiaoqing Song, and Trina Williams Shanks, "Do Single Mothers in the United States Use the Earned Income Tax Credit to Reduce Unsecured Debt?," *Review of Economics of the Household* 11 (2013): 659–80.

14. Vanetta is a pseudonym.

15. Mary Jo Bane and David Ellwood, *Welfare Realities: From Rhetoric* *to Reform* (Cambridge, Mass.: Harvard University Press, 1994), 33, 40, 95–96; Greg Duncan, Martha Hill, and Saul Hoffman, "Welfare Dependence Within and Across Generations," *Science* 239 (1988): 467–71; La-Donna Pavetti, *The Dynamics of Welfare and Work: Exploring the Process by Which Women Work Their Way Off Welfare*, PhD Dissertation (Cambridge, Mass.: Harvard University, 1993), 29.

16. Desmond, "House Rules"; Jay Shambaugh, Lauren Bauer, and Audrey Breitwieser, "Who Is Poor in the United States? Examining the Characteristics and Workforce Participation of Impoverished Americans," Brookings Institution, October 2017, 1–10.

17. Gilbert Crouse and Suzanne Macartney, *Welfare Indicators and Risk Factors: Eighteenth Report to Congress* (Washington, D.C.: U.S. Department of Health and Human Services, 2021), 21; Internal Revenue Service, "EITC Participation Rate by States Tax Years 2011 Through 2018," January 15, 2021; Jennifer Haley et al., "Medicaid/CHIP Participation Reached 93.7 Percent Among Eligible Children in 2016," *Health Affairs* 37 (2018): 1194–99, 1194; Pamela Herd and Donald Moynihan, *Administrative Burden: Policymaking by Other Means* (New York: Russell Sage Foundation, 2019), 6–7; Sarah Lauffer and Alma Vigil, *Trends in Supplemental Nutrition Assistance Program Participation Rates: Fiscal Year 2016 to Fiscal Year 2018* (Washington, D.C.: U.S. Department of Agriculture, 2021), 3.

18. Mettler, *Government-Citizen Disconnect*, 49; Robert Moffitt, "An Economic Model of Welfare Stigma," *American Economic Review* 73 (1983): 1023–35.

19. These dollar values assume that the average claim amount of eligible households that didn't claim benefits would have been the same as those that did. I used program participation numbers and benefit amounts prior to program and enrollment changes that occurred during the COVID-19 pandemic. EITC participation rates are from tax year 2018; program participation and average benefit amounts are from tax year 2019. SNAP participation rates and average benefit amounts are from fiscal year 2018. "Government Health Insurance" indicates 2019 participation rates for Medicaid/Children's Health Insurance Program (CHIP)—Child Medicaid, inclusive of CHIP participation; median benefit amounts are also from 2019 but do not include CHIP. Enrollment data are from December 2019 and include data from the forty-nine states that reported enrollment by age group. Adult Medicaid participation rates are estimated from parent participation in Medicaid/CHIP in

2019; median benefit amounts are from 2019 for nondisabled adults under sixty-five not covered under Medicaid expansion. Enrollment data are for adults from December 2019 and include data from the forty-nine states that reported enrollment by age group. Disabled adults, elderly individuals, and those covered under expansion have higher median per-enrollee expenditures, which means the estimated total of unclaimed government health insurance is an underestimate. Unemployment insurance participation rates are averaged from 2002 to 2015; benefit amounts are from 2019. Participation was decreasing over time in this period, which means my estimate of unclaimed unemployment insurance also likely undershoots the true mark. SSI participation rates are from 2016, and enrollment data and average benefit amounts are from 2019.

Combining survey and administrative data, which I have done here, can overestimate take-up rates, which likely makes my estimate of the total value of unclaimed benefits conservative. See Stéphane Auray and David Fuller, "Eligibility, Experience Rating, and Unemployment Insurance Take-Up," *Quantitative Economics* 11 (2020): 1059–107, 1061; Centers for Medicare and Medicaid Services, "Medicaid Per Capita Expenditures," October 2021; Centers for Medicare and Medicaid Services, "Medicaid and CHIP Enrollment Trends Snapshot Through June 2020," August 31, 2020; Crouse and Macartney, *Welfare Indicators and Risk Factors,* 23; Herd and Moynihan, *Administrative Burden,* 6; Internal Revenue Service, "Statistics for Tax Returns with the Earned Income Tax Credit (EITC)—2019 Tax Returns Processed in 2020 by State with EITC Claims," March 10, 2022; Internal Revenue Service, "EITC Participation Rate by States Tax Years 2011 to 2018," March 10, 2022; Jennifer Haley et al., "Uninsurance Rose Among Children and Parents in 2019," Urban Institute, 2021, table B.1; Sarah Lauffer and Alma Vigil, *Trends in Supplemental Nutrition Assistance Program Participation Rates: Fiscal Year 2016 to Fiscal Year 2018* (Washington, D.C.: U.S. Department of Agriculture, 2021), xiii; Social Security Administration, "SSI Monthly Statistics, 2019," January 2020, table 1; U.S. Department of Agriculture, "SNAP Data Tables," August 12, 2022; Ben Sommers et al., *Understanding Participation Rates in Medicaid: Implications for the Affordable Care Act* (Washington, D.C.: Department of Health and Human Services, 2012), 4–5; U.S. Department of Labor, "Monthly Program and Financial Data," July 7, 2022.

20. Arthur Delaney and Michael McAuliff, "Paul Ryan Wants 'Welfare Reform Round 2,'" *Huffington Post,* March 20, 2012.

21. Here, "homeowner subsidies" refers to the mortgage interest deduction ($24.73 billion), the deduction of state and local property taxes on owner-occupied homes ($6.45 billion), the exclusion for capital gains ($39.45 billion), and the exclusion for imputed rent ($123.21 billion) for fiscal year 2020. Office of Management and Budget, *Analytical Perspectives: Budget of the U.S. Government Fiscal Year 2022* (Washington, D.C.: Office of Management and Budget, 2021), 109; Office of Management and Budget, "Historical Tables," table 3.2. See also Desmond, "House Rules"; Joint Committee on Taxation, *Estimates of Federal Tax Expenditures for Fiscal Years 2020–2024* (Washington, D.C.: Joint Committee on Taxation, 2020), 27–35.

22. Mettler, *Government-Citizen Disconnect,* 4, 45, 48. See also Christopher Howard, *The Welfare State Nobody Knows: Debunking Myths About US Social Policy* (Princeton, N.J.: Princeton University Press, 2008), chap. 1. For international welfare state comparisons, see also Irwin Garfinkel, Lee Rainwater, and Timothy Smeeding, *Wealth and Welfare States: Is America a Laggard or Leader?* (New York: Oxford University Press, 2010); Jacob Hacker, *The Divided Welfare State: The Battle over Public and Private Social Benefits in the United States* (New York: Cambridge University Press, 2002); Jacob Hacker, "Bringing the Welfare State Back In: The Promise (and Perils) of the New Social Welfare History," *Journal of Policy History* 17 (2005): 125–54.

23. Mettler, *Government-Citizen Disconnect,* 67, 71; Heather McGhee, *The Sum of Us: What Racism Costs Everyone and How We Can Prosper Together* (New York: One World, 2021), 45.

24. Congressional Budget Office, *Federal Subsidies for Health Insurance Coverage for People Under 65: 2022 to 2032* (Washington, D.C.: Congress of the United States, June 2022); Congressional Research Service, *Worker Participation in Employer-Sponsored Pensions: Data in Brief* (Washington, D.C.: U.S. Government Printing Office, 2021), 4; Gilens, *Why Americans Hate Welfare,* 3; Jonathan Gruber, "The Tax Exclusion for Employer-Sponsored Health Insurance," *National Tax Journal* 64 (2011): 511–30; Kaiser Family Foundation, *Health Insurance Coverage of the Total Population* (Washington, D.C.: Kaiser Family Foundation, 2019); Mettler, *Government-Citizen Disconnect,* 4, 37, 58–61, 63; Mettler, *Submerged State,* 10; Nicholas Turner, "Tax Expenditures for Education," Department of the Treasury, Office of Tax Analysis, Working Paper 113, November 2016, table 1.

25. Congressional Budget Office, *The Budget and Economic Outlook: 2021 to 2031* (Washington, D.C.: Congress of the United States, 2021), 19–20; Congressional Budget Office, *Health Care* (Washington, D.C.: Congress of the United States, 2021); Kaiser Family Foundation, *Health Insurance Coverage of the Total Population;* Social Security Administration, *FY 2021 Congressional Justification* (Washington, D.C.: Social Security Administration, 2021); "Gross Domestic Product for Russian Federation," FRED, Federal Reserve Bank of St. Louis, 2022.

26. By "middle-class families" I mean those in the middle quintile of the income distribution. Congressional Budget Office, *The Distribution of Major Tax Expenditures in 2019* (Washington, D.C.: Congress of the United States, 2021). The FY 2023 military and national defense budget is expected to exceed $838 billion. Congressional Budget Office, "Congressional Budget Office Cost Estimate: H.R. 7900, National Defense Authorization Act for Fiscal Year 2023, at a Glance," July 6, 2022.

27. Congressional Budget Office, *The Budget and Economic Outlook: 2021 to 2031,* 19–20; Congressional Budget Office, *Health Care;* Kaiser Family Foundation, *Health Insurance Coverage of the Total Population;* Social Security Administration, *FY 2021 Congressional Justification;* Congressional Budget Office, *Distribution of Major Tax Expenditures in 2019;* Congressional Research Service, *Worker Participation in Employer-Sponsored Pensions,* 4; Molly Michelmore, *Tax and Spend: The Welfare State, Tax Politics, and the Limits of American Liberalism* (Philadelphia: University of Pennsylvania Press, 2012), 1; Richard Reeves, *Dream Hoarders: How the American Upper Middle Class Is Leaving Everyone Else in the Dust, Why That Is a Problem, and What to Do About It* (Washington, D.C.: Brookings Institution, 2017).

28. Emmanuel Saez and Gabriel Zucman, *The Triumph of Injustice: How the Rich Dodge Taxes and How to Make Them Pay* (New York: Norton, 2019), 13–16; Internal Revenue Service, *IRS Provides Tax Inflation Adjustments for Tax Year 2020* (Washington, D.C.: U.S. Department of the Treasury, 2019).

29. Howard, *Welfare State Nobody Knows;* Christopher Howard, *The Hidden Welfare State* (Princeton, N.J.: Princeton University Press, 1999); Suzanne Mettler, "Making What Government Does Apparent to Citizens: Policy Feedback Effects, Their Limitations, and How They Might be Facilitated," *The Annals of the American Academy of Political and Social Science* 685 (2019): 30–46, 35; Mettler, *Submerged State,* 42–43.

30. Mettler, "Making What Government Does Apparent to Citizens," 40–41, 45; Mettler, *Submerged State,* 18.

31. Reeves, *Dream Hoarders,* 5–6.

32. Daniel Kahneman and Amos Tversky, "Prospect Theory: An Analysis of Decision Under Risk," *Econometrica* 47 (1979): 263–92.

33. Monica Prasad, "Filing Your Taxes Is an Expensive Time Sink. That's Not an Accident," *The Atlantic,* April 4, 2019.

34. Following Okun (*Equality and Efficiency,* 99), we can view both tax breaks and welfare stipends as "negative taxes," since both function as government payments to spur private spending.

35. With Jacob Haas, a research specialist in Princeton's Eviction Lab, I drew on data from 2018, using the Congressional Budget Office's report, *The Distribution of Household Income, 2018,* Supplemental Data, August 4, 2021. After dividing the population into five income groups (quintiles), based on their incomes before taxes and transfers, the average family in the middle of the distribution (the third quintile) had an income of $63,900. Here, income refers to "market income" and consists of labor income, business income, capital income (including capital gains), income received in retirement for past services, and other nongovernmental sources of income. Social insurance benefits consist of benefits from Social Security (Old-Age, Survivors, and Disability Insurance), Medicare (measured as the average cost to the government of providing those benefits), unemployment insurance, and workers' compensation. Means-tested transfers are cash payments and in-kind services provided through federal, state, and local government assistance programs. Federal taxes consist of individual income taxes, payroll taxes, corporate income taxes, and excise taxes. (In this analysis, taxes for a given year were the amount a household owed on the basis of income received that year, regardless of when the taxes are paid.) Taxes from these four sources accounted for 93 percent of federal revenues in fiscal year 2018. The remaining federal revenue sources not allocated to U.S. households include states' deposits for unemployment insurance, estate and gift taxes, net income earned by the Federal Reserve, customs duties, and miscellaneous fees and fines. As such, this is a replication of Mettler's analyses on data from 2011 (*Government-Citizen Disconnect,* table 3.2).

36. These estimates come from adding up the country's major social programs, tax benefits, and higher education aid in 2018, 2019, and 2016, respectively, recorded by the Congressional Budget Office (CBO). See Congressional Budget Office, *The Distribution of Household Income, 2018* (Washington, D.C.: Congressional Budget Office, 2021), Supplemental Data tables 1 and 3; Congressional Budget Office, *The Distribution of Major Tax Expenditures in 2019* (Washington, D.C.: Congressional Budget Office, 2021), figure 2; Congressional Budget Office, *The Budget and Economic Outlook: 2019 to 2029* (Washington, D.C.: Congressional Budget Office, 2019), figure 4-4; Congressional Budget Office, *Distribution of Federal Support for Students Pursuing Higher Education in 2016* (Washington, D.C.: Congressional Budget Office, 2018), table 5.

I include means-tested transfers, social insurance benefits, and tax expenditures. I account for social insurance benefits from Social Security (Old-Age, Survivors, and Disability Insurance), Medicare (measured as the average cost to the government of providing those benefits), unemployment insurance, and workers' compensation. I account for means-tested transfers, both cash payments and in-kind transfers, from federal, state, and local government assistance programs. I also account for the following tax expenditures: exclusion for employment-based health insurance, exclusion for pensions and retirement savings accounts, net preferential tax rates on capital gains and dividends, Child Tax Credit, Earned Income Tax Credit, premium tax credit, charitable contribution deduction, qualified business income deduction, exclusion of capital gains on assets transferred at death, exclusion of Social Security and railroad retirement benefits, exclusion of capital gains on the sale of principal residences, mortgage interest deduction on owner-occupied residences, and state and local tax deductions. Regarding higher education programs, I account for spending on Pell Grants, Federal Supplemental Educational Opportunity Grants, student loan subsidies, veteran benefits, work study, tax credits for education, exclusions from taxable income for education, and deductions for student loan interest, tuition, and fees. Income distribution data and number of households are from 2018 while tax expenditure data is from 2019. Tax expenditure amounts for 2019 and higher education amounts for 2016 are divided by the number of households in each quintile from 2018 CBO estimates.

The CBO data capture the bulk of government aid allocated for programs serving low-income families as well as most tax expenditures, but they are not comprehensive. Specifically, the data appear to capture roughly 84 percent of all income tax expenditures. At the same time, the data also leave out several programs that primarily serve low-income Americans, including Job Corps and Head Start. The data on means-tested programs comprise roughly 87 percent of federal spending on low-income families (excluding tax expenditures), based on the Congressional Research Service's report *Federal Spending on Benefits and Services for People with Low Income: FY2008–FY2018* (Washington, D.C.: Congressional Research Service, 2021). Accordingly, the reported amounts of government benefits received by both rich and poor families are likely underestimated by similar margins.

37. Desmond, "Why Work Doesn't Work Anymore"; Seth Holmes, "'Oaxacans Like to Work Bent Over': The Naturalization of Social Suffering Among Berry Farm Workers," *International Migration* 45 (2007): 39–68.

38. The dominant terms of the poverty debate in wide circulation today emerged in the 1930s in response to New Deal programs that regulated banks and businesses and provided support for the poor and vulnerable. Consider this 1947 editorial in the *Milwaukee Sentinel:* "Under the New Deal," the editorial read, "a shift from the free enterprise kind of private spending toward the totalitarian kind of government spending has been steadily in progress. Under free enterprise the citizen wants his own money for the kind of living he wants. Under the tyranny of collectivism, the government confiscates a very great share of the citizen's money through taxation, and does the spending itself." The author attempted to not only hide our mutual dependence and shared community but to aggressively denigrate it.

"Free enterprise," writes the historian Lawrence Glickman in his book by that title, "was a reactionary discourse that clothed itself in the respectability of the business community." The discourse involved, first, employing apocalyptic terms. The New Deal wouldn't simply expand the American welfare state. It would lead to "tyranny" or "serfdom" or a "totalitarian kind of government spending." Second, the antipoverty programs were framed as a frontal assault on a besieged free enterprise system. And third, you had to choose: capitalism or socialism, freedom or tyranny; there was no middle ground. The New Deal passed. But, ironically, as New Deal programs like Social Security have grown in popularity, so too has antigovernment rhetoric first deployed in opposition to those very programs. Today, those who oppose expanding welfare spending still use language that is *polarizing*. In 2020, a Fox News commentator told his audience that progressive Democrats believe "the only way to end poverty in America is to destroy the economic system that made the U.S. the most powerful and prosperous country on earth." And *embattled*. Senate Minority Leader Mitch McConnell recently described the Republican Party as "the firewall that saves the country from socialism." And *seditious*. Fox News commentator Sean Hannity once described Senator Bernie Sanders's platform as a "radical brand of Soviet-style socialism [that] is about one thing and one thing only: that is government control and takeover of every aspect of our lives." There is a word for this kind of language: propaganda.

"Your Money and Your Freedom," *Milwaukee Sentinel*, November 17, 1947; Lawrence Glickman, *Free Enterprise: An American History* (New Haven, Conn.: Yale University Press, 2019), 7, 14, 44, 81–82, 87, 100, 107, 235; Justin Haskins, "Sanders, AOC and Other Socialists Are Wrong—Socialism Is a Cause of Poverty, Not the Cure," Fox News, February 8, 2020; Sean Hannity, "Bernie Sanders Isn't a Socialist, He's a Marxist," Fox News, February 25, 2020; Kelsey Snell, "McConnell's 2020 Plan: Cast GOP as 'Firewall' Against Socialism," National Public Radio, April 11, 2019.

39. Pew Research Center, "Most Americans Point to Circumstances, Not Work Ethic, for Why People Are Rich or Poor," March 2, 2020; Spencer Piston, *Class Attitudes in America: Sympathy for the Poor, Resentment of the Rich, and Political Implications* (New York: Cambridge University Press, 2018), 3, 33, 46; Leslie McCall, *The Undeserving Rich: American Beliefs About Inequality, Opportunity, and Redistribution* (New York: Cambridge University Press, 2013), 7, 99, 119, 152–54.

40. Congressional Budget Office, *The Distribution of Major Tax Expenditures in 2019* (Washington, D.C.: Congressional Budget Office, 2021), figure 2; Desmond, "House Rules"; Christopher Ellis and Christopher Faricy, *The Other Side of the Coin: Public Opinion Toward Social Tax Expenditures* (New York: Russell Sage Foundation, 2021), 37; Joint Committee on Taxation, *Estimates of Federal Tax Expenditures for Fiscal Years 2020–2024*, JCX-23-20 (Washington, D.C.: Joint Committee on Taxation, November 5, 2020), 42–43; Barbara Ransby, *Ella Baker and the Black Freedom Movement: A Radical Democratic Vision* (Chapel Hill: University of North Carolina Press, 2003), 305.

CHAPTER 6

1. Paul Krugman, "For Richer," *The New York Times,* October 20, 2002; "City Life in the Second Gilded Age," *The New York Times Magazine,* October 14, 2007. Writers are beginning to expand critiques of inequality beyond the very richest Americans. See Reeves, *Dream Hoarders;* Matthew Stewart, *The 9.9 Percent: The New Aristocracy That Is Entrenching Inequality and Warping Our Culture* (New York: Simon & Schuster, 2021).

2. Bhutta et al., *Changes in U.S. Family Finances from 2016 to 2019,* 16; Thomas Colson, "English Homes Are Nearly a Third of the Size of American Homes," *Business Insider,* October 14, 2017; National Marine Manufacturers Association, "U.S. Boat Sales Reached 13-Year High in 2020, Recreational Boating Boom to Continue Through 2021," January 6, 2021; Debbie Phillips-Donaldson, "US Pet Food Sales Rose 10% in 2020, 5% Projected for 2021," Petfood Industry, March 26, 2021; Joe Pinsker, "Why Are American Homes So Big?," *The Atlantic,* September 12, 2019; U.S. Travel Association, "Travel: The Hardest-Hit U.S. Industry," June 11, 2021.

3. In his famous essay "Economic Possibilities for Our Grandchildren," penned in 1930, John Maynard Keynes predicted that in the near future—a future we now inhabit—science and economic growth would free us from "pressing economic cares" and that our focus would turn to the question of "how to occupy [our] leisure." Writing a generation before Keynes, Thorstein Veblen's speculations were far less cheerful. Veblen understood that leisure attaches itself to a specific class—the propertied class—not to a mass of people, no matter how advanced their economy or technologies. "In the sequence of cultural evolution the emergence of a leisure class coincides with the beginning of ownership," Veblen wrote in *Theory of the Leisure Class,* 22. If there is to be a service economy, he understood, there must be somebody doing the serving. See Daniel Bell, *The Coming of Post-Industrial Society: A Venture in Social Forecasting* (New York: Basic Books, 1973), 456–74; John Maynard Keynes, *Essays in Persuasion* (London: Palgrave Macmillan, 1930), 321–32.

4. Scholastica (Gay) Cororaton, "The Impact of Russia-Ukraine Tensions on the U.S. Housing Market," National Association of Realtors, March 7, 2022; Brenda Medina, "Are Oligarchs Hiding Money in US Real Estate? Ownership Information Is a Missing Link, Researchers Say," *International Consortium of Investigative Journalists*, April 1, 2022; Tom Namako, "New York City's Mayor Says He's Not Sure What to Do About Rich Russians Buying Up All the Nice Apartments," *BuzzFeed News*, October 27, 2021.

5. Stuart Middleton, "'Affluence' and the Left in Britain, c. 1958–1974," *The English Historical Review* 129 (2014): 107–38.

6. John Kenneth Galbraith, *The Affluent Society* (Boston: Houghton Mifflin, 1998 [1958]), 64, 186–99.

7. Ibid., chap. 17.

8. Monica Prasad, *Starving the Beast: Ronald Reagan and the Tax Cut Revolution* (New York: Russell Sage Foundation, 2018), 1; Eric Scorsone and Nicolette Bateson, *Long-Term Crisis and Systemic Failure: Taking the Fiscal Stress of America's Older Cities Seriously* (East Lansing: Michigan State University Extension, 2011).

9. National data was adjusted for inflation using the Personal Consumption Expenditures Price Index. U.S. Bureau of Economic Analysis, "Real Personal Income [RPI]," FRED, Federal Reserve Bank of St. Louis; Office of Management and Budget, "Historical Tables," table 1.3; Office of Management and Budget, "Historical Tables," table 3.2. For individual state data, personal income data was inflation-adjusted using CPI rather than PCE to stay consistent with National Center for Education Statistics (NCES) data. NCES data is 1989–90 and 2017–18, current primary and secondary education expenditures in constant 2020–21 dollars. National Center for Education Statistics, "Digest of Education Statistics," 2020, table 236.25; U.S. Bureau of Economic Analysis, "Personal Income by State," Interactive Data Tables; U.S. Bureau of Economic Analysis, "Personal Consumption Expenditures: Chain-type Price Index [PCEPI]," FRED, Federal Reserve Bank of St. Louis; U.S. Bureau of Labor Statistics, "Consumer Price Index for All Urban Consumers: All Items in U.S. City Average [CPIAUCSL]," FRED, Federal Reserve Bank of St. Louis.

10. U.S. Bureau of Economic Analysis, "Shares of Gross Domestic Product: Government Consumption Expenditures and Gross Investment," FRED, Federal Reserve Bank of St. Louis, 1950–2021; U.S. Bu-

reau of Economic Analysis, "Shares of Gross Domestic Product: Personal Consumption Expenditures," FRED, Federal Reserve Bank of St. Louis, 1950–2021; U.S. Bureau of Economic Analysis, "Shares of Gross Domestic Product: Gross Private Domestic Investment," FRED, Federal Reserve Bank of St. Louis, 1950–2021.

11. Committee for a Responsible Federal Budget, "Is President Trump's Tax Cut the Largest in History Yet?," October 25, 2017; Prasad, *Starving the Beast*, 2, 137–45; Alex Schwartz, *Housing Policy in the United States*, 4th ed. (New York: Routledge, 2021); Jerry Tempalski, *Revenue Effects of Major Tax Bills, Updated Tables for All 2012 Bills* (Washington, D.C.: Office of Tax Analysis, Department of the Treasury, 2013).

12. Ben Christopher, "Why Do We Keep Voting on This? Exploring Prop. 13's 'Tax Revolt Family Tree,'" *Cal Matters*, October 21, 2020; Thomas Edsall with Mary Edsall, *Chain Reaction: The Impact of Race, Rights, and Taxes on American Politics* (New York: Norton, 1991), 18, 129–31; Clyde Haberman, "The California Ballot Measure That Inspired a Tax Revolt," *The New York Times*, October 16, 2016; Prasad, *Starving the Beast*, 5. On tax cuts as an issue that cuts across party lines, see also Isaac Martin, *The Permanent Tax Revolt: How the Property Tax Transformed American Politics* (Stanford, Calif.: Stanford University Press, 2008), 23.

13. Edsall and Edsall, *Chain Reaction*, 130; Haberman, "The California Ballot Measure That Inspired a Tax Revolt."

14. Edsall and Edsall, *Chain Reaction*, 5–6, 13–14, 135; Kevin Kruse, *White Flight: Atlanta and the Making of Modern Conservatism* (Princeton, N.J.: Princeton University Press, 2005), 106–7; McGhee, *The Sum of Us*, 38.

15. Georgia Department of Education, *Atlanta Public Schools (761) Enrollment by Ethnicity/Race, Fiscal Year 2022—Data Report;* Kruse, *White Flight*, 106, also 15, 123–25, 169–71, 178, 239–40; McGhee, *The Sum of Us*, 28; U.S. Census Bureau, "Quick Facts: Atlanta City, Georgia." See also Dan Carter, *The Politics of Rage: George Wallace, the Origins of the New Conservatism, and the Transformation of American Politics*, 2nd ed. (Baton Rouge: Louisiana State University Press, 2000 [1995]); Michael Goldfield, *The Color of Politics: Race and the Mainsprings of American Politics* (New York: New Press, 1997).

This pattern was prefigured during the Great Migration (1940–70), when northern whites abandoned neighborhoods to Blacks coming from the South. See Ellora Derenoncourt, "Can You Move to Opportunity? Evidence from the Great Migration," *American Economic Review* 112 (2022): 369–408. And before that, Du Bois wrote of Reconstruction (1860–80) being about "the new American industrial elite" who sought "not national well-being, but the individual gain . . . through the power of vast profit on enormous capital investment." W.E.B. Du Bois, *Black Reconstruction in America, 1860–1880* (New York: Free Press, 1998 [1935]), 586.

16. Somewhat ironically, proposals to privatize underfunded public goods often fail because those institutions have fallen into a state of disrepair. As Paul Pierson shows in his classic book, *Dismantling the Welfare State?*, during the 1980s, Prime Minister Margaret Thatcher was able to privatize public housing in Britain because so much of it was in good condition, but President Reagan was unable to do the same in the United States because nobody wanted to buy our run-down public housing stock. Meanwhile, public institutions on which affluent Americans disproportionately rely—one thinks of the Federal Aviation Administration—avoid both disinvestment and calls for privatization.

17. David Grusky and Alair MacLean, "The Social Fallout of a High-Inequality Regime," *The Annals of the American Academy of Political and Social Science* 663 (2016): 33–52; Charles Varner, Marybeth Mattingly, and David Grusky, "The Facts Behind the Visions," *Pathways*, Spring 2017, 3–8.

18. Congressional Budget Office, *The Budget and Economic Outlook: 2018 to 2028* (Washington, D.C.: Congress of the United States, 2018), 106; Conor Dougherty, "California's 40-Year-Old Tax Revolt Survives a Counterattack," *The New York Times*, November 10, 2020.

19. I first encountered the term "opportunity hoarding" in Charles Tilly's book *Durable Inequality* (Berkeley: University of California Press, 1998), chap. 5. On variation in public investments across cities, see Jessica Trounstine, "Segregation and Inequality in Public Goods," *American Journal of Political Science* 60 (2016): 709–25.

20. On the results of "moving to opportunity" policies, see Xavier de Souza Briggs, Susan Popkin, and John Goering, *Moving to Opportunity: The Story of an American Experiment to Fight Ghetto Poverty* (New York: Oxford University Press, 2010); Raj Chetty, Nathaniel Hendren, and Lawrence Katz, "The Effects of Exposure to Better Neighborhoods on Children: New Evidence from the Moving to Opportunity Experiment," *American Economic Review* 106 (2016): 855–902; William Clark,

"Intervening in the Residential Mobility Process: Neighborhood Outcomes for Low-Income Populations," *Proceedings of the National Academy of Sciences* 102 (2005): 15307-12.

21. Alexander Sahn, "Racial Diversity and Exclusionary Zoning: Evidence from the Great Migration," Princeton University Center for the Study of Democratic Politics, Working Paper, November 23, 2021; Brentin Mock, "The Housing Proposal That's Quietly Tearing Apart Atlanta," *Bloomberg*, November 22, 2021; Jessica Trounstine, *Segregation by Design: Local Politics and Inequality in American Cities* (New York: Cambridge University Press, 2018).

22. Emily Badger and Quoctrung Bui, "Cities Start to Question an American Ideal: A House with a Yard on Every Lot," *The New York Times*, June 18, 2019; Nico Calavita and Alan Mallach, eds., *Inclusionary Housing in International Perspective* (Cambridge, Mass.: Lincoln Institute of Land Policy, 2010); Justin Fox, "Single Family Zoning Is Weird," *Bloomberg*, January 18, 2020; Sonia Hirt, "To Zone or Not to Zone: Comparing European and American Land-use Regulation," PNDonline, 2019, 1-14, 4-5, 7-8; Sahn, "Racial Diversity and Exclusionary Zoning." An alternative measure of the reach of single-family zoning comes from the American Community Survey (2015-19), which finds that 62 percent of all homes in the United States are single-family detached.

23. Edward Glaeser and Joseph Gyourko, "The Economic Implications of Housing Supply," *Journal of Economic Perspectives* 32 (2018): 3-30; Joseph Gyourko, Albert Saiz, and Anita Summers, "A New Measure of the Local Regulatory Environment for Housing Markets: The Wharton Residential Land Use Regulatory Index," *Urban Studies* 45 (2008): 693-721; Matthew Kahn, "Do Liberal Cities Limit New Housing Development? Evidence from California," *Journal of Urban Economics* 69 (2011): 223-28; Sahn, "Racial Diversity and Exclusionary Zoning," 31.

24. Democrats' commitment to environmentalism does not explain this finding. Jerusalem Demsas, "60 Percent of Likely Voters Say They're in Favor of Public Housing. So Why Isn't There More of It?," *Vox*, January 26, 2021; William Marble and Clayton Nall, "Where Self-Interest Trumps Ideology: Liberal Homeowners and Local Opposition to Housing Development," *The Journal of Politics* 83 (2021): 1747-63. See also Demis Glasford, "The Privileged Liberal Principle-Implementation Gap: How the Personal Behavior of Privileged Liberals Contributes to Social Inequality," *Journal of Applied Social Psychology* 52 (2022): 865-85.

25. Edsall and Edsall, *Chain Reaction,* 12, 282–83; Lily Geismer, *Don't Blame Us: Suburban Liberals and the Transformation of the Democratic Party* (Princeton, N.J.: Princeton University Press, 2015), 173–200; Kruse, *White Flight,* 106–7, 125, 178, 196–204.

26. McGhee, *The Sum of Us,* chap. 1. See also Du Bois, *Black Reconstruction,* chaps. 1 and 2; Anne Case and Angus Deaton, *Deaths of Despair and the Future of Capitalism* (Princeton, N.J.: Princeton University Press, 2020); Jonathan Metzl, *Dying of Whiteness: How the Politics of Racial Resentment Is Killing America's Heartland* (New York: Basic Books, 2019).

27. In 2021, when the residents of the affluent area of northern Atlanta known as Buckhead discovered that the city was working on a proposal to permit more multifamily housing in several neighborhoods, they formed a committee to secede from the city. See Mock, "The Housing Proposal That's Quietly Tearing Apart Atlanta." Durable, racially integrated neighborhoods are becoming more common, but they are still the exception to the rule of segregation. See Kyle Crowder, Jeremy Pais, and Scott South, "Neighborhood Diversity, Metropolitan Constraints, and Household Migration," *American Sociological Review* 77 (2012): 325–53.

28. From the expansive body of research regarding the impact of school and classroom poverty on educational outcomes, let me stress three points. The first is that policies that attempt to expand poor children's opportunities only by integrating their classrooms along class lines—allowing those children over the wall only when school is in session—while doing nothing to address the poverty they face at home and in their neighborhoods will have limited results. The second is that students who are smart and driven, or who have parents who care deeply about education, or both, still shine in the classroom (and on standardized tests) even in the nation's poorest schools, a fact to which the best teachers in those schools can attest. But in America—my third conclusion—that's not enough to get you into college; what really helps on that score is attending a rich high school. See David Armor, Gary Marks, and Aron Malatinszky, "The Impact of School SES on Student Achievement: Evidence from U.S. Statewide Achievement Data," *Educational Evaluation and Policy Analysis* 40 (2018): 613–30; Douglas Downey, *How Schools Really Matter: Why Our Assumptions About Schools and Inequality Is Mostly Wrong* (Chicago: University of Chicago Press, 2019);

Jennifer Jennings et al., "Do Differences in School Quality Matter More Than We Thought? New Evidence on Educational Opportunity in the Twenty-first Century," *Sociology of Education* 88 (2015): 56–82; Douglas Lee Lauen and S. Michael Gaddis, "Exposure to Classroom Poverty and Test Score Achievement: Contextual Effects or Selection?," *American Journal of Sociology* 118 (2013): 943–79; Ann Owens, "Income Segregation Between School Districts and Inequality in Students' Achievement," *Sociology of Education* 91 (2017): 1–27; Robert Sampson, Patrick Sharkey, and Stephen Raudenbush, "Durable Effects of Concentrated Disadvantage on Verbal Ability Among African-American Children," *Proceedings of the National Academy of Sciences* 105 (2008): 845–52.

In an email exchange with me, Ruth López Turley, a sociologist of education at Rice University, used the phrase "social status preservation machine." I've borrowed it with her permission.

29. Tressie McMillan Cottom, *Thick and Other Essays* (New York: New Press, 2019), 106.

CHAPTER 7

1. Leo Tolstoy, *What Then Must We Do?*, trans. Aylmer Maude (Ford House, Hartland, UK: Green Books, 1991 [1886]), 1, 63.

2. Ibid., 63.

3. Bhutta et al., *Changes in U.S. Family Finances from 2016 to 2019*, 18, 40; Edward Glaeser, Joseph Gyourko, and Raven Saks, "Why Have Housing Prices Gone Up?," *American Economic Review* 95 (2005): 329–33; Jennifer Surane et al., "Bank Overdraft Fees Are Costing American Consumers $8 Billion," *Bloomberg*, July 26, 2022.

4. John Guyton et al., "Tax Evasion at the Top of the Income Distribution: Theory and Evidence," National Bureau of Economic Research, Working Paper 28542, March 2021.

5. The term "wealth trap" comes from Gary Solon, "What We Didn't Know About Multigenerational Mobility," *Ethos*, February 14, 2016.

6. Sampson, *Great American City;* Patrick Sharkey and Jacob Faber, "Where, When, Why, and for Whom Do Residential Contexts Matter? Moving Away from the Dichotomous Understanding of Neighborhood Effects," *Annual Review of Sociology* 40 (2014): 559–79; Wilson, *Truly Disadvantaged.*

7. We forget, sometimes, that Veblen's concept of "conspicuous consumption" was never far from his less remembered notion of a "predatory life." Veblen, *Theory of the Leisure Class*, 43, 57.

8. Okun, *Equality and Efficiency*, 16.

9. See Janet Currie, "The Take-up of Social Benefits," in *Public Policy and the Income Distribution*, ed. Alan Auerbach, David Card, and John Quigley (New York: Russell Sage Foundation, 2006), 80–148; Moffitt, "Economic Model of Welfare Stigma," 1023–24. For SNAP participation rates by state, see USDA, Food and Nutrition Service, *SNAP Participation Rates by State, All Eligible People* (Washington, D.C.: U.S. Department of Agriculture, 2021). Estimates of SNAP take-up rates are imperfect, calculated by combining administrative data to get the number of people enrolled in the program with survey data that measures the eligible population. But those estimates are imperfect everywhere. A state's exact enrollment estimate might be imprecise, but differences in enrollment between states remain meaningful. See Stacy Dickert-Conlin et al., "The Downs and Ups of the SNAP Caseload: What Matters?," *Applied Economic Perspectives and Policy* 43 (2021): 1026–50; Peter Ganong and Jeffrey Liebman, "The Decline, Rebound, and Further Rise in SNAP Enrollment: Disentangling Business Cycle Fluctuations and Policy Changes," *American Economic Journal: Economic Policy* 10 (2018): 153–76; Caroline Ratcliffe, Signe-Mary McKernan, and Kenneth Finegold, "Effects of Food Stamp and TANF Policies on Food Stamp Receipt," *Social Service Review* 82 (2008): 291–334; U.S. Department of Agriculture, *State Options Report*, 14th ed. (Washington, D.C.: U.S. Department of Agriculture, 2018), 6–33, 49.

10. Raj Chetty and Emmanuel Saez, "Teaching the Tax Code: Earnings Responses to an Experiment with EITC Recipients," *American Economic Journal: Applied Economics* 5 (2013): 1–31; Manasi Deshpande and Yue Li, "Who Is Screened Out? Application Costs and the Targeting of Disability Programs," *American Economic Journal: Economic Policy* 11 (2019): 213–48, 232–33; Colin Gray, "Leaving Benefits on the Table: Evidence from SNAP," *Journal of Public Economics* 179 (2019): 1–15; Tatiana Homonoff and Jason Somerville, "Program Recertification Costs: Evidence from SNAP," National Bureau of Economic Research, Working Paper 27311, June 2020, 3. For a study that finds no effect on take-up rates from behavioral nudges, see Elizabeth Linos et al., "Can Nudges Increase Take-up of the EITC? Evidence from Multiple Field Experi-

ments," National Bureau of Economic Research, Working Paper 28086, 2020.

11. Saurabh Bhargava and Dayanand Manoli, "Psychological Frictions and the Incomplete Take-Up of Social Benefits: Evidence from an IRS Field Experiment," *American Economic Review* 105 (2015): 3489–529; Amy Finkelstein and Matthew Notowidigdo, "Take-Up and Targeting: Experimental Evidence from SNAP," *The Quarterly Journal of Economics* 134 (2019): 1505–556.

12. There were 7.29 million families living in poverty in 2020, with the average family needing $11,318 to no longer be considered officially poor. It would have taken $82.55 billion to lift all those families out of poverty. There were an additional 11.92 million "unrelated individuals," people who weren't living with relatives, who needed on average $7,802 to no longer be poor, totaling $92.97 billion. And there were 143,000 poor "unrelated subfamilies"—the government's strange term for families living with another, unrelated family—who on average sat $11,731 below the poverty threshold. That's an additional $1.68 billion to pull them all up. Add that up, and you get $177.2 billion. The Current Population Survey's Annual Social and Economic Supplement produces yearly estimates of the number of families below the poverty threshold and the average deficit of these families. U.S. Census Bureau, Current Population Survey, 2021 Annual Social and Economic Supplement, CPS Detailed Tables for Poverty, POV-28. All figures are in 2020 dollars. In this way, I updated and expanded on Matt Bruenig's analysis "How Much Money Would It Take to Eliminate Poverty in America?," *The American Prospect,* September 24, 2013.

13. The U.S. Food and Drug Administration estimated that $161 billion worth of food was wasted in 2010. Assuming this rate of loss remains constant, that amounts to $191.67 billion in 2020, adjusting for inflation. U.S. Food and Drug Administration, "Food Loss and Waste," November 19, 2021. Other studies have supported this finding. See Zach Conrad, "Daily Cost of Consumer Food Wasted, Inedible, and Consumed in the United States, 2001–2016," *Nutrition Journal* 19 (2020): 1–9.

14. Alan Rappeport, "Tax Cheats Cost the U.S. $1 Trillion Per Year, I.R.S. Chief Says," *The New York Times,* October 13, 2021.

15. Guyton et al., "Tax Evasion at the Top of the Income Distribution"; Saez and Zucman, *Triumph of Injustice,* 60–62; Gabriel Zucman and Gus Wezerek, "This Is Tax Evasion, Plain and Simple," *The New*

York Times, July 7, 2021. See also Tax Justice Network, *The State of Tax Justice 2021* (Bristol, England: Tax Justice Network, 2021), 27.

16. Heather Boushey, *Unbound: How Inequality Constricts Our Economy and What We Can Do About It* (Cambridge, Mass.: Harvard University Press, 2019), 91, 94–95, 104.

17. Emmanuel Saez and Gabriel Zucman, "How to Tax Our Way Back to Justice," *The New York Times,* October 11, 2019; Tax Policy Center, "Historical Highest Marginal Income Tax Rates," February 9, 2022; Tax Policy Center, "Corporate Top Tax Rate and Bracket," February 14, 2022; Tax Foundation, "Historical U.S. Federal Corporate Income Tax Rates & Brackets, 1909–2020," August 24, 2021.

18. Boushey, *Unbound,* chap. 3; Ross Douthat, *The Decadent Society: How We Became the Victims of Our Own Success* (New York: Avid Reader, 2020).

19. The Editorial Board, "The Democrats' Wealth-Tax Mirage," *The Wall Street Journal,* October 25, 2021.

20. Okun (*Equality and Efficiency,* 59) once said that a core commandment of public policy is that "once something is given, it shall not be taken away." It's true that once the government bestows a certain benefit, no matter how regressive and ridiculous that benefit may be, it becomes increasingly difficult to reverse course. Then again, the government has shown little restraint in breaking this commandment when it comes to aid directed at the poor. Washington helped to build union power, then it helped take it away. It constructed towering public housing complexes then dynamited them. It expanded cash welfare then abruptly ended the program. Or consider how the government extended bold relief to low-income Americans during COVID-19, in the form of beefed-up unemployment insurance and a bigger Child Tax Credit, before withdrawing aid once the pandemic began to recede. It seems to me that Okun's commandment applies more to welfare for the rich, but even those benefits are not set in stone. When I began stumping for affordable housing policy in Washington, many fellow advocates told me that no elected official would go near the mortgage interest deduction. *It's the third rail of politics,* they told me. *Impervious to reform.* But during the first year of Donald Trump's presidency, Congress reformed it. To help ease the deficit hit caused by the Tax Cuts and Jobs Act of 2017, the Trump administration capped the mortgage interest deduction at $750,000, down from $1 million, a change for which liberal housing activists had been lobbying for years. I have begun viewing overconfident claims about the impossibility of reform with skepticism. As Susanna Blankley, an organizer for the Right to Counsel NYC Coalition, once told me, "Everything is impossible—until it's not."

21. Chye-Ching Huang and Brandon DeBot, "Corporate Tax Cuts Skew to Shareholders and CEOs, Not Workers as Administration Claims," Center on Budget and Policy Priorities, August 16, 2017; Congressional Budget Office, *Options for Reducing the Deficit: 2021 to 2030* (Washington, D.C.: Congressional Budget Office, 2020), 75, 77; Lucas Goodman et al., "How Do Business Owners Respond to a Tax Cut? Examining the 199A Deduction for Pass-through Firms," National Bureau of Economic Research, Working Paper 28680, April 2021, 8; Samantha Jacoby, "Repealing Flawed 'Pass-Through' Deduction Should Be Part of Recovery Legislation," Center on Budget and Policy Priorities, June 1, 2021; Joint Committee on Taxation, *Estimates of Federal Tax Expenditures for Fiscal Years 2020–2024* (Washington, D.C.: Joint Committee on Taxation, 2020), 28, 42; Chuck Marr, "JCT Highlights Pass-Through Deduction's Tilt Toward the Top," Center on Budget and Policy Priorities, April 24, 2018; Gordon Mermin et al., *An Updated Analysis of Former Vice President Biden's Tax Proposals* (Washington, D.C.: Tax Policy Center, 2020), 9; Saez and Zucman, *Triumph of Injustice*, 19; Tax Policy Center, "T20-0137—Tax Benefit of the Preferential Rates on Long-Term Capital Gains and Qualified Dividends, Baseline: Current Law, Distribution of Federal Tax Change by Expanded Cash Income Percentile, 2019," April 22, 2020.

22. Abby Goodnough, "As Some Get Free Health Care, Gwen Got Squeezed: An Obamacare Dilemma," *The New York Times*, February 19, 2018.

23. Sarah Donovan, *Universal Basic Income Proposals for the United States* (Washington, D.C.: Congressional Research Services, 2018); Hilary Hoynes and Jesse Rothstein, "Universal Basic Income in the US and Advanced Countries," National Bureau of Economic Research, Working Paper 25538, February 2019, 2, 5–6, 13–14, 17.

24. "EITC Fast Facts," Internal Revenue Service, January 14, 2022; Robert Greenstein, *Targeting, Universalism, and Other Factors Affecting Social Programs' Political Strength* (Washington, D.C.: The Hamilton Project, June 2022), 1–8, 10.

25. john a. powell, Stephen Menendian, and Wendy Ake, *Targeted Universalism: Policy and Practice* (Berkeley, Calif.: Haas Institute for a Fair and Inclusive Society, 2019). See also Theda Skocpol, *Social Policy in the United States: Future Possibilities in Historical Perspective* (Princeton, N.J.: Princeton University Press, 2020 [1995]), chap. 8.

26. Justin Elliott, Patricia Callahan, and James Bandler, "Lord of the Roths," *ProPublica,* June 24, 2021; Harrington, *Other America,* 157–58.

27. Thomas Blanchet, Emmanuel Saez, and Gabriel Zucman, "Real-Time Inequality," National Bureau of Economic Research, Working Paper 30229, July 2022, 4, 25; Bernard Yaros et al., *Global Fiscal Policy in the Pandemic* (New York: Moody's Analytics, 2022).

28. Desmond, "'The Moratorium Saved Us'"; U.S. Department of Housing and Urban Development, *Fiscal Year 2020: Budget in Brief* (Washington, D.C.: U.S. Department of Housing and Urban Development, 2020); Kay Jowers et al., "Housing Precarity and the COVID-19 Pandemic: Impacts of Utility Disconnection and Eviction Moratoria on Infections and Deaths Across US Counties," National Bureau of Economic Research, Working Paper 28394, January 2021; Jasmine Rangel et al., "Preliminary Analysis: 11 Months of the CDC Moratorium," The Eviction Lab, August 21, 2021.

29. Chris Arnold and Kenny Malone, "The Rent Help Is Too Damn Slow," *Planet Money,* October 1, 2021; Annie Nova, "Just a Sliver of Assistance Has Reached Renters, with Eviction Ban About to Expire," July 13, 2021; Ron Lieber, "Why Do We Make Things So Hard for Renters?," *The New York Times,* August 6, 2021.

30. Eviction filing estimates are drawn from the Eviction Lab's "Eviction Tracking System," developed by Peter Hepburn and Renee Louis. Emily Benfer et al., "The COVID-19 Eviction Crisis: An Estimated 30–40 Million People in America Are at Risk," Aspen Institute, August 7, 2020; U.S. Department of the Treasury, *Emergency Rental Assistance Program (ERA1) Interim Report,* January 1–November 30, 2021.

31. Gromis et al., "Estimating Eviction Prevalence Across the United States."

32. Walter Brueggemann, *The Prophetic Imagination,* 40th Anniversary ed. (Minneapolis: Fortress Press, 2018 [1978]), 4, 39.

33. "Evaluating the Success of the Great Society," *The Washington Post,* May 17, 2014; "A Short History of SNAP," U.S. Department of Agriculture, Food and Nutrition Service, 2018; Melody Barnes and Julian Zelizer, "What Democrats Can Learn from Lyndon Johnson's Great Society," CNN, February 3, 2020; Economic Opportunity Act of 1964,

Pub. L. No. 88-452, 78 Stat. 508 (1964); Lucy Danley, "A Brief History and Overview of the Head Start Program," First Five Years Fund, October 16, 2020.

34. Guyton et al., "Tax Evasion at the Top of the Income Distribution," 4.

35. In 1959, 22.4 percent of Americans lived below the official poverty line. In 1970, 12.6 percent did. Market and government forces combined to generate this significant reduction in poverty. Government spending on the poor increased dramatically. For one, Social Security expanded. In 1950, only 16 percent of elderly Americans claimed the benefit. By 1965, 75 percent did. Congress increased Social Security payments during the 1960s, and elderly poverty rates plummeted. Through the War on Poverty and Great Society, Congress rolled out other forms of critical aid as well: Between 1965 and 1970, federal investments in health, education, and welfare more than tripled. Crucially, this happened during a time of sustained economic growth that boosted the incomes of typical American workers. Between 1960 and 1973, median annual earnings for men rose from $37,600 to $53,300. Widespread income growth combined with expanded government support to release millions of Americans from poverty. But after 1973, wages began to stagnate, and the poverty-reducing power of the labor market has since diminished. This has led to today's current regime of economic growth that does not result in broad prosperity and increased government spending that does not result in considerable poverty reduction.

See Rebecca Blank, "Why Were Poverty Rates So High in the 1980s?," in *Poverty and Prosperity in the USA in the Late Twentieth Century*, eds. Dimitri Papadimitriou and Edward Wolff (London: Macmillan, 1993), 25–26; Martha Bailey and Sheldon Danziger, eds., *Legacies of the War on Poverty* (New York: Russell Sage Foundation, 2013); Ajay Chaudry et al., *Poverty in the United States: 50-Year Trends and Safety Net Impacts* (Washington, D.C.: U.S. Department of Health and Human Services, 2016), 4–5; Sheldon Danziger and Peter Gottschalk, *America Unequal* (New York: Russell Sage Foundation, 1995), 102–3; Gary Engelhardt and Jonathan Gruber, "Social Security and the Evolution of Elderly Poverty," National Bureau of Economic Research, Working Paper 10466, May 2004; Eli Ginzberg and Robert Solow, *The Great Society: Lessons for the Future* (New York: Basic Books, 1974); Kathleen McGarry, "The Safety Net for the Elderly," in *Legacies of the War on Poverty*, eds. Martha

Bailey and Sheldon Danziger (New York: Russell Sage Foundation, 2013), 181–88; Semega et al., *Income and Poverty in the United States: 2019*, 61, table B-5; U.S. Census Bureau, Current Population Survey, Historical Poverty Tables: People and Families—1959 to 2020, table 2; Wimer et al., "Progress on Poverty?," Jane Waldfogel, "Presidential Address: The Next War on Poverty," *Journal of Policy Analysis and Management* 35 (2016): 267–78, 267.

36. Jaime Dunaway-Seale, "U.S. Rent Prices Are Rising 4x Faster Than Income (2022 Data)," Real Estate Witch, May 16, 2022. See also Alicia Mazzara, "Rents Have Risen More Than Incomes in Nearly Every State Since 2001," Center on Budget and Policy Priorities, December 10, 2019.

37. There is evidence that the EITC suppresses wages, particularly for workers with the lowest education levels. This is particularly harmful to childless workers who receive much lower benefits. See Margot Crandall-Hollick, *The Earned Income Tax Credit (EITC): A Brief Legislative History* (Washington, D.C.: Congressional Research Service, 2018 [2020]); Andrew Leigh, "Who Benefits from the Earned Income Tax Credit? Incidence Among Recipients, Coworkers and Firms," *The B.E. Journal of Economic Analysis and Policy* 10 (2010): 1–41; Jesse Rothstein, "Is the EITC as Good as an NIT? Conditional Cash Transfers and Tax Incidence," *American Economic Journal: Economic Policy* 2 (2010): 177–208; Jesse Rothstein and Ben Zipperer, "The EITC and Minimum Wage Work Together to Reduce Poverty and Raise Incomes," *Economic Policy Institute Report* (2020): 1–10.

There is also evidence that families with housing vouchers are charged significantly more than unassisted renters in comparable units and neighborhoods. Robert Collinson and Peter Ganong, "How Do Changes in Housing Voucher Design Affect Rent and Neighborhood Quality?," *American Economic Journal: Economic Policy* 10 (2018): 62–89; Matthew Desmond and Kristin Perkins, "Are Landlords Overcharging Housing Voucher Holders?," *City and Community* 15 (2016): 137–62.

CHAPTER 8

1. Xavier de Souza Briggs and Russell Jackson, "How a $15 Minimum Wage Could Help Restaurants and Other Hard-Hit Small Businesses," Brookings Institution, February 22, 2021; U.S. Bureau of Labor Statistics, *Characteristics of Minimum Wage Workers, 2020* (Washington, D.C.:

BLS Reports, February 2021); Drew DeSilver, "The U.S. Differs from Most Other Countries in How It Sets Its Minimum Wage," Pew Research Center, May 20, 2021; One Fair Wage, *The Key to Saving the Restaurant Industry Post–COVID 19,* 2022.

2. Desmond, "Dollars on the Margins"; Leigh et al., "Minimum Wages and Public Health."

3. Sharon Block and Benjamin Sachs, *Clean Slate for Worker Power: Building a Just Economy and Democracy* (Cambridge, Mass.: Labor and Worklife Program, Harvard Law School, 2020), 2, 16–18; Desmond, "Capitalism," 181–83; Dray, *There Is Power in a Union,* 184; Rayford Whittingham Logan, *The Betrayal of the Negro: From Rutherford B. Hayes to Woodrow Wilson* (New York: Collier, 1965 [1954]), 142.

4. Specifically, most union drives do not end in a successful contract agreement. A study of union drives that took place between 1999 and 2004 found that only about one-fifth of the petitions filed to the National Labor Relations Board ended in a contract within two years of an election's certification. John-Paul Ferguson, "The Eyes of the Needles: A Sequential Model of Union Organizing Drives, 1999–2004," *ILR Review* 62 (2008): 3–21.

5. Block and Sachs, *Clean Slate for Worker Power,* section 3B; Farber et al., "Unions and Inequality over the Twentieth Century"; Gordon Lafer and Lola Loustaunau, *Unlawful.*

6. Kate Andrias, "The New Labor Law," *The Yale Law Journal* 126 (2016): 1–100; Block and Sachs, *Clean Slate for Worker Power,* section 3B; David Rolf, *A Roadmap to Rebuilding Worker Power* (New York: The Century Foundation, 2018).

7. DeSilver, "The U.S Differs from Most Other Countries in How It Sets Its Minimum Wage."

8. Kate Andrias, "Union Rights for All: Toward Sectoral Bargaining in the United States," in *The Cambridge Handbook of U.S. Labor Law for the Twenty-First Century,* Richard Bales and Charlotte Garden, eds. (New York: Cambridge University Press, 2020), chap. 6; Block and Sachs, *Clean Slate for Worker Power,* section 3B; Martin Rama, "Bargaining Structure and Economic Performance in the Open Economy," *European Economic Review* 38 (1994): 403–15. For a critique of sectoral bargaining in the American context, see Veena Dubal, "Sectoral Bargaining Reforms: Proceed with Caution," *New Labor Forum* 31 (2022): 11–14.

9. Orwell, *Road to Wigan Pier,* 227.

10. Sonya Acosta and Erik Gartland, "Families Wait Years for Housing Vouchers Due to Inadequate Funding," Center on Budget and Policy Priorities, July 22, 2021; U.S. Department of Housing and Urban Development, *Picture of Subsidized Housing, 2020* (Washington, D.C.: HUD, 2021).

11. Wells Dunbar, "No Room at the Complex," *The Austin Chronicle*, September 14, 2007; Michael Kimmelman, "In a Bronx Complex, Doing Good Mixes with Looking Good," *The New York Times*, September 26, 2011.

12. Jacqueline Chiofalo et al., "Pediatric Blood Lead Levels Within New York City Public Versus Private Housing, 2003–2017," *American Journal of Public Health* 109 (2019): 906–11; Andrew Fenelon et al., "The Impact of Housing Assistance on the Mental Health of Children in the United States," *Journal of Health and Social Behavior* 59 (2018): 447–63; Jeehee Han and Amy Ellen Schwartz, "Are Public Housing Projects Good for Kids After All?," Annenberg Institute, Brown University, Working Paper 21-437, July 2021; Henry Pollakowski et al., "Childhood Housing and Adult Outcomes: A Between-Siblings Analysis of Housing Vouchers and Public Housing," *American Economic Journal: Economic Policy* 14 (2022): 235–72.

13. Alanna McCargo et al., "The MicroMortgage Marketplace Demonstration Project," Urban Institute, December 2020.

14. Alanna McCargo, Bing Bai, and Sarah Strochak, "Small-Dollar Mortgages: A Loan Performance Analysis," Urban Institute, December 2020, 1, 6; McCargo et al., "The MicroMortgage Marketplace Demonstration Project," 8; National Rural Housing Coalition, "Rural Housing Success Story: Section 502 Direct Loans," January 2011; USDA spokesperson, email correspondence, March 15, 2022.

15. Matthew Desmond, "The Tenants Who Evicted Their Landlord," *The New York Times Magazine*, October 13, 2020.

16. Amanda Huron, *Carving Out the Commons: Tenant Organizing and Housing Cooperatives in Washington, DC* (Minneapolis: University of Minnesota Press, 2018), 77–78; Ronald Lawson, ed., *The Tenant Movement in New York City, 1904–1984* (New Brunswick, N.J.: Rutgers University Press, 1986), 221–22.

17. Huron, *Carving Out the Commons*, 2–3, 55.

18. See Bhattarai et al., "Rents Are Rising Everywhere." For estimates of homeless schoolchildren, see Advocates for Children in New York,

"New Data Show Number of NYC Students Who Are Homeless Topped 100,000 for Fifth Consecutive Year," December 2020; National Center for Homeless Education, *Federal Data Summary, School Years 2016–17 Through 2018–19* (Greensboro, N.C.: National Center for Homeless Education, April 2021).

19. Baradaran, *How the Other Half Banks*, 141–43; Aluma Zernik, "Overdrafts: When Markets, Consumers, and Regulators Collide," *Georgetown Journal on Poverty Law and Policy* 26 (2018): 1–45, 4.

20. Neil Bhutta, Jacob Goldin, and Tatiana Homonoff, "Consumer Borrowing After Payday Loan Bans," *The Journal of Law and Economics* 59 (2016): 225–59; Jialan Wang and Kathleen Burke, "The Effects of Disclosure and Enforcement on Payday Lending in Texas," *Journal of Financial Economics* 145 (2022): 489–507.

21. Bhutta et al., "Consumer Borrowing After Payday Loan Bans"; Consumer Federation of America, "Payday Loan Information for Consumers," 2022; Wang and Burke, "The Effects of Disclosure and Enforcement on Payday Lending in Texas," 489–507.

22. Jonathan Macey, "Fair Credit Markets: Using Household Balance Sheets to Promote Consumer Welfare," *Texas Law Review* 100 (2022): 683–745; Frederick Wherry, "Payday Loans Cost the Poor Billions, and There's an Easy Fix," *The New York Times*, October 29, 2015.

23. Martha Bailey, "Reexamining the Impact of Family Planning Programs on US Fertility: Evidence from the War on Poverty and the Early Years of Title X," *American Economic Journal: Applied Economics* 4 (2012): 62–97; Thomas Carper, Andrea Kane, and Isabel Sawhill, "Following the Evidence to Reduce Unplanned Pregnancy and Improve the Lives of Children and Families," *The Annals of the American Academy of Political and Social Science* 678 (2018): 199–205; Jocelyn Finlay and Marlene Lee, "Identifying Causal Effects of Reproductive Health Improvements on Women's Economic Empowerment Through the Population Poverty Research Initiative," *The Milbank Quarterly* 96 (2018): 300–322; Lawrence Finer and Mia Zolna, "Declines in Unintended Pregnancy in the United States, 2008–2011," *New England Journal of Medicine* 374 (2016): 843–52; Stefanie Fischer, Heather Royer, and Corey White, "The Impacts of Reduced Access to Abortion and Family Planning Services on Abortions, Births, and Contraceptive Purchases," *Journal of Public Economics* 167 (2018): 43–68; Claudia Goldin, "The Quiet Revolution That

Transformed Women's Employment, Education, and Family," *American Economic Review* 96 (2006): 1–21.

24. Kathryn Kost, Isaac Maddow-Zimet, and Ashley Little, "Pregnancies and Pregnancy Desires at the State Level: Estimates for 2017 and Trends Since 2012," Guttmacher Institute, September 2021; Margot Sanger-Katz, "Set It and Forget It: How Better Contraception Could Be a Key to Reducing Poverty," *The New York Times,* December 18, 2018; Upstream USA, Delaware Contraceptive Access Now.

25. Roberts, *Killing the Black Body;* Sanger-Katz, "Set It and Forget It"; Kim Severson, "Thousands Sterilized, a State Weighs Restitution," *The New York Times,* December 9, 2011.

26. Diana Greene Foster, *The Turnaway Study: Ten Years, a Thousand Women, and the Consequences of Having—or Being Denied—an Abortion* (New York: Simon & Schuster, 2021); Diana Greene Foster et al., "Comparison of Health, Development, Maternal Bonding, and Poverty Among Children Born After Denial of Abortion vs. After Pregnancies Subsequent to an Abortion," *JAMA Pediatrics* 172 (2018): 1053–60; Diana Greene Foster et al., "Socioeconomic Outcomes of Women Who Receive and Women Who Are Denied Wanted Abortions in the United States," *American Journal of Public Health* 108 (2018): 407–13; Sarah Miller, Laura Wherry, and Diana Greene Foster, "The Economic Consequences of Being Denied an Abortion," National Bureau of Economic Research, Working Paper 26662, January 2020.

27. "Employers Are Begging for Workers. Maybe That's a Good Thing," *The Ezra Klein Show,* June 8, 2021; C. Wright Mills, *The Power Elite* (New York: Oxford University Press, 2000 [1956]), 335.

28. Union Plus, a benefits program for union members, has curated lists of union-made products. See also Sarah Reinhardt, "During Pandemic, It's All Tricks and No Treats for Mars Wrigley Workers," Union of Concerned Scientists, October 26, 2020; Mercedes Streeter, "UPS Is Winning the Delivery Wars with Its Unionized Workers," *Jalopnik,* November 8, 2021.

29. Lawrence Glickman, *Buying Power: A History of Consumer Activism in America* (Chicago: University of Chicago Press, 2009), 5–6, 14–15, 31–32, 69–71, 306, 390.

30. James Bessen, "Everything You Need to Know About Occupational Licensing," *Vox,* November 18, 2014; Jamie Lauren Keiles, "The

Man Who Turned Credit-Card Points into an Empire," *The New York Times Magazine,* January 5, 2021; Scott Schuh, Oz Shy, and Joanna Stavins, "Who Gains and Who Loses from Credit Card Payments? Theory and Calibrations," Federal Reserve Bank of Boston, Discussion Paper 10-3, November 2010.

31. Elizabeth Levy Paluck and Donald Green, "Deference, Dissent, and Dispute Resolution: An Experimental Intervention Using Mass Media to Change Norms and Behavior in Rwanda," *American Political Science Review* 103 (2009): 622–44; Elizabeth Levy Paluck and Donald Green, "Prejudice Reduction: What Works? A Review and Assessment of Research and Practice," *Annual Review of Psychology* 60 (2009): 339–67.

32. James Alm, Kim Bloomquist, and Michael McKee, "When You Know Your Neighbour Pays Taxes: Information, Peer Effects and Tax Compliance," *Fiscal Studies* 38 (2017): 587–613; Jörg Paetzold and Hannes Winner, "Tax Evasion and the Social Environment," Center for Economic Policy Research, December 17, 2016.

33. Gallup, "Labor Unions," 2021.

34. B Lab, "Best for the World 2022: Workers"; Teamsters Local 332, "Union Made."

35. James Baldwin, "Fifth Avenue, Uptown," *Esquire,* July 1960.

CHAPTER 9

1. Raj Chetty and Nathaniel Hendren, "The Impacts of Neighborhoods on Intergenerational Mobility I: Childhood Exposure Effects," *The Quarterly Journal of Economics* 133 (2018): 1107–62; Raj Chetty, Nathaniel Hendren, and Lawrence Katz, "The Effects of Exposure to Better Neighborhoods on Children: New Evidence from the Moving to Opportunity Experiment," *American Economic Review* 106 (2016): 855–902; Eric Chyn, "Moved to Opportunity: The Long-Run Effects of Public Housing Demolition on Children," *American Economic Review* 108 (2018): 3028–56; Patrick Sharkey, *Stuck in Place: Urban Neighborhoods and the End of Progress Toward Racial Equality* (Chicago: University of Chicago Press, 2013).

2. Friedrich Nietzsche, *Thus Spoke Zarathustra,* trans. R. J. Hollingdale (London: Penguin UK, 1974), 2.

3. Ryan Enos, *The Space Between Us: Social Geography and Politics* (New York: Cambridge University Press, 2017).

4. Derrick Bell, *Silent Covenants: Brown v. Board of Education and the Unfulfilled Hopes for Racial Reform* (New York: Oxford University Press, 2004); Mary Pattillo, "Black Middle-Class Neighborhoods," *Annual Review of Sociology* 31 (2005): 305–29. The statistic about Cherry Hill comes from a personal correspondence with Adam Gordon of the Fair Share Housing Center, March 25, 2022.

5. Nikole Hannah-Jones, "Choosing a School for My Daughter in a Segregated City," *The New York Times Magazine,* June 9, 2016; Rucker Johnson, *Children of the Dream: Why School Integration Works* (New York: Basic Books, 2019), chap. 2.

6. Richard Kahlenberg, "From All Walks of Life: New Hope for School Integration," *American Educator,* Winter 2012–13, 4–5; Heather Schwartz, *Housing Policy Is School Policy: Economically Integrative Housing Promotes Academic Success in Montgomery County, Maryland* (Washington, D.C.: The Century Foundation, 2010).

See also Kendra Bischoff and Ann Owens, "The Segregation of Opportunity: Social and Financial Resources in the Educational Contexts of Lower- and Higher-Income Children, 1990–2014," *Demography* 56 (2019): 1635–64; Ann Owens, Sean Reardon, and Christopher Jencks, "Income Segregation Between Schools and School Districts," *American Educational Research Journal* 53 (2016): 1159–97; Jennifer Jennings et al., "Do Differences in School Quality Matter More Than We Thought? New Evidence on Educational Opportunity in the Twenty-First Century, *Sociology of Education* 88 (2015): 56–82; Ann Owens, "Income Segregation Between School Districts and Inequality in Students' Achievement," *Sociology of Education* 91 (2017): 1–27.

7. Ann Owens, "Inequality in Children's Contexts: Income Segregation of Households with and without Children," *American Sociological Review* 81 (2016): 549–74; Owens, Reardon, and Jencks, "Income Segregation Between Schools and School Districts," 1159–97; Sean Reardon et al., "Has Income Segregation Really Increased? Bias and Bias Correction in Sample-Based Segregation Estimates," *Demography* 55 (2018): 2129–60; Sean Reardon and Ann Owens, "60 Years After *Brown:* Trends and Consequences of School Segregation," *Annual Review of Sociology* 40 (2014): 199–218.

8. Grounded Solutions Network, *Inclusionary Housing,* 2022; Emily Hamilton, "Inclusionary Zoning and Housing Market Outcomes," *Cityscape* 23 (2021): 161–94; Office of Policy Development and Research,

Inclusionary Zoning and Mixed-Income Communities (Washington, D.C.: U.S. Department of Housing and Urban Development, Spring 2013).

9. Calavita and Mallach, *Inclusionary Housing in International Perspective*, 8, 11.

10. Len Albright, Elizabeth Derickson, and Douglas Massey, "Do Affordable Housing Projects Harm Suburban Communities? Crime, Property Values, and Taxes in Mount Laurel, NJ," *City and Community* 12 (2013): 89–112; Mai Nguyen, "Does Affordable Housing Detrimentally Affect Property Values? A Review of the Literature," *Journal of Planning Literature* 20 (2005): 15–26.

11. Richard Rothstein, *The Color of Law: A Forgotten History of How Our Government Segregated America* (New York: Liveright, 2017), 201.

12. Katherine Levine Einstein, David Glick, and Maxwell Palmer, *Neighborhood Defenders: Participatory Politics and America's Housing Crisis* (New York: Cambridge University Press, 2019), 36, 97, 106; Alexis de Tocqueville, *Democracy in America*, ed. J. P. Mayer, trans. George Lawrence (New York: Perennial Classics, 2000 [1835]), 511; Jesse Yoder, "Does Property Ownership Lead to Participation in Local Politics? Evidence from Property Records and Meeting Minutes," *American Political Science Review* 114 (2020): 1213–29.

13. Einstein, Glick, and Palmer, *Neighborhood Defenders*, 4–5, 17, 106.

14. I thank Alexandra Murphy of the University of Michigan for first showing me this brochure.

15. H. Robert Outten et al., "Feeling Threatened About the Future: Whites' Emotional Reactions to Anticipated Ethnic Demographic Changes," *Personality and Social Psychology Bulletin* 38 (2012): 14–25; Lincoln Quillian, "Prejudice as a Response to Perceived Group Threat: Population Composition and Anti-Immigrant and Racial Prejudice in Europe," *American Sociological Review* 60 (1995): 586–611; Rachel Wetts and Robb Willer, "Privilege on the Precipice: Perceived Racial Status Threats Lead White Americans to Oppose Welfare Programs," *Social Forces* 97 (2018): 793–822; Clara Wilkins and Cheryl Kaiser, "Racial Progress as Threat to the Status Hierarchy: Implications for Perceptions of Anti-White Bias," *Psychological Science* 25 (2014): 439–46.

16. Larry Bartels, *Unequal Democracy* (Princeton, N.J.: Princeton University Press, 2016); Derek Brown, Drew Jacoby-Senghor, and Isaac Raymundo, "If You Rise, I Fall: Equality Is Prevented by the Misperception That It Harms Advantaged Groups," *Science Advances* 8 (2022): 1–18; Pis-

ton, *Class Attitudes in America,* 6, 56–62; McCall, *Undeserving Rich,* 35, 47, 217.

17. Jenny Schuetz, *Fixer-Upper: How to Repair America's Broken Housing Systems* (Washington, D.C.: Brookings Institution Press, 2022); Neil Smith and Peter Williams, eds., *Gentrification of the City* (London: Routledge, 2013).

18. Greenstein, *Targeting, Universalism, and Other Factors Affecting Social Programs' Political Strength,* 17.

19. Oliver Cromwell Cox, *Caste, Class, and Race: A Study in Social Dynamics* (New York: Doubleday, 1948), 345. See also Desmond, "Capitalism"; Du Bois, *Black Reconstruction.*

20. This concept was also popular among some Depression-era economists. See Stuart Chase, *The Economy of Abundance* (New York: MacMillan, 1934); Albert Newman, *Enough for Everybody* (Indianapolis: Bobbs-Merrill, 1933).

21. Desmond, "The Tenants Who Evicted Their Landlord"; Robin Wall Kimmerer, "The Serviceberry: An Economy of Abundance," *Emergence Magazine,* December 10, 2020; E. P. Thompson, "The Moral Economy of the English Crowd in the Eighteenth Century," *Past and Present* 50 (1971): 76–136.

22. James Baldwin, "Faulkner and Desegregation," in *The Price of the Ticket: Collected Nonfiction, 1948–1985* (New York: St. Martin's Press, 1985), 147.

23. Martin Luther King, Jr., *Why We Can't Wait* (New York: Penguin, 1964), 65.

24. Kimmerer, "Serviceberry"; Franklin D. Roosevelt, "State of the Union Message to Congress," January 11, 1944.

25. "Happiness Among Americans Dips to Five-Decade Low," *UChicago News,* June 16, 2020.

26. Alex Bell et al., "Who Becomes an Inventor in America? The Importance of Exposure to Innovation," *The Quarterly Journal of Economics* 134 (2019): 647–713; Plato, *The Republic* (New York: Penguin Classics, 1987), 312.

27. Antipoverty investments have often been motivated by broader national concerns. In 1946, General Lewis Hershey, who had overseen the draft board during World War II, testified in front of Congress that during the war every sixth recruit failed the Army's physical examination, and that in 40 to 60 percent of cases, malnutrition or underfeeding played a role. In neglecting to ensure that its people were eating well, the country had seriously hindered its ability to raise a standing army. Food scarcity and poor nutrition, General Hershey told Congress, put democracy and national security at risk. Washington responded by establishing the National School Lunch Program, which today serves meals to tens of millions of children, many of them from low-income families. The military also hired nutritionists, conducted numerous studies on human physiology, and produced propaganda films about healthy meals. These efforts gave rise to things like Recommended Dietary Allowances, which included caloric counts and daily vitamin regimens, and even the food pyramid. The country as a whole became healthier and more knowledgeable when it addressed a problem that primarily affected low-income Americans. Peter Hinrichs, "The Effects of the National School Lunch Program on Education and Health," *Journal of Policy Analysis and Management* 29 (2010): 479–505; Hannah Findlen LeBlanc, *Nutrition for National Defense: American Food Science in World War II and the Cold War,* PhD Dissertation (Stanford, Calif.: Stanford University, 2019).

EPILOGUE

1. Reformers resemble mountain climbers who plot a course and attempt to ascend to the summit, step by grueling step. There are others who prefer to remain at base camp and sit around the fire, talking continuously about blowing the mountain up. *All routes to the top are corrupt,* the base campers say. But "life is a corrupting process," as Saul Alinsky writes. "The most unethical of all means is the non-use of any." Saul Alinsky, *Rules for Radicals: A Pragmatic Primer for Realistic Radicals* (New York: Vintage, 1971), 24, 26.

2. Dray, *There Is Power in a Union,* 192, 255, 383, 433–46; Nelson Lichtenstein, *State of the Union* (Princeton N.J.: Princeton University Press, 2013), 25, 35–36, 39.

3. James Farmer, *Freedom—When?* (New York: Random House, 1965), 40–41; Lyndon B. Johnson, "Special Message to the Congress: The American Promise," March 15, 1965; Lawson, ed., *The Tenant Movement in New York City, 1904–1984,* 20; Frances Fox Piven and Richard Cloward, *Poor People's Movements: Why They Succeed, How They Fail* (New York: Vintage, 1977), 244–46, 254–55; Julian Zelizer, *The Fierce Urgency of Now:*

Lyndon Johnson, Congress, and the Battle for the Great Society (New York: Penguin, 2015), chaps. 1–2.

4. Desmond, "The Tenants Who Evicted Their Landlord"; Poor People's Campaign, "About the Poor People's Campaign: A National Call for Moral Revival."

5. Desmond, "Capitalism," 185; Dray, *There Is Power in a Union*, 183–84.

6. The Reverend Dr. William Barber II, *The Third Reconstruction: How a Moral Movement Is Overcoming the Politics of Division and Fear* (Boston: Beacon Press, 2016), chap. 9; Alicia Garza, *The Purpose of Power: How We Can Come Together When We Fall Apart* (New York: One World, 2020), 216; George Goehl, "If Progressives Don't Try to Win Over Rural Areas, Guess Who Will," *The New York Times*, October 19, 2019.

7. Amina Dunn, "Most Americans Support a $15 Federal Minimum Wage," Pew Research Center, April 22, 2021; Amina Dunn and Ted Van Green, "Top Tax Frustrations for Americans," Pew Research Center, April 30, 2021; Ruth Igielnik and Kim Parker, "Most Americans Say the Current Economy Is Helping the Rich, Hurting the Poor and Middle Class," Pew Research Center, December 11, 2019.

8. U.S. Census Bureau, Current Population Survey, 2021 Annual Social and Economic Supplement, HINC-01. See also PolicyLink, *100 Million and Counting*.

9. Amartya Sen, *Development as Freedom* (New York: Anchor Books, 1999), chap. 4.

INDEX

MATTHEW DESMOND is a professor at Princeton University, where he holds the Maurice P. During chair of Sociology and serves as the founding director of the Eviction Lab. His last book, *Evicted: Poverty and Profit in the American City,* won the Pulitzer Prize for General Nonfiction, the National Book Critics Circle Award, the Carnegie Medal, and the PEN/John Kenneth Galbraith Award for Nonfiction. A *New York Times* bestseller, *Evicted* was selected as one of the best books of 2016 by more than two dozen news outlets, was named one of the best books of the 2010s by *Time* and *Vox,* and was listed among the fifty best nonfiction books of the past one hundred years.

A contributing writer for *The New York Times Magazine,* Desmond focuses his research and writing on politics, the economy, and inequality in America. He is the recipient of a MacArthur Fellowship, the American Bar Association's Silver Gavel Award, and the Harriet Beecher Stowe Prize for Writing to Advance Social Justice, and has been selected among the *Politico* 50, as one of "fifty people across the country who are most influencing the national political debate."

This book was set in Dante, a typeface designed by Giovanni Mardersteig (1892–1977). Conceived as a private type for the Officina Bodoni in Verona, Italy, Dante was originally cut only for hand composition by Charles Malin, the famous Parisian punch cutter, between 1946 and 1952. Its first use was in an edition of Boccaccio's *Trattatello in laude di Dante* that appeared in 1954. The Monotype Corporation's version of Dante followed in 1957. Though modeled on the Aldine type used for Pietro Cardinal Bembo's treatise *De Aetna* in 1495, Dante is a thoroughly modern interpretation of that venerable face.